MOUNTAIN MIDSUMMER

MOUNTAIN MIDSUMMER

Climbing in Four Continents

MICHAEL GILL

Mountain midsummer; the sun's bright burning glass
Hovering westward over the peaks of the Darrans,
High yet in heaven, the snow-touched airs still;

Charles Brasch

HODDER AND STOUGHTON
LONDON AND AUCKLAND

Printed in Great Britain
for Hodder and Stoughton Limited,
London and Auckland,
by Cox & Wyman Ltd, London, Fakenham and Reading

FOREWORD
BY
SIR EDMUND HILLARY

MIKE GILL is typical of nothing except himself. His slim, almost frail-looking exterior conceals powerful arms and shoulders. His long thin legs carry him at a pace most of us cannot match. He can display extraordinary strength and endurance, or lie on a mountainside in the sun and revel in lethargy.

He is one of those unusual people who is more than competent at everything he does, be it in his medical work, as a movie cameraman, paddling a canoe, or cooking some exotic Indian curry. Liberal in his views and perhaps a little cynical about human motives, he never becomes fully involved in the rat-race of human life.

A skilful and experienced climber, Mike will take more risks than most—or at least do things that would be risky for a less competent individual. On a great Himalayan climb he is sound and exceptionally safe.

If an Antarctic blizzard is trying to demolish your tent or you're camped on an uncomfortable ledge at 20,000 ft and don't know whether to go up or down . . . then Mike is a magnificent companion. He'll cook any meal, do any miserable job that needs doing, and if you feel like mental stimulation he'll argue any abstruse point you want—then drop off to sleep like a baby and let the blizzard rage on.

ACKNOWLEDGEMENTS

IN 1963 PHIL HOUGHTON and I spent a summer in the Himalayas, living in a small stone house attached to the Kumjung Monastery while we looked after the medical needs of the Sherpas. We were not overworked. Phil was writing a novel at the time and eventually I was provoked into starting this book. What I wrote then was unusable but at least I had made a beginning. Most of the work has been done over the past year or so. Writing in one's spare time can be a long weary task and I would thank those mentioned below for their much-needed encouragement as well as for more specific assistance. Ed Hillary, besides supplying half my material, has read the manuscript and his trenchant comments have led to some substantial improvements. I am grateful to Charles Brasch for some valuable comments on the manuscript and for permission to quote from *The Estate*, without which I would have no title. John Pascoe has generously allowed me to use his splendid photo of Mt Whitcombe and I have quoted both from his writing and that of Lindsay Stewart.

I would like to thank also: The Pegasus Press for allowing me to use extracts from A. R. D. Fairburn's *Collected Poems*, a fruitful source of quotations; the College Book Company, Ohio, for passages from M. A. and F. A. Hitchcock's excellent translation of Paul Bent's *Barometric Pressure*; A. H. and A. W. Reed, for permission to quote from *Beyond the Southern Lakes*; Stru Ensor for photos of Tutoko; Barbara Goodfellow for persuading me to strike out a very large number of semi-colons; the Hocken Library, Dunedin, for a reproduction of John Buchanan's *Mitre Peak and Milford Sound*; and the author of *The Ascent of Rum Doodle*—I realised how much that classical work had influenced me when I read the proofs of my Chapter 13. Elizabeth Carnachan kindly typed the manuscript as it appeared chapter by chapter and her interest was always encouraging.

Finally my thanks to the publishers; to Neil Robinson and Ron Coombes in Auckland who have helped me from the beginning; and to those distant people in London who have laboured to finish the book in time despite delays from this end.

Auckland   MICHAEL GILL
March, 1969

CONTENTS

ILLUSTRATIONS

ACKNOWLEDGEMENTS
[1] The Hocken Library, Dunedin
[2] Stru Ensor
[3] *Chicago Daily News*
[4] John Pascoe

LIST OF MAPS

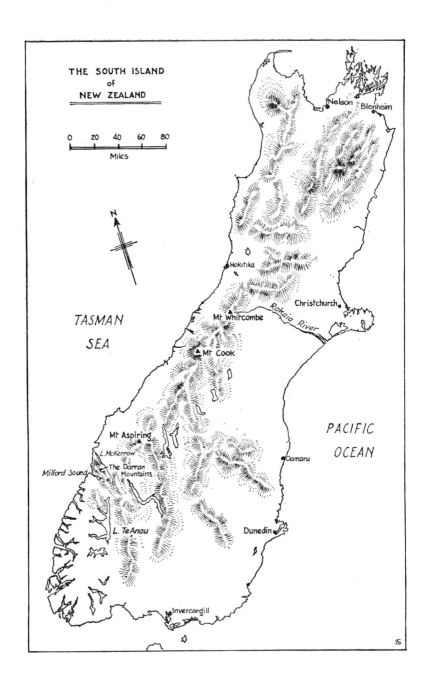

THE SOUTH ISLAND
of
NEW ZEALAND

0   20   40   60   80
Miles

N

TASMAN
SEA

PACIFIC
OCEAN

Nelson
Blenheim

Hokitika

Christchurch

Mt Whitcombe

Rakaia River

Mt Cook

Mt Aspiring

L.McKerrow

Milford Sound

The Darran
Mountains

Oamaru

L. TeAnau

Dunedin

Invercargill

1

THE DARRANS: AN UNKNOWN ARRAY

Land of mountains and running water
rocks and flowers
and the leafy evergreen, O natal earth,
the atoms of your children
are bonded to you for ever:
A. R. D. Fairburn

FALLING IN love with mountains is like any other love. You may, before, have been stirred by a voice or an alluring shape seen in a crowd, but there comes a moment when you are suddenly aware of someone uniquely and bewitchingly different. So it is with mountains —when I first saw the peaks of the Darrans I was smitten hopelessly. And though there was no sign of acceptance on their part, no sly wink from Madeline, no gesture from the old warrior Te Wera, I felt that I would see more of them.

I was on the summit of Mitre Peak in December 1955. With a friend I had set out early that morning from a camp near Milford Hotel and in a canoe we had crossed the Sound, its walls rising like the battlements of a fortress from a moat. Dominating the scene was the rock wedge of Mitre, sheer from the sea on its northern side but with a bush-covered ridge dropping more gently to the east. At its foot, in a small cove, we pulled the canoe ashore and set off. The ridge was long, much longer than we had thought, and in the bush we were held back by the vines, the fallen trees and the fern, which lay in a tangle over the cliffs and tumbled boulders of the mountain. It was 3 o'clock before we reached the bush-line and above us still was a steep rock ridge. From there I went on alone.

At 5 o'clock I stood on the summit. Below were the black waters of the Sound and the hotel, dwarfed by the surrounding precipices; westwards the Tasman Sea gleamed pale bronze in the later afternoon sun, and to the south was a host of lesser peaks.

But my attention was held by the mountains to the north-east, the Darrans, an unknown array of ridges and ice-falls and grey rock faces.

At 5,000 feet I was on a level with tussock ledges and expansive snow fields, above the gloom and oppression of the valleys. Two of Captain Cook's officers had climbed such a peak: they reported that "inland nothing was to be seen but barren mountains with huge craggy precipices frightful to behold . . ." That was nearly two hundred years ago. They were men who had been sailing in unknown seas for months on end and they longed, no doubt, for green fields and open forests, not that inhospitable tract of Fiordland which lay before them, spreading to the horizon. But in the mid-twentieth century when there is hardly a corner of our overcrowded earth that has not been thrown open, it is only in these last, remote, areas that the urge to explore the unknown can be satisfied. To me those mountains were not barren or frightful to behold, for in there, I knew, were the places I dreamed of, the unclimbed ridges, the lakes, the pockets of land where no one had been.

The descent to the Sound that evening was long and it was near midnight when we were paddling home. The sea lay sleek and black in the moonlight. And then, bringing that perfect day to a close, above the silence we heard a soft splashing sound as a school of porpoises glided out of the darkness, sliding effortlessly around the canoe as if to escort us back.

Next day I found a map to identify the peaks I had seen. The Darrans are at the northern apex of Fiordland. Their north-eastern boundary is the Hollyford Valley; Milford Sound and the road leading to it lie south, and to the west is the Tasman Sea. The highest peak is Tutoko (9,042 feet) with Madeline beside it, and south of these is a less accessible group, the Central Darrans, with Te Wera amongst them. Fiordland itself occupies the whole south-western corner of the South Island. The configuration of the valleys is different from those farther north, for the rock is uniquely hard, and where the glaciers of a past ice-age have ground down into it they have left U-shaped valleys with vertical walls and level floors. It is a land on which one can shower superlatives: the greatest precipices are there, the heaviest rainfall, the thickest bush; the rock is harder than that of other regions and the rock-climbing better; there are more sandflies and fewer people.

On his second voyage in 1773 Cook made his landfall in Fiordland at Dusky Sound where he spent a month. His impressions have been echoed by all those who have come after him. Of the rain and the sandflies he wrote: "The most mischievous animal is the small black sandfly which are exceedingly numerous and are so troublesome that they exceed everything of the kind I ever met with. Wherever they light they cause a swelling and such an intolerable itching that it is not possible to refrain from scratching and at last ends in ulcers like

Small Pox. The almost continual rain may be reckoned, another ilconveniency attending this Bay . . ." And of the topography: "the Country is exceedingly mountainous, not only about Dusky Bay but all the southern parts of this eastern coast and exhibits to our view nothing but woods and barren craggy precipices, no meadows or havens are to be seen nor plains, flat land of any extent; the land near the Sea, the shores of the Bay and all the Islands are thickly covered with wood of various sorts . . ."

From 1956 to 1961 I studied medicine in Dunedin, an aging city two hundred miles east of the Darrans. Though I knew I wanted to climb in Fiordland, it seemed I had no one to go with nor any easy way of getting there. But then I met Phil Houghton. At the time I hardly realised what a stroke of good fortune this was. For one thing Phil had a car. Friendships have been founded on less but there was more to our association than that. Our attitude towards life in Dunedin was the same. We preferred climbing to football, and bivvy rocks to ski huts; we believed that climbing took precedence over other activities and so had a cavalier attitude towards the medical course—and if an anticyclone formed over the Tasman Sea on a Thursday we were there to meet it in the Darrans on the Friday. Each of us had an independent streak and together we resisted such limitations as early marriage or the more cautious precepts of mountaineering.

We met at the hostel where we both stayed. On the door of the room next to mine was the name P. Houghton, and when the door lay open—as often as not, a pile of books, clothes, sleeping bags, records and old boots (many of them his own) made it impossible to shut—I saw on the wall a map of the mountain area around Mt Cook. Occasionally we passed in the corridor. He was of medium height, strongly built, with a tanned face and steady blue eyes, and he had an air of mature self possession which gave the impression of someone older than eighteen. For three weeks we barely glanced at each other —his nickname "Rock" seemed unusually apt. And then one day I saw a new ice-axe being delivered to his room. I could contain my curiosity no longer. Cautiously poking my head round the door I nodded at the map.

"See you do a bit of climbing," I said. "I do a bit myself."

Briefly we exchanged notes on where we'd been.

"We may as well go off together one of these weekends," suggested Phil.

"Good idea," I replied—and the matter was settled.

So began a climbing partnership which took us through the Darrans from end to end. Two is not the ideal number in terms of safety,

B

but then safety is not the only consideration. We found we worked well together and in the course of weekend excursions we learned something of the art of climbing and of living in the hills. By the end of the year we had reached a few minor summits and felt ready for something bigger.

We chose Tutoko for our first long summer trip together.

2

CROSSING THE RANGE

Blessed are you whose worthiness gives scope,
Being had to triumph, being lack'd to hope.
William Shakespeare

As it turned out we failed to climb Tutoko or even set foot on it, for we were side-tracked on to another climb which in the end was more rewarding than the big peak itself. Nevertheless we learned something of the approaches, and on Tutoko that is half the battle. Unlike most mountains there is no really easy route. From the south the walk-in is short but the routes to the summit are not; from the north, on the other hand, though the ridges are easy, to reach them is a task of Himalayan proportions.

All the early expeditions were from the south, starting from Milford Sound. Three names stand out: Ross, Grave and Turner. Malcolm Ross, a journalist and founding member of the New Zealand Alpine Club, led the first expedition in 1895. There were rumours then that Tutoko was a volcano for a plume of grey cloud had often been seen streaming from its summit, and there were reports of ash settling, and pumice in the rivers. By a piece of inspired route-finding they discovered the only easy way out of Tutoko Valley and in a long day climbed almost to the top of Mt Madeline, under the impression that it was Tutoko. To anyone who climbs Madeline there is little doubt that Tutoko, which rears up two miles away, is considerably higher (and more difficult), and there must have been a growing uneasiness in the party that they had, so to speak, backed the wrong horse.

But Ross was not a journalist for nothing, and in his account of "the first ascent of Tutoko" he mentions in passing, "A magnificent snow-clad peak, adjoining Tutoko on the west, was named Mt Fosberry . . ." Fosberry however was never heard of again—and Tutoko was still unclimbed. The reports of smoke from the summit were no more than a sad commentary on the constancy with which storm-cloud is seen there.

Two years later, William Grave, a schoolteacher from Oamaru,

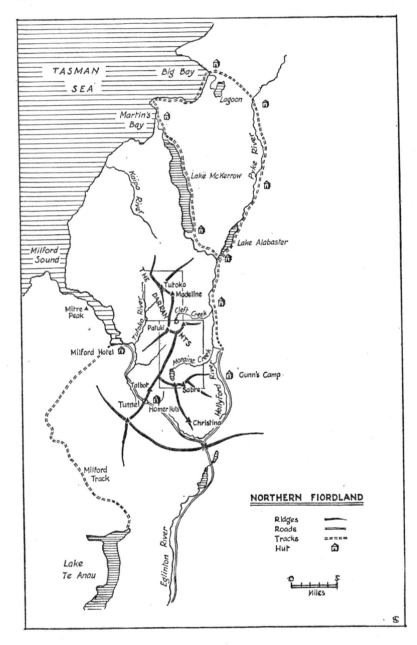

NORTHERN FIORDLAND

Ridges	▬▬▬
Roads	▭▭▭
Tracks	=====
Hut	⌂

0   5
Miles

chose Tutoko Valley for the first of his explorations in Fiordland. In spite of the bad weather and a hazardous first ascent of Grave Couloir, there was something about Fiordland which caught hold of his imagination. In the next thirty years he returned to the area again and again in a series of formidable (and wet) expeditions, during which he explored much of the Darrans and the region immediately south. Well would he have deserved the first ascent of Tutoko—but that awaited the Turner expeditions.

Samuel Turner was a remarkable man in many ways and he attacked Tutoko with determination. His first ascent in 1924, with the guide Peter Graham, was preceded by five lengthy and expensive expeditions. The first three of these are described in his book *The Conquest of the New Zealand Alps* which, as he points out in the Foreword, "is a frank description of actual pioneering, exploration and climbing of New Zealand's most difficult mountains". It is an entertaining book, not only as a record of his climbs but also for an unusual sense of humour and a degree of imagination not always found in mountain writers. His account of the summit rocks of Tutoko (in a later publication) is an example: "I ran up the last hundred feet of its snow cap only to come face to face with a wall of rock . . . We tackled this precipice, in some cases climbing overhanging rocks . . . There were no footholds, but only smooth rock, along which we worked for 15 to 20 feet until we reached a 1 in. by 3 in. ledge for the right foot."

And of fitness in climbing: "The best respect a climber can show the mountains is to keep himself in the peak of condition by all kinds of exercises when mountains are not available. As an example of this I beat the one hour non-stop skipping record on the R.M.S. *Tainui*, at sea, near Panama, on December 16th, 1921, by skipping with both feet together, no change of skip and no pause of the rope, 10,100 times in one hour, counted by the ship's doctor and a passenger."

Turner left his name behind him not only as conqueror of Tutoko, but on Turner Pass, Lake Turner, Turner Falls and last but not least, Turner's Bivvy. Phil and I, after reading accounts of the climbs on the mountain (there are now seven different routes), decided to use Turner's Bivvy as our base and attempt the south-east ridge. We left Dunedin, mid-February 1956, in Phil's car, a poor maltreated Morris Minor called Doodle whose scarlet and cream paintwork showed dimly through dust accumulated on back-country roads. On the back seat and in the boot there was always a litter of primuses, old food, plastic bags, pitons, fragments of rope and sometimes a dead rabbit. There was little doubt that Doodle was functional rather than kept for her good looks, but she could reach the Darrans in six hours and that was all we asked of her. The road from Dunedin runs east for 180 miles to Lake Te Anau and from there north up the Eglinton Valley, which is separated by a low saddle from the Hollyford. Though we did the trip often, we never tired of it. The road approaches Te Anau over dry, undulating, tussock country. Slowly the lake draws nearer, a broad band of water from which, on the western shore, the peaks of Fiordland rise with startling abruptness; the lake divides the plains from the mountains, the grassland from the forest, the dryness from the rain.

As we drove into Te Anau township that February there were clouds on the tops and in the Hollyford we struck rain. There was water everywhere. It roared in the flooded rivers and drummed on the roof of the car; the creeks, the road, the screes, the flanks of the mountains, all streamed and ran with water as only Fiordland can. Darkness had closed in by then and where the road ran under Mt Christina, waterfalls loomed out of the night, white threads plunging thousands of feet down its great precipices. "Welcome to Fiordland" read a sign beside the road.

But by morning the rain had eased and we drove on through the Homer Tunnel to the lower end of Tutoko Valley. Where the road crosses Tutoko River there is an old orange bridge with tall beech forest around it overhanging the water. The track up-valley starts on the Milford side of the bridge and traverses the bush for four miles before emerging on to the flats where we hoped to camp. We parked the car by the side of the road, swung up our loads and pushed through the fern into the dripping forest. After a search we found the track, overgrown but recognisable by the old blazes on the trees. Hodgkins in 1895 described the near-by Cleddau track as "old" and "much disused", and this one too we decided was "much disused".

Fiordland bush, in the rain, is curiously dismal. There is a cloying smell of dank vegetation in the air, and the light filtering through the overlying beech canopy is green and yellow, almost lurid; moss covers the trunks and branches; the forest floor is thick with crown fern and rotting trunks, and pools of water lie stagnant around bared roots or under rocks. The track was never easy to find and at times it disappeared completely in swamp or a chaos of wind-fallen trees. After four hours we came to the flats, an open area, perhaps a mile long, of lichen-covered boulders, low scrub and tussock. With an air of finality Phil planted an ice-axe in the centre of the first camp-site we came to, and there in silence we pitched our tent. It was early in the afternoon to be stopping, but the continuing drizzle made travelling unpleasant, and besides, we were exhausted. As sandflies fell on us in swarms we began wondering what perversity it was that inspired Grave on his explorations. The answer came in the morning. We rose early to find the sky clear and the mountains in full view, a scene splendid enough to make small any discomforts. The southern bluffs of Tutoko rose from the farther end of the flats, forming one wall of the deep canyon enclosing Leader Creek and the Age Glacier. Our route lay there, up the creek and up steep bluffs to the bivvy 5,000 feet higher.

Rejoicing in the warmth and stillness of the morning we crossed Tutoko River and scrambled up a dry creek bed to Leader Falls. The half flooded creek was still waist deep—too high to cross—and we retraced our steps to Dave's Cave, a bivvy rock near the falls. Next morning with a hard frost to shrink the flow of water from the ice and snow above, we crossed easily and moved up towards the snout of the glacier. Here we stopped for an hour to light a fire for breakfast and a billy of tea; then we started up the bluffs.

As the Age fell away below we saw it more clearly—a slab of grey ice, scarred by rockfall, withdrawn from the sun, lying deep in the rock trench it has gouged for itself. I wondered who had given it so apt a name, for to look on the Age is to catch a glimpse of a time when there was no life there and those regions were a desolation of rock and ice. But alas, it is named after a newspaper Ross wrote for—there is no more to it than that. We pushed our way through thick scrub at first, then followed tussock ledges winding up through the bluffs. As the confinement of the valley receded we emerged into a more spacious world of big snow-fields and dry tussock thick with seed-heads. A few hundred feet below the Madeline Snow Plateau we came to our bivvy, a large boulder placed there by the Age when it still filled the valley. It rests on top of smaller boulders so as to leave a space beneath where four people can live in comfort (relatively speaking) or two in luxury. Early in the season it is buried by snow, but in February there is only tussock.

We had hardly put down our loads when a pair of keas dropped in to see who the newcomers were. The leader hopped up to a pack, one eye cocked shrewdly at us, the other inspecting a root he was holding in one claw, as a feint perhaps to conceal his interest in the pack. Keas are likeable birds, but they are also diabolically destructive, and throwing rocks at them is a protective reflex one soon learns. Usually they duck these with ease but this one was strangely slow. To the astonishment of us both my third throw hit him squarely amidships and in the twinkling of an eye he was on his back with his toes in the air. For a moment, like the Ancient Mariner, I was dismayed, but a moment's reflection showed that this was no more than natural selection at work—for any kea unable to dodge a slow-thrown stone at ten feet is unfit to survive in the mountains. In the end, with only a trace of regret, we made him into a stew.

That evening we discussed plans for the next day. Our proposed

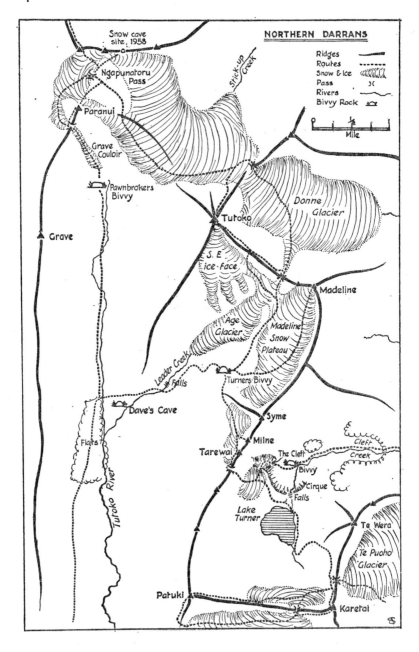

NORTHERN DARRANS

Ridges
Routes
Snow & Ice
Pass
Rivers
Bivvy Rock

Mile

Snow cave
site, 1958

Ngapunatoru
Pass

Stick-up Creek

Paranui

Grave
Couloir

Pawnbrokers
Bivvy

Grave

Donne
Glacier

Turoko

S. E.
ice-face

Madeline

Age
Glacier

Madeline
Snow
Plateau

Leader Creek

Falls

Turners Bivvy

Dave's Cave

Syme

Flats?

Milne

Tarewai

The Cleft

Cleft
Creek

Bivvy

Cirque
Falls

Turoko River

Lake
Turner

Te Wera

Te Puoho
Glacier

Patuki

Karetai

route on Tutoko was not easy, we decided, and with unusual warmth
we both approved an alternative plan to climb Madeline. As it turned
out this was a mistake, for if Tutoko is intimidating from the bivvy,
from the summit of Madeline it is terrifying. This however we were
not to know. The weather stayed fine and next morning we climbed
up to the big plateau above and across it to the foot of the dazzling
snow-face of Madeline. On crampons we made short work of it and
soon were on the summit. We sat there feeling lazy and sucking snow
and chocolate. The broad valley of the Hollyford lay below, running
north, the river winding in big loops down to Lake McKerrow and
beyond was a long white beach with surf rolling in from the sea. Westwards however the view was sobering for there, a couple of miles
away, was the tumbled ice of the Tutoko face with a line of vertical
black buttresses beside it. That was our route! We looked at it for
a long time, sucked a few more pieces of snow and chocolate and
decided to postpone any firm decision.

Back at the bivvy we spent an indolent afternoon. There was a pile
of dry grass to be collected for the sleeping bench, but most of the
time we lay amongst the tussock in the sun, reading, or watching
avalanches drop off the ice-face. Broken tongues of ice cling to the
face, and all through the day and night the intermittent thunder of
avalanches echoes down-valley.

Late in the afternoon ominous high cloud began moving across from
the north-west. The wind rose during the night and by morning
heavy rain was beating on our rock. The change of scene was complete. Though we still heard avalanches the ice-face was blotted out
by the storm, the tussock bent before the wind, and water pouring
down the bluffs was whipped off by gusts in a smoking mist. Warm
in sleeping-bags, we settled in to our cave under the rock to withstand
the siege. The day was enlivened by Phil's readings from *Arabia
Deserta*: "The summer's night at end, the sun stands up as a crown of
hostile flames from that huge covert of inhospitable sandstone bergs
. . . the hot sand-blink is in the eyes, and there is little refreshment
to find in the tents' shelter; the worsted booths leak to this fiery rain
of sunny light. Mountains looming like dry bones through the thin
air . . ." Phil pointed out the similarities: the leaking of the booth,
the looming mountains. And then from a stream near by, a tributary
came gurgling down the floor of the bivvy between our sleeping bags,
"calling with blithesome chuckle over the extreme waterless desolation," added Phil with approval.

All day and that night the storm continued before it began to ease.
Late on the second afternoon it stopped altogether as the wind swung
through west to the south and patches of watery blue appeared through
rifts in the cloud. Snow fell in the night and with the cycle of the

nor'-wester completed, the third day dawned fine. All was white; snow covered tussock and rock but so thinly that the sun had soon dispersed it. We began to have covetous thoughts about a virgin we had heard of south of Madeline on the Main Divide.

After a leisurely breakfast we ambled up to the gentle snow-field south of the Madeline Plateau. A brief look and we sat down, puzzled —which one was the virgin? Ahead was a collection of unpretentious summits, low grey humps spaced along the divide like a row of elephants trunk to tail. Syme was identified first as the larger shattered northern hump. A quick ascent of a truncated peak farther south revealed an elaborately constructed cairn—so that was Milne—and the next was our virgin.

If it could be likened to an elephant then our route was up its back end, steep at first, almost vertical, but easing off to a long flat summit. We roped up and I started on the first (and only) pitch. The air was still, as if exhausted by the storm; nothing about us but grey rock, snow and silence, or the tinkle of an icicle dropping off in the heat of the sun. The rock was smooth in contour but rough in texture and wrinkled into holds—the hide of our elephant was a pleasure to climb on, and where the route eased out to the left over a drop, there was a satisfying element of exposure. I had never climbed on such rock before. What delight it was to poise myself, in the sun, scanning the rock above, resolving it into a ladder of holds; and then the easy rhythm of climbing—it was all over too soon. In half an hour we were moving together up the easy stretch to the top.

Our first new climb! And how incomparably more satisfying than any other summit it was. Tutoko alone, flaunting his ice-clad buttresses, refused to look benignly on our small triumph, and we turned our back on him to look east. It was true Darran country. Along the sky-line ranged the shapely summits of the Central Darrans buttressed by a tantalising array of unclimbed ridges. We knew their names—Te Wera, Karetai, Patuki, Taiaroa—and nestling in their midst was a lake, utterly remote, its midnight-blue waters sparkling in the sun. A stream running from it through tussock-covered hummocks, plunged 1,200 feet into a great cirque. They could only be Lake Turner and Turner Falls. The cirque enclosed the head of an unknown valley with a river meandering gently over grassy flats before entering a gorge leading to the Hollyford. It looked infinitely inviting. Tomorrow according to our plans, we should attempt Tutoko. We looked back at the ice-face and ridge without enthusiasm—why not, suggested Phil, explore the delectable valley?

Why not indeed! And as we looked more closely we saw a route down the great cirque enclosing the head of the valley. Below our peak (which we called Tarewai) was a spacious shelf abutting on a

great cleft which split the vertical wall of the cirque, thus giving access
to the valley below. And we could reach the shelf itself by traversing
Tarewai to the col south of us.

We decided to attempt the traverse next day. There was no time
to lose and in what was left of the day we raced down the bluffs to
Dave's Cave with our tent, ice-pitons and surplus food, for our packs
would have to be light for the crossing. We arrived back at the bivvy
just on dark. Next day we were up before dawn for a breakfast of
bacon, potatoes, bread and a pint of tea. In our packs, now down to
thirty-five pounds each, we carried sleeping-bags, rope, pitons and
three days' food. Then we were off, through the frosted tussock, up
the rock and across the snow-field to the foot of Tarewai.

Now the sun was up to take the chill off the rock. We rested a
while, then climbed the ridge, using the rope to haul our loads up the
first steep pitch. A pause on the summit; across the southern horizon
was a crowd of lesser peaks and valleys, grey, green, and purple, and
snow-fields whose whiteness was muted by the haze. Mixed snow and
rock lead down to the col as we continued the traverse and there we
turned left down a snow-slope to reach the shelf.

By midday we stood on the lip of the cleft. From close up it looked
fearful. There was no sun down there, nothing but steep black rock,
soaked by the spray of a cataract which rushed down in the V where
the opposing walls of the cleft met. The other wall was higher than
ours, in shadow, smooth and overhanging; a stream of snow water
running over the lip fell clear, only to disperse and dissolve in the
breeze blowing up from below. Our wall, however, still held the sun;
it slipped down gently at first but at an ever steepening angle. Yet
the floor of the valley looked close enough. "Only a stone's throw,"
suggested Phil reflectively.

It was midday. "Lunch?" I looked down and momentarily had a
vision of us sitting in the sun on those grassy flats beside a driftwood
fire. "Let's have it down there," I said. Phil shrugged his shoulders
and we set off. To begin with we stepped down the sloping slabs with
ease on our rubbers but as the angle steepened we slowed to an insecure shuffle. We began to have to search out zig-zagging lines of
cracks and ledges to make any progress at all, and at length the
descent became too precarious to continue unroped.

And how comforting that slender link of nylon between us was. We
moved one at a time, one anchored to the rock while the other sought
out the best line of holds. Finally we could make no further progress
for below us, and on either side, the rock was holdless and almost
vertical. By now we were about half-way down; only a rope length
below us the water pitched down in the V of the cleft in a series of
falls. We were out of the warmth, the air damp, the rock sheer and

slimy, and overhead loomed the overhanging north wall. There were
two alternatives: either retrace our steps, which was not to be considered, or rappell down to the stream bed. Finding a suitable crack
for a piton we looped the rope through its eye, then sliding down the
doubled rope, pulled it down after us. There was no going back, anyway.

It was the only impassable piece of rock we found. For short
stretches the stream-bed could be used; very soon we were wet. When
we came to a waterfall there was usually a ledge out to the left and
various combinations of cracks and chimneys led us down. Slowly
the terminal scree fan at the foot of the cleft drew closer, but it was
6 o'clock before we reached it. The sun had already fled from the
valley though the mountains above were still bathed in light. Cold,
weary and hungry, we trudged down the scree towards the first
flats. A mob of deer milling around a boulder paused to watch us and
a few, after ambling off in leisurely fashion, turned to stare, so tame
that we could almost have moved amongst them. Ten minutes
farther on we came to the first of the tussock flats. Had we not been
so tired we might have felt a mild glow of elation but that did not come
till the morning. After gathering some wood we made a fire and
cooked a meal; then throwing down our sleeping-bags in the grass
we fell deeply asleep.

When we woke in the morning the valley was drenched in dew. Our
sleeping-bags were wet and beads of water weighed down each blade
of tussock so that one could almost have bathed in it. The wood was
damp enough to give us trouble lighting the fire but soon we had it
blazing and some bacon sizzling in the pan. Over breakfast we talked
about the day ahead. The way home was down the valley (later we
named it Cleft Creek) to the Hollyford. Meanwhile, however, we had
some exploration to do.

We started by walking up-stream for twenty minutes to the foot of
Turner Falls. There was a pool there and around it the air was thick
with whirling spray and the noise of the water thundering down the
cirque from the lake above. Off to one side were some deer, many
more of them than we had seen yesterday, and one of them, a big
fourteen-point stag, cantered up some ledges at the base of the cirque
until he reached a commanding outcrop of rock farther up; there he
stood barking his disapproval at us, a strange noise that echoed across
the valley. We looked about us. Under the cliffs, the valley was
littered with boulders of all sizes. Hunting out bivvy rocks, like
beach-combing, is always a satisfying occupation and we set off towards a likely one. It was as big as a house, and the cave beneath it,
bone-dry, was roomy enough for a dozen people. Perhaps we would
return to the valley some time so we tossed in a heap of firewood and

some pads of moss for a sleeping bench. Above us the sky was clear but the sun had not yet penetrated to the depths of the valley. Slowly the line between shadow and light moved down the cirque; the first rays touched the tops of the beech trees beside our camp and crept down the trunks till the beads of dew on the tussock were glistening in the sun and the sombre greens were alive with colour.

We packed up and set off down the flats with the warmth of the sun gathering about us. At first we stayed beside the creek where it rippled over shingle or swelled into deep pools separated by rapids. Expertly negotiating his way down one of these was a blue duck whistling at us as he spun in the eddies. A startled doe bounded out of the scrub towards the creek; away she went, splashing into the water, till suddenly curiosity stopped her and she turned to watch us.

Half a mile farther on in a patch of bush the creek ran into a short rocky gorge before emerging on to lower flats, a minor obstacle easily avoided by following a deer-trail skirting the bush. Soon we were strolling across the flats. Where the main gorge began, the walls of the valley closed in. We looked back at the way we had come, the flats, the forest, Tarewai on the sky line and the great cleft down which we had climbed yesterday—two flawless days. We turned down into the bush, our next stop the Hollyford. Even in the gorge luck stayed with us. After a brief tussle with a bluff we came on a deer trail which lead down 1,500 feet with surprising ease. Early in the afternoon we emerged on the west bank of the Hollyford and plunging in waist-deep, we waded across. On the other side we took off our clothes to dry, and lit a fire for a ceremonial brew of tea.

We had completed the crossing.

3

FLOOD AND FIRE

Those two old Bachelors without loss of time
The nearly purpledicular crags at once began to climb;
Edward Lear

FOR OUR first major sortie, the Darrans had been at their most benevolent. But the mountains have two faces, the one warm in the sun, welcoming, the other clouded by storm, indifferent, dealing harshly with those who regard them lightly. And when I returned to Cleft Creek two months later, bursting with confidence, I came within a hair's-breath of being drowned.

It happened in Easter 1957. We were to attempt a peak east of Te Wera, the highest virgin in the Darrans—almost the only one for that matter—and we chose Cleft Creek as our line of attack. Searching through back numbers of the *Alpine Journal* I found that Cleft Creek had been visited before—by Lindsay Stewart in 1939. He too, was a medical student and he fell under the spell of the Darrans just as we did twenty years later. Then, however, the prize was greater: the Central Darrans were untouched, their peaks unclimbed, their ridge systems unknown. As I re-read his accounts of those climbs I seemed to find the same enthusiasm and sense of wonder that inspired Phil and me, the same awareness of the magic of the landscape, the same zeal for exploring its landmarks and byways. On the last day of what must have been a memorable trip (in November 1936) he and his two companions used their newly-discovered route up the Korako Glacier to make the first ascent of Revelation. "Soon we stood on the summit with not a breath of air to disturb us. The whole system of the ridges of the Darran Peaks was revealed to us . . . We could see for miles and miles—Aspiring, Earnslaw, the Dart and Barrier Peaks, the Remarkables, Hollyford Peaks, Milford Peaks, and all the Darran giants. It was the most majestic scene any of us had ever gazed upon. Lying flat on the edge, we looked directly into the head of the Donne Valley, thousands of feet beneath us, while two glaciers lay on either side of our peak. It was one of those days which fills one with that indescribable feeling of exaltation which only a climber can know. It was now 5 o'clock, so we ran down the snow slopes back to the Te Puoho Glacier, down and round this, when an obvious route up Taiaroa Peak struck us, and we climbed it . . ."

The following year he made first ascents of Te Wera, Underwood and Karetai, leaving Patuki the only major peak unclimbed. As an approach to this he decided to explore Cleft Creek in Easter 1939 to see if any route led out of the head of it. They forced a route up the gorge and from the flats noted "with suitable awe, the great precipices at the head of the valley". Late in the afternoon (too late) they started up the great cleft which we used later: "We attacked the western wall at the most likely spot—a deep chasm which splits the wall from top to bottom. It seemed likely to succeed, but we were late, and returned to camp . . ." Though they missed their main objective, the weather was fine, and they enjoyed the beauty of the flats. "The valley is filled with every variety of flower, and must be a virtual botanists' paradise. It has not yet been desecrated by deer, though hens and ducks abound . . . from a scenic point of view the valley is splendidly awesome with its savage black precipices frowning down."

Our plans in 1957 were not dissimilar; the time of year was the same and we too were aiming to reach an unclimbed peak from the head of the valley. We felt sure now, after pondering the matter, that a route could be forced up the cleft (few climbs seem difficult from an armchair by the fire) and without doubt Lake Turner was accessible from the top of the cleft. All we needed was fine weather . . .

There was one complication: on Easter Saturday I was rowing in the University Tournament, and rather than waste three days Phil decided to go on ahead with a friend deer-stalking. I would walk in alone to join them as soon as I could. Rowing has a good many obvious disadvantages—the training is punishing, the scenery limited and there is no great variety of movement. It does however breed stoicism, and when I set off down the Hollyford that Easter Monday I felt fit enough to tackle any number of clefts and gorges.

The point of departure is Gunn's "Hollyford Camp", a cluster of rusty-red corrugated-iron huts standing uneasily between bush and road as if resisting the encroachment of fern and bush-lawyer on one side and civilisation on the other. Beside the camp a huge roughly painted sign bore the stern command: NO SHOOTING HORSES. It was early morning when I started and the river in high flood following a day of torrential rain—not the best conditions for a long solo dash up Cleft Creek, but the rain had eased off to a misty drizzle and might clear later. The bush was at its gloomiest, bathed in a water-green light and sodden. In low-lying areas close to the river the brown water had spilled over the banks to drift sluggishly, waist-deep, across the track and through the stands of beech so that in places only the blazed trunks showed where the track lay. I saw with misgiving that even the smallest tributaries had become torrents— clearly a few formidable river crossings lay between me and the Cleft Creek bivvy.

The first was High Falls Creek. I stood on the bank watching the greenish-brown water pouring past till, twenty yards downstream, it emerged from the bush to join the tossing flood of the Hollyford. I could not afford to risk a slip—and only the rope would secure me against that. Fifteen yards upstream a big tree stood out from the bank. Having looped the rope round its trunk and tied the ends into a waist-loop I worked across the current, pendulum fashion, making the doubled rope absorb the power of the water.

So far all was well. Farther on I came to a creek draining a swamp, a black seemingly bottomless moat but moving so slowly that I could safely swim across. At midday, cold and wet but still feeling strong, I reached the wire cable which spans the Hollyford near Cleft Creek. The wire supported a decrepit iron cage, scarcely ever used, and the floor boards had rotted out of it. Seated on one of its ribs, pack on my knees, I released the mooring wire, and with the pulleys overhead squealing rustily, ran down to the sag in the middle of the cable; then the long pull up to the far bank and I was clambering down to solid earth again.

Next was the crossing of Cleft Creek itself. I was feeling less and less happy about the risks I was taking. Reaching the bank I looked across the flood, wider than High Falls and deeper. Was it worth the risk? The exuberant strength of early morning had left me—probably it wasn't worth it. I wandered unhappily up the bank for a while wondering if I mightn't chance on a good ford farther up. And then I found something I hadn't thought of: a huge beech-tree had fallen across the creek, bridging it from bank to bank. This was an un-expected stroke of luck and soon I was on the far side heading up the gorge with renewed energy.

Surely nothing could stop me now. For had I not only one month earlier, written a route-guide for the gorge? "There is a good deer-trail all the way to the flats on the north bank, at first away from the river, then on a flat area beside it. Above this a small bluff is climbed before entering on the open flats." Alas! I have tried twice since then to follow my instructions, and though I have found at least two more bluffs, that good deer-trail and the flat area have eluded me. I con-tinued the familiar struggle with bush-lawyer, windfalls and trails which led nowhere. Through breaks in the beech canopy high over-head I caught glimpses of the black side-walls of the valley rearing up; sometimes there was the crashing of a frightened deer breaking through the undergrowth, and once I came close to a young stag nibbling foliage from a tree. Suddenly aware of me, he took a startled pace backwards, gazed at me a moment with head thrown back, then with a bound was off downhill. All through the afternoon I pushed on, tiring a little but not to the point of slowing down. I let myself day-dream of pleasanter things, of the warmth of a fire in the bivvy, the orange light flickering on the rock walls, of fat venison steaks sizzling in the pan and of the comfort of a sleeping-bag.

It was dusk when I stepped out of the bush on to the tussock of the lower flats. Scattered about were deer skins weighted with stones—so the shooting had been successful. With the darkness gathering quickly I pressed on. Though the creek was still high, here, as it meandered across the flats, it had no power and I crossed at will. Being anxious to move fast I had not eaten all day, and now that I was almost there I began to feel the effects. I was tired and hungry, moving carelessly, stumbling and slipping on the rocks in the creek-bed where they were covered by slimy lichen. At the head of the lower flats I paused to put on a head-lamp for now it was completely dark. Only 300 yards of bush-covered moraine separated me from the bivvy. In February we had taken a wide detour to avoid the moraine but now I was under the influence of that apathetic optimism which one slips into when weary. Why not go straight up the stream-bed? Why bother with that long detour? Soon I was regretting the choice. The moraine boulders on either side were huge, with caverns under and between them, the bush was a tangle of stunted trees, and the stream-bed a series of deep pools linked by cataracts. Cursing my folly in choosing so bad a route I reached the edge of the upper flats half an hour later, exhausted. Ahead of me there was only darkness; no glow of fire, no answering cry as I shouted hopefully above the noise of the stream.

I was standing at the point where the stream left the flat to plunge down into the pools and waterfalls of the moraine and I had to cross to the other side. At my feet the water curved smoothly over the brink of the first fall and in the centre was a stepping-stone, a rock showing just beneath the surface. I stepped across to it using my ice-axe for balance.

But I had misjudged. My boot glanced off the rock, and for a terrifying moment I was falling backwards into the void. Then I was in a tumult of water sliding down with frightening speed.

"Get out!" I said to myself—but the rocks I clutched at were smooth and holdless. Now the water had me. The pack held me spread-eagled, its straps binding me. Then I was falling backwards again down another waterfall, plunging head-first, the water pouring about me, thrusting me under, hammering at my ears. I came to the surface, and tried frantically to roll over, to get off my back, use my arms, get my feet on the bottom—but I was tied down, helpless. And

C

then I was falling, a confusion of water in my eyes and ears, swallowing it, breathing it—"This is how people drown," I thought. And yet again I bobbed to the surface, gasping, but with the noise of the water now strangely muffled.

I have no clear recollection of what happened next. My pack came off somehow. I rolled over on my front and remember seeing in the swinging arc of the still shining head-lamp, the black forest, the gleaming, rounded rocks, and my pack, ten feet away, poised for an instant on the brink of a fall. Then it was gone. I was fumbling, clutching at a rock, hauling myself clear of the current, clambering up the bank. The lamp gave a last flicker and I was left alone in the dark.

I sat down to recover, blowing up water like a porpoise. An incongruous collection of thoughts passed though my mind. The ice-axe had been the first piece of equipment to go and I wondered if there'd be any chance of improvising something. What about sleeping-out at Lake Turner without a sleeping-bag?—cold probably. And thinking again of the creek, what a fool of a place to slip after what I'd been through earlier in the day! A pity about the food too: a bag of potatoes, hot cross buns, an Easter egg, a cabbage. I got up and set off towards the bivvy in total darkness. The more I stumbled the more I grew exasperated at what I'd done. I was moving like a blind man with hands in front of me, hesitantly feeling a way round every tree and boulder.

Up on the flats I moved faster for I knew the ground was level. The bivvy lay off to the right through a small grove of beech trees and across a hundred yards of open moraine. I began to shout out to Phil and John, but there was no reply. Soon I was into the moraine stumbling and having to feel my way again. I shouted once more. No reply. Strange I thought, for surely I was close now—and for the first time I began to have misgivings. I pressed on with increasing urgency. Suddenly the hulking shape of the rock loomed out of the darkness only twenty feet away. With a sinking feeling I looked—no fire, no sound, no sleeping figures. I stepped under the big overhang: warm ashes lay in the fireplace, and a slab of fresh meat beside it—but there was no pack, no clothes or sleeping-bag, no dry wood even. There was something uncanny about it—for why should they have moved out so early? And where to? I began to feel uncomfortably naked and alone for all I had on was a woollen singlet, shorts, boots and socks— all soaked. Hopefully I looked around for a deer-skin but there was none. Like a rat going into its hole, I crawled as far under the rock as I could and there for some reason I felt more secure. I shifted aside some rocks to make a hollow, filled it with what dry grass and moss I could find and curled up amongst it.

Seldom has a night passed so slowly. Though I had whiled away
the monotonous hours of tramping earlier in the day by dreaming of
food and a warm fire, the trick no longer worked. Quarter hour by
quarter hour I counted out the passing of time by the luminous dial
of my watch. I experimented with the relative comforts of various
positions, occasionally adjusted a rock. What on earth had made Phil
leave, I wondered—and I thought out a few choice phrases for when
I caught up with him. Surprisingly the cold was never a serious discomfort. I shivered as I never have before or since—not the usual
mild quivering, but a coarse shaking of my whole body, as if I were
hanging on to a rock drill. It went on intermittently all night, starting
and stopping abruptly as if controlled by a switch. Somewhere inside
me some physiological mechanism was working admirably well. Near
midnight I rose to stretch my legs and saw that the rain had stopped.
Then at about 6 o'clock came a bleak dawn. I crawled out stiffly,
glanced around to see that I had missed nothing in the dark and set
off down valley almost at a run.

Within five minutes I had reached the point where I slipped in—how
innocuous it looked now that the rain had stopped and there was some
light, dim though it was. I carried on beside the creek looking for signs
of my pack. Now that I was relieved of its bulk and weight I could
travel fast, leaping from boulder to boulder or slipping between close-
set timber where yesterday the pack-frame would have caught. Of
ice-axe, pack, rope or clothing there was no sign—well, it was insured
anyway. I took off down valley as fast as I could. I no longer felt
hungry or even tired—only one thing was of importance and that was
getting out.

Down at the cable across the Hollyford I caught up with Phil and
John. They hardly looked in better shape than I was: wet, smeared
with mud, stubbly chins, and they carried huge loads of meat, skins,
and a pair of fourteen-point heads. With some surprise they turned
to see me loping out of the bush, unladen, in shorts and singlet, like
some mad marathon runner. I sat down on the bank immeasurably
relieved. Here were food, clothes, company—

"Where were you last night?" I asked as casually as I could.

"Walking down the gorge. Where were you?"

"Walking up the gorge," I replied. "Didn't I tell you I was coming
in?"

"We didn't think you'd be crazy enough to come in with the rivers
like that. Can't understand how we missed you in the gorge anyway.
We were following that good deer track you mentioned in your route-
guide—couldn't you find it?"

"Go to hell!" I said, "I nearly drowned in the creek last night."

"So did I," replied Phil. "Fell in just where it joins the Hollyford and lost my rifle. Then John fell ten feet down the bank of one of those small tributaries. So we both had wet gear. Pretty cold night wasn't it?"

"Yes!" I said feelingly but before I could enlarge on this someone produced a cake of chocolate and some biscuits and I set about the more serious business of eating.

Back in Dunedin that night I lay soaking luxuriously in a hot bath. I noticed for the first time that my legs were covered with a multitude of scratches and bruises, most of them acquired that morning, no doubt, when the urgency of my descent had made me unaware of such things. I thought back to those few dark moments when I was being carried down the flooded creek. Surprising how mundane my thoughts had been when I was close to drowning—a feeling of vexation that I should have been so foolish as to slip there, a momentary reflection on the peaceful nature of death by drowning. No fear at the end, no panic except for that first fraction of a second. Often enough I'd been more frightened than that simply looking at a flooded river . . . Really, it had been quite an Easter.

There was an interesting sequel to this episode. The following August I was again down the Hollyford with Phil, this time tramping out to the coast. Though the Darrans were still packed with winter snow, the weather was perfect day after day as it so often is in August. With no rain and the snow frozen in the grip of winter frosts, the Hollyford was lower than I had ever seen it, hardly more than ankle deep in some fords. We decided to go for a quick run up Cleft Creek to see how the flats looked at this time of the year.

In its winter setting the valley was hardly recognisable. The surrounding ridges, under a thick blanket of snow, sparkled in the bright light of the upper air, but not a ray of sun penetrated to the depths of the valley. There all was frozen; no stream flowed down the creek-bed, Turner Falls had vanished and the tussock and shingle flats lay white under a carpet of frost. It was a less friendly aspect but in its own way no less beautiful.

Wondering if I might find something of my lost pack I started up the empty creek-bed. Before I had gone far I saw a flash of yellow amongst the rocks: a piece of plastic groundsheet. And a little farther up I came on a shred of tartan shirt. Then nothing till I came to where I slipped and there I found the nylon rope, coiled amongst the rocks. Above this was the ice-axe lying on the shingle exactly where I had dropped it. Of the pack itself there was no sign.

Higher up we found deer still roaming the flats despite the ice-bound vegetation, and as planned Phil shot a small hind for meat. The rest of the day we spent improving the bivvy—dragging out unwanted rocks, laying down a thick cushion of moss on the sleeping bench and collecting firewood. That night we dined well and slept in comfort till late next morning. We were awakened by the deafening roar of an avalanche that had us scurrying out of our sleeping-bags. From the direction of the cleft a billowing wall of white was bearing down on us like a tidal wave. For one wild moment I thought the top of the main divide must have fallen off and was about to engulf us, but then it hit the bivvy, a wind laden with snow-dust that swept across the valley and up the opposite wall for a thousand feet.

When we returned to the Hollyford that evening we met some friends in the hut. One of them examined my ice-axe with a critical eye. "I'll show you how to test the shaft," he said. Taking the axe he laid it against a stool. I was just starting to grasp the implication of this when with an air of great determination he leapt into the air, all of 180 pounds, and landed squarely on the mid-point of the shaft. There was a rending sound as the solid hickory reluctantly splintered into two halves. "Water must have got into it," he explained, handing the two pieces to me.

However, I had little to complain about financially, for an All Risks insurance policy had replaced most of my equipment. The ice-axe and crampons had been too heavy anyway, the rope had had a couple of chafed areas (all right provided you don't fall, someone had remarked) and the sleeping-bag was acquiring the pungency of old age. The new gear was quite an improvement I thought. The insurance man, sitting in an ugly varnished office smelling of floor polish, had listened to my story with growing disbelief. "Cleft Creek you say it's called. And no one else ever goes there? By yourself? At night!" The details were taken down and after swearing to the truth of it before a Justice of the Peace I signed the document and duly received a cheque for £116. The following February I was back in the same office as a result of an unfortunate slip in a river. I had lost nothing, but the camera around my neck had dipped underwater momentarily—and the cleaning of it was paid for by the insurance company at a cost of £6.

Two months later it was Easter again and we were out to claim the Te Wera virgin, this time using an approach from Moraine Creek. By the evening of Black Friday we were settled in the hut at the head of the valley planning a climb for the next day. The hut is built beside a small stream which occasionally swells enough to flow into the hut itself—or so we deduced from the quantity of wet silt on the floor and some sodden sacks under the sleeping-bench.

Next morning it was still dark when I crawled out of my sleeping-bag to cook breakfast. After lighting a candle I began to fill the primus with white spirits. Carefully done this is unspectacular, but this time the fuel flowed over my hand and on to the sleeping-bench. Clumsily I reached out for the candle to shift it but instead I knocked it sideways into the spreading pool of petrol. With an explosive pop half the sleeping-bench and my hand sprang into flame. Out of the corner of one eye I saw Phil, still wrapped in his sleeping-bag, sleepily retreating into one corner. By now I was thoroughly awake. I hurled the primus out of the door and seizing a wet sock from under the bench doused the remaining spirit. Why I didn't treat my still burning hand in the same way I don't know—but instead I rushed out side shaking the arm violently, with the intention of plunging it in the stream. Before I could reach the water the flame had died, leaving me with an exquisitely painful blistered hand. And while brandishing my arm I had shaken off my watch.

Five days later I was back in the insurance company's ugly little room to explain the circumstances of the loss of my watch.

"Fallen into another river?" suggested the claims officer to open the discussion.

"No, no," I said, "I set my hand on fire and when I was trying to put it out I shook my watch off . . .!"

When I finished the story he shook his head sadly.

"I don't think you'll get this one," he said.

But I did. A fortnight later I received a letter:

Dear Sir,

We enclose our cheque for £8.10.0. in settlement of your claim for a lost watch and strap.

In view of the fact that this is your third claim within twelve months we have to advise that we cannot continue this policy beyond Wednesday, 14th May, 1958, at 4 p.m.

The hazards to which the interests insured are exposed are very great as shown by your claim record.

Yours faithfully,

4

TAKE TWO HATS

Always begin to train a climber as soon as it is possible; do not wait for it to start to climb.

Star Guide to New Zealand Gardening

CLEFT CREEK was nearly the end of my climbing career. The beginning was less dramatic. I have always wanted to climb mountains. I began by climbing trees for sparrows' nests, and cliffs for kingfishers' eggs, by climbing hills because I wondered what lay on the other side, by climbing anything steep or inaccessible simply because I enjoyed climbing. Once in the South Island when I was six, I caught a glimpse of a real mountain, an immense shadowy massif of glacier and rock veiled in storm-cloud—it stands as clear in my memory as the day I saw it.

At boarding school I dreamt of mountains and wondered how I could get into them. I scoured the school library for mountaineering books and read whatever I found. Eric Shipton's *Nanda Devi* was one that caught my imagination, John Pascoe's *Unclimbed New Zealand* another. Both had superb photos and they, I found, could be as much of an inspiration as a whole chapter of text. I moved on to accounts of other Himalayan expeditions, mainly on the early Everest attempts, for at that time, in the 1950s, Nepal had only just been opened to visitors and high-altitude climbing was in its infancy. Then there were the tales of death and disaster on the big faces of the Alps. Of alpine books there was no end; it seemed that everyone who had been into the mountains had written about them. As the years go by one reads less of them, for accounts of expeditions can be repetitive, but a few authors—Tilman is one—can still hold me. Books on the technique of mountaineering gave me an extensive theoretical knowledge, much of it irrelevant to a New Zealander. "If a leader takes guides or porters he has to know how to manage them," wrote Geoffrey Winthrop Young in *Mountaincraft*, the bible of an earlier generation of mountaineers. "Keep your stomach warm as it furnishes heat to the rest," wrote one climber. "Take two hats," warned another.

Reading about mountains is one thing; getting into them is more difficult and as a substitute I joined the school Bird Club, a unique organisation run by an equally unique schoolmaster, R. B. Sibson, who combined ornithology with a love of the Classics. Sib was one of those rare masters with the ability to inspire affection in his pupils and under his guidance we escaped in weekends to near-by tidal estuaries in search of godwits and wry-bill plovers and to bush ranges for forest birds; and each Christmas holiday he took us to one of the remote and beautiful bird islands of the Hauraki Gulf.

Bird watching, however, was getting me no closer to the mountains, and in 1953 a friend, Noel Johnson, and I founded a Tramping Club. Although Noel and I both had a sense of adventure, in appearance and temperament we were utterly dissimilar: Noel was short, of burly fleshy build, with ginger hair, an impudent aggressive manner and a boisterous sense of humour. I was taller, thinner, a good deal less articulate, blond, introverted and at school drably virtuous. We made an unlikely sort of combination but along with the others we attracted to the club, we went on some good trips together. Being keen on the idea of climbing I would hopefully write letters to mountaineers, seeking encouragement for a variety of improbable trips:

Dear Sir—We are hoping to make a winter crossing of the Ruahines starting from Rangiwahia. Could you please give us some idea of how difficult this is and what sort of conditions we . . .

Dear Michael Gill—I am sorry to have to act the part of a wet blanket, particularly as I started on the Tararuas myself at the age of seventeen, but however competent your party one just cannot have acquired the experience at that age and this country is nothing to sneeze at under bad conditions . . .

There was however no shortage of alternatives. Within a small area New Zealand has all that the adventurous school-boy might wish for, and we made the most of our opportunities. We explored caves in the Waikato, crawling through narrow passages, and wading underground rivers. We went tramping along the black-sand ocean beaches that separate the bush of the Waitakere Ranges from the stormy seas of the west coast. We ventured into parts of the Ruahine and Tararua ranges in winter, ploughing through snow on the open tops, shooting red deer, and gleefully rolling boulders down the big slips. We slept out in the rain, soaked and hungry; we were initiated into the crossing of mountain rivers and learnt something of their terrifying power when swollen by rain. Though everyone was against us climbing, we met no objections to the equally dangerous sport of river exploration and two of our best trips were in rubber dinghies down the Mokau and Wanganui rivers.

It was through canoeing, oddly enough, that I found my way into mountaineering, at Auckland University in 1955. Early in the first term I joined the University Canoe Club. At that time Jim Mason, the president, was concentrating his energies on building a hut near the highest part of the Waitakere Ranges, an odd sort of place for a canoe club to be establishing itself but Jim's activities were never predictable. Late one Saturday evening after a day's work there, Jim suggested a quick trip to Onuku, headquarters of the University Tramping Club. We arrived at the hut shortly after midnight. Inside, packs and sleeping bags were scattered untidily about the room, there were people sleeping, others sat around a large fire eating, and a third noisier group were talking in a corner. I joined the eating group for a while and listened to the talkers before falling asleep. There were more, and better weekends in Onuku and other huts in the bush ranges of the North Island. There were tough trips and easy trips and always a good fire to sit by at the end of the day and plans to discuss for the coming Christmas. It was a good club to belong to for its members had an enthusiasm that took them the length and breadth of the country. Through them I began climbing.

I remember my first climb clearly for it was also my first experience of an avalanche. We were in a hut on Mt Ruapehu, an easy volcanic peak of 9,000 feet, and after a lot of pleading I had inveigled myself into a party climbing one of the minor summits. Our leader was Ivan Pickens, a tall dark and silent individual, much respected in the club. By mid-morning we were on the upper snow-fields with the crater lake steaming gently a few hundred feet below. Above us stretched what little climbing there was to reach our summit, some 300 feet higher. Ivan seemed taken aback to learn that I had never used a rope before, but never a man to waste words, he helped me tie in to the middle position and set off plugging a row of steps up a soft snow-face. We had moved barely a rope length when I became aware of an unsteadiness. Strange I thought, and the snow seemed to move a little. Looking up I saw a rapidly widening breach in the snow-face above and I realised that this was an avalanche. Rising gently as we slid downwards, the snow swelled and crumpled up past knees to waist and finally almost shoulder high. A couple of hundred feet farther down the mass of wet snow came to a halt. As we dug ourselves out Ivan wryly observed that conditions on the peak were unsuitable. And so ended the day's climbing.

The Christmas holidays were drawing nearer and still I had no plans. Because there seemed little chance of getting into the mountains I decided to join Jim's canoeing expedition to Milford Sound and the Clutha River. And then, out of the blue, came an invitation to join a three-man varsity party in the Otago Alps—my enthusiasm had not passed unnoticed after all.

The initiative for the trip came from Bob Barrack and Stru Ensor. Bob, completing a B.Sc. in chemistry, was powerfully built, resourceful, a generous and reliable friend and, like most of us, more at home in the hills than the city. Stru Ensor was a primary schoolteacher, lightly built, but strong and wiry, with a wide experience of tramping. Then came the fascinating problem of where to climb. Stru and Bob were keen on an attempt on Mt Aspiring, followed by a crossing from the Matukituki Valley to the Dart and Rees Valleys and perhaps a look at Mt Earnslaw. This sounded like a good start. Aspiring and Earnslaw are two of a superb trio of 9,000 foot peaks (the third is Tutoko) which dominates the ranges south of the Mt Cook region. Aspiring, though a beautiful mountain, is easy under the right conditions; nevertheless with its spectacular appearance it is generally regarded as unsuitable fare for beginners and our more cautious advisers recommended something less ambitious. Though Bob and Stru had a season behind them I was incontestably a beginner—apart, that is, from the avalanche on Ruapehu.

But first there was the canoeing venture. It was a trip that showed Jim's eccentric genius as a leader. As planned, we assembled at the South Island rail-head in mid-December. Immediately we were faced with a crisis: most of the canoes had not arrived. Jim rose to the occasion, and for the next fortnight, until the canoes arrived, we covered the ground on foot. The weather at Milford was flawless giving me the chance to climb Mitre Peak; and the tramp across to Lake Wakatipu, where we found our canoes waiting, was a good introduction to South Island valleys. The main part of the trip was the descent of the Clutha River. The biggest river in New Zealand, it flows swift and turbulent in a gorge through the hot barren hills of Central Otago; everywhere by the river are old diggings, miners' huts and disused tracks. Now the wealth of the region lies not in gold but in orchards, for where water can be brought to the soil it is richly fertile.

Jim believed in publicity and had released to the local papers a schedule of our arrival times at the townships down river. So when we came to the head of the first big rapid beside the town of Cromwell, we found a crowd of holiday-makers on the bridge which crosses the river there. As the first canoe swung into view the crowd fell silent. Down it went, riding the big pressure waves, but there was trouble somewhere and suddenly the boat was upside down with the occupants clinging to bow and stern. The next canoe was more successful and the next. Last came our leader Jim; with assurance he swept down the V of smooth water leading to the first big wave. And then a gasp went up from the crowd for the canoe had suddenly swung through 180° and now was advancing in to the roughest water stern first. Somehow Jim brought it through. "What skill," everyone was saying, and there was a round of applause as he drifted into the calm water beyond, the first person to shoot the Cromwell Rapids backwards.

We paddled on into a gorge where the two biggest rapids awaited us, remote from the road and without spectators. The leading canoe shot through, then it was my turn. For a hundred yards the water was white and a series of high, breaking pressure waves stretched across the river from one bank to the other. The bow of the canoe climbed each wave, broke through the crest with a rush of water over the decking, and slid down the other side into the trough. It was exciting stuff, but half-way down I felt the stern go under. Before I knew what was happening I was under water. Frantically I tried to push myself out of the cockpit, my legs tangled in a pile of gear under the deck. Half-way out, I reached a hand up to the keel, hauled myself to the surface and slipped back to the stern.

For rescuing those who capsized there was a rubber dinghy in the rear. I was dragged ashore, the canoe emptied, and colder and less confident, I paddled on. But we all got through the second rapid, leaving only ten miles of gorge between us and the diversion canal of the Roxburgh dam under construction downstream. Cold and eager to get ashore, some of us paddled ahead. The river, darkening in the late afternoon, flowed erratically between steep walls; currents surged unpredictably from side to side, boiled against the cliffs or without warning formed whirlpools. We reached the dam and waited for Jim to catch up and lead us in procession through the diversion canal to the accompaniment of cheers from the assembled onlookers who had been waiting now for some four hours. An hour later, as we were growing worried, Jim's canoe appeared, upside down. Of Jim there was no sign. In silence the spectators watched the grey, shark-like canoe, almost submerged, sweep through the slot of the diversion canal. Then an hour later the rubber dinghy appeared with Jim, blue and shivering. The whirlpools had been as sinister as they looked and one had sucked the boat down and capsized it. A few months later the two biggest rapids on the river and the Roxburgh gorge along with its gold tailings and stone huts, were submerged by the rising waters of the dam. We were there only just in time.

.   .   .

The mountaineer's road to Aspiring is the Matukituki Valley. It is the archetype of the Otago mountain valleys, and on that sunny day in mid-January when we set off up the grass flats it was at its best. On either side dark-green forested slopes rise easily to the mountains; golden tussock clothes the valley floor and across it spread groves of open beech forest as if planted in a park. From near the head of the valley we followed the spur which leads to the French Ridge Hut at 5,000 feet and there in a nor'-wester, we waited for fine weather. Then early one morning we rose to find the clouds swept from a starlit sky. At dawn we stood on the edge of an expansive névé beyond which rose the noble pyramid of Aspiring.

Our route to the top, the north-west ridge, looked easy enough, but before the day was out Aspiring had taught me two short sharp lessons in mountaineering. Having crossed the névé, we were standing in shadow below the ridge looking for a route up to its snow-covered crest. A band of slabby rock separated us from the snow crest above. It looked ridiculously easy. Even the rope seemed unnecessary. Confidently I led up thirty feet with Bob following. It was not so easy now: the rock in some strange way had suddenly steepened and the smooth grey slabs, still deep in shadow, felt cold and insecure under my fingers. I moved up on small holds. And then suddenly I was slithering downwards. Before I could grasp what was happening I had come to rest on a small ledge ten feet below. Then behind me came the same jumpy slithering sound and there was Bob, spread-eagled, vanishing into the schrund between rock and snow. Ruefully rubbing one knee he hauled himself back to the surface. We looked up, puzzled more than afraid, as a blind man, when struck, might wonder where the blows were coming from. Yet again I tried, and again I slipped, this time coming to rest on another ledge with torn trousers and trembling knees. There was something mysterious and sinister about the whole business, as if some mountain hobgoblin was dancing about the rock knocking our feet from under us.

But there was of course nothing mysterious about it. We looked closely at the rock and found ice, a thin almost invisible film of it, showing patchily here and there where water had leaked out of cracks or run down the face. Ah, yes! Now I remembered the warning of the book: "Beware of verglas on sunless rock in the early morning." It was abundantly clear, too, that the route was a bad one even without verglas ("beware of fore-shortening," echoed in my mind) and we moved left on to an easy snow slope leading up to the ridge. Soon we were on its crest, a broad snow and shingle highway up which we climbed to the summit. We spent an hour on top and then began the descent. After belaying carefully down the steeper snow slopes and trudging across the now soft névé, we moved away from the morning's trail, down the Breakaway ice-fall which seemed to offer a more direct route back to the hut. Almost there, I thought.

But the mountain had not finished with me yet. We came to a point where there were two alternative routes. The first was easy but required a detour; the second, a thirty-foot snow slope leading to a crevassed area, was direct but steep. Weariness urged me to try the direct route and without further thought I started, unroped, down the initial slope. It was too steep. Soon I was slipping, gathering speed while I braked hard with the axe shaft. I remembered the text book instructions: "Roll over to face the slope, grasp the head of the ice axe firmly, and brake with the pick . . ." Taking my weight off the shaft, I grasped the head of the axe, rolled over to face the slope. Out of control I accelerated down the slope, sailed across the first crevasse and dropped into the gaping mouth of the second.

From above the others watched in dismay but at length an ice-axe appeared waving feebly. Down in the crevasse I was sorting myself out, moving painfully from astride the wedged boulder on which I had come to rest. Make a note of that, I said to myself—steep snow on ice can be dangerous.

The rest of the trip was uneventful. The consequences of these falls on Aspiring could easily have been serious but I learnt well: it was five years before I fell again on a mountain. Meanwhile, I had climbed a big peak and with growing confidence began looking for something more difficult.

The peaks we climbed next season were bigger and more dangerous, but not a great deal more difficult. For most of the trip there were three of us, Bob, Paul Bieleski and I, and we climbed in the Hermitage area, the central high region of the New Zealand Alps. The peaks have big faces and shattered ice-falls and in the valleys, instead of tussock and beech forest, there are long glaciers and barren moraines. Much of the rock is rotten.

We arrived in mid-January. The season till then had been a bad one with a succession of nor'-westers keeping the big peaks out of condition. When we started, the Christmas–New Year rush of climbers had already returned, with little to talk of but the frustrations of sitting in a hut in bad weather. But no sooner had we arrived than the weather changed and a succession of relentlessly clear days, combined with the deep soft snow covering the mountains, drove us daily to exhaustion.

An ascent of De la Bêche and the Minarets gave us a taste of what was ahead: the reluctant rising from a warm bed at 2 a.m., the unpalatable breakfast; and then the delicious hours of dawn and sunrise when we and the mountains came alive. There followed the decline of enthusiasm in the heat of the day, the interminable descent down slopes of knee-deep wet snow; and finally billyfuls of sweet drink back at the hut as we collapsed on to a bunk in the fierce heat of the afternoon.

Our climb of Elie de Beaumont followed the same pattern but the traverse to its West Peak was something different. The ridge is high with a level crest, a fragile corniced ice arête dropping away sharply on either side, and for two hours we chipped a line of steps along it, revelling in the exposure. While we were climbing the weather was turning bad, with mist slowly thickening around us. In the milky light the snow was featureless and to see better I removed my goggles —no danger of snow-blindness I thought. But that evening and all next day I lay in bed, my eyes burning as if packed with hot sand. At least it gave us a rest.

But the day after we were climbing again, this time on Douglas and Glacier Peak. We were traversing below the summit rock face of Douglas at the most dangerous time of day, the two hours after sunrise. Rocks loosened by the morning thaw scattered around us; I remember ramming in a belay as a great shower of them went flying past Paul, one of them, the size of a football, large enough to have knocked his head off. But the view of the huge Fox and Franz Joseph névés, the gorges of Westland, and the Tasman Sea were reward enough.

We moved to Malte Brun, traditionally the classic rock climb of the Southern Alps. The first ascent by Tom Fyfe in 1894 was a solo climb. Fyfe, who later made the first ascent of Cook, was by all accounts, an admirable mountaineer, a man who took to the hills easily. I remember reading with approval the opening paragraph of his account of the ascent of Malte with its indignant rejection of current attitudes to solo mountaineering. "To most mountaineers an apology for climbing alone will appear necessary, but I have none to offer, and fail to see that solitary climbing is, on rock peaks, so foolhardy as authorities would have us believe. Foolhardy or not, it has a fascination that is entirely wanting when climbing in company."

Malte's rock is good but nowhere very demanding by modern standards. The famous cheval ridge, a narrow exposed section, was no problem and Paul swaggered along the crest taking in the coils as he went. "We found it came quite up to our expectations, and experienced not a few thrills as we negotiated this remarkable icy knife-edge," said an early account. But standards have changed since then.

After so successful a round of peak-bagging where could we go to next? There was only one place: Haast Hut for an attempt on Cook itself. Cook is a massive and beautiful mountain with three summits, five faces and seven ridges; all, except for the mighty Caroline ice-face, have been climbed. Our route up the Linda Glacier was the easiest. We left the hut at 1.15 a.m. loaded down by a huge meal I had prepared, rice fried with bacon and cheese. In spite of the breakfast we climbed at a good fast clip through a foot of soft snow freshly fallen the day before. At dawn we had left the crevasses of the lower Linda and were in the cwm beyond, a gloomy ice-bound canyon menaced on three sides by ice-falls. Back at Haast Hut was a brass plaque with the names of a party killed there by an ice avalanche and it required no stretch of the imagination to see how it had happened. As swiftly as possible we pressed on, changing the lead frequently till we were on to the steep snow leading to the foot of the summit cone. Suddenly an explosive crack split the silence and our eyes shot upwards to that ominous hanging ice. A dense white cloud was mushrooming out from the face and below it a wave of snow and tumbling ice was hissing down. Across the smooth surface of the cwm it went, across our tracks, and then we were enveloped in a billowing cloud of snow dust. Ten minutes later the white dust had settled and we saw the swept cwm. There, two hundred feet below, our steps disappeared into the ploughed snow and shattered ice to reappear far below.

"Nearly another brass plaque," muttered Bob and we moved on up to the summit rocks. By now our greasy breakfast was making its presence felt. It seemed to have given us a good turn of speed but now its influence was spreading. All of us had queasy stomachs and as we halted at the foot on the summit rocks Bob moved to one side. "My insides seem to have gone crazy," he explained apologetically and began hacking a hole in the snow with his axe. There was a splintering sound and Bob ruefully held up the two halves of a snapped shaft. Then he was sick.

"It's the altitude," I explained.

"It's your damn breakfast," said Paul.

The ice-cap was covered in bare sastrugi and we cramponed easily upwards. At 9 a.m. we were on top. It was good to be there so early, before the heat of the day, before the sun had risen high enough to burn out the shadows on the ranges stretching north and south. Most spectacular of all was the summit ridge running south to the middle and low peaks, with the brown tussock hills of Canterbury beyond and the milky blue water of Lake Pukaki.

With more speed than caution we stormed back to the hut by 11 a.m. to find unexpectedly that our time of nine and three-quarters was the fastest in the book. At mid-day two climbers arrived at the hut, having swagged up from the glacier below.

"I thought you blokes would have been out climbing on a day like this," said one of them.

"We have," we said. "We've climbed Cook."

It was a satisfactory season, but something was missing. Partly it was the lack of any real difficulties. Partly it was the conditions, for no one really enjoys plugging steps in deep wet snow for hours at a stretch. But there was something else too. There used to be a theory that one should approach the Hermitage region gradually. First a season or two tramping the valleys and passes to become familiar with rivers and rock-bluffs and nor'-westers; then a taste of mountains on French, or Bevan or Leary, followed by a season on Aspiring or the Sealy Range. And then, taking stock of your experience and ability (and age), you could decide if you were ready for the big stuff. There is merit in this approach, even if the assumptions behind it (that Hermitage climbs need great skill and experience) are questionable — for the allure and atmosphere of the New Zealand hills lie in their close association of forested valley and mountain. The Hermitage area, with its ice and desolate moraines, is like a meal without wine — one's appetite is too soon satisfied, there is no temptation to linger and relax after the main course.

Now attitudes are changing. Season by season the Hermitage huts carry more climbers while those of the back-country are empty by comparison. For the ice technician the high peaks are, of course, incomparably the best. And the beginner, if he has good weather and avoids a fatal accident, may learn the elements of mountaineering more quickly there than anywhere else. But there are many who will always find more lasting satisfaction in the remote valleys. Perhaps more climbers will go to the back country when competition for new routes is more fierce. The major routes from the Tasman, apart from the Caroline Face (good luck!), have now been climbed. For the rest the ambitious climber will have to start from more remote valleys, the Callery, the la Pérouse, the Landsborough or some other area away from roads and air-strips.

As for me, what did I want? A month after the climb of Cook, Phil and I crossed from Tutoko River to Cleft Creek. And there in the Darrans, like two fishermen amongst a shoal of trout, we found all that we wanted.

5

A SEASON OF STORMS

And every fair from fair sometime declines,
By chance, or nature's changing course, untrimm'd;
William Shakespeare

THE WEATHER in Fiordland has the reputation of being the worst in the world, with the exception, perhaps, of Tierra del Fuego. I have never agreed with this. There are, at times, storms and floods (is there any part of the Southern Alps that is not plagued by them?) but as I look back over a succession of summer trips I see little but sun. Except, of course, for that Christmas season of 1957, the trip to Ngapunatoru Pass.

In the New Zealand mountains, the weather is little more than a succession of nor'-westerly storms linked by fine intervals of uncertain length. The cycle is predictable, from the first crystallising of the high, hump-backed warning clouds, through the days of gale-force winds and rain, to the final swing south of the dying wind. Next morning, in a clear dawn, the climber scurries from his camp knowing that he has only a day or two before those hump-backed clouds are coming in again though occasionally wind settles in the east and the fine weather lasts longer.

But that season there were no fair intervals and all summer the wind, rain and snow blew in relentlessly from the west. Perhaps Phil had been the good fairy waving a magic ice-axe to drive away the nor'-westers, for that season I was climbing again with Bob Barrack, Paul Bieleski and Stru Ensor of the Auckland University Tramping Club. By then we had all left the Club, but the *espirit de corps* of that excellent institution was such that its members kept together, no matter what part of the country they were in.

That year it was my turn to do the organising. I was eloquent about the virtues of the Darrans, the beauty of the valleys, the surpassing hardness of the rock, the profusion of new routes to be climbed, the sunny camps in the tussock—and the others were impressed. How lucky we were that I should have discovered this hidden paradise! And how strange that so few knew of it! I drew up an itinerary: start

D

from Tutoko Valley—climb Grave Couloir—snow-cave on Ngapunatoru Pass—climb Tutoko—circle round it on the big northern névés—
south to Lake Turner—the Te Wera virgin (at last!)—and exit via
Moraine Creek. A nice, neat ring round the Darrans.

The scene, as was loaded up at the beginning of the Tutoko Valley
track was strikingly like that of the year before when I had been with
Phil: the river was high, the bush dripping, and of the mountains
nothing was visible but their immense wet walls vanishing into the
mist. I caught up with Bob to find him crashing about in the bush
looking baffled. "Where's the track?" he asked. "Not always easy to
find," I explained apologetically, as I fossicked about for the line of
old blazes which I knew was there somewhere. In a moment I found
them and led off into the almost familiar maze of windfalls and fern.
Up at the flats, soaked, and aching under our eighty-pound loads, we
were greeted by the sandflies which are always thick there. A cloud
of them descended on us out of the mist, little black nits busily crawling into hair, nostrils, mouth, ears, and biting wherever they found
bare flesh. The whole valley had an unfriendly atmosphere and
momentarily I realised that for those who had not the eye of faith,
as I had, the Darrans might not be making a favourable impression.
Leader Creek and the lower part of the Age were just visible and I
pointed out with enthusiasm where we had been the year before. Bob
spat out a sandfly. "It's terrific," he said, determined to be loyal.

"It isn't like the Matuki is it?" suggested Stru hesitantly.

"No bloody wonder the peaks aren't climbed," added Paul, bringing the conversation to a close, and there was a long silence broken
only by the swatting of sandflies.

"Well, I guess there's not much point in standing about round
here," I said, and as no one disputed this we set off across the flats,
forded the river, and settled down for the night in Dave's Cave.

On the following day, leaving behind us a cache of food to be picked
up later, we moved up to the head of the main valley. More and more
I saw the valley through the eyes of the others and up here, I realised,
the scene was utterly desolate. To compare it with Cleft Creek, as I
saw it that first morning, was like comparing winter with summer.
And though I pointed this out, I was aware that the place looked
irremediably dark and gloomy. The floor of the valley, cramped by
the walls of the big cirque, was littered with straggly vegetation,
avalanche debris and boulders, and a drizzle of rain still fell from a
grey sky.

"Let's quit sunbathing and find the bivvy," suggested someone,
and we dropped our packs and began looking over the likely boulders.
Pawnbroker's Bivvy was discovered by Roland Rodda in 1949 on a
trip to Ngapunatoru Pass; it can be identified, he wrote, by "its tus-

sock-bearing top, on which three flax bushes are prominently arranged like the pawnbroker's balls". The description was accurate enough, for under the overhang of a large rock bearing three flax bushes, we found a dry rock platform, clearly man-made. The platform was too small for four of us and we enlarged it: in my diary I find the bald entry, "While enlarging bivvy, hit Bob in back with rock and squashed aluminium plate."

That evening after the usual meal of rice and bacon-stew, we sat in our sleeping-bags talking about the peaks we hoped to climb and what we had seen of the Grave Couloir. It was quite black outside and apart from the patter of light rain there was no sound. It was not silent a century ago for then the Westland valleys were alive with ground-birds, kakapos, kiwis, wekas, "screeching and yelling like a lot of demons". Even when the West Coast explorer, Charlie Douglas, wrote this nearly a hundred years ago, their numbers had been decimated by cats, dogs and weasels, and now the valleys are silent. Or so we thought. But we had just blown out the candle and curled up for the night when from the blackness outside came a mysterious noise, a scratching, and rustling of leaves. "It's a kakapo," I thought, suddenly awake. We were all sitting up by then, Bob fumbling for a torch: the beam lit up the boulders, the thicket of wet scrub, the rotting leaves—and unconcernedly scratching about amongst them, a kiwi. He was grey, larger than I had imagined kiwis were and he had small beady eyes. Around the root of his beak was a growth of whiskers which gave him a seedy unshaven look and he moved jerkily, probing the leaf-mould and turning it over, snuffling through his long nostril-tipped beak as he did so. Even if there was no thrill of pride as we watched our national emblem—"the Kiwi's intelligence is on about the same level as a spider," wrote Charlie Douglas, and ours certainly looked stupid enough—he was fascinating to watch as he scratched around, quite undisturbed by the spotlight turned on him.

The next day and the next it rained hard, but late that evening the clouds lifted, and for the first time we could look south and see the full length of Tutoko Valley. We were optimistic about our chances of climbing Grave Couloir, but when the dawn came, though patches of watery blue sky showed through, the wind was still westerly. Should we take a chance on the weather and make a dash for Ngapunatoru Pass? We hesitated for a while but eventually, spurred on mainly by Bob's enthusiasm, we decided to give it a go.

Grave Couloir splits the Tutoko cirque in exactly the same way as the cleft of Cleft Creek divides the rock wall there, but with the important difference that the Grave Couloir, 4,000 feet of it, is filled with snow from top to bottom. When Grave made the first ascent in 1897 he and his three companions knew almost nothing about climbing on snow and ice. They had lost some of their equipment in transit, and their ice-axes had been improvised at Milford, "from a couple of oars and some old augers, fossickers' picks, files and a gun barrel". It must have been an exciting climb: "Crevasses and ice bridges now became more numerous. Being unskilled in mountaineering, we found the rope often a source of danger, and used it only when we had to. We were thus moving along, unroped, close under the cliff, near-ing the top of the couloir, when we heard a crack. There was a cry of 'Avalanche!' Each of us started to rush away from the wall, but after the first step or two, to our horror, Gifford slipped, and shot rapidly down towards the crevasses below. After going down sixty yards he received a momentary check, managed to get his axe into the ice, and thus stayed his headlong course. We had forgotten the avalanche in our excitement. It was, however, a small one. We moved no more after this unroped."

For us, the snow of the couloir was in perfect condition, neither too soft nor frozen, and we moved steadily up, at 1,000 feet an hour; the occasional rock came whirring past, bounding from side to side of the couloir, but we had little difficulty dodging these. By midday we were on top in a gathering storm. On the far side a snow slope dropped away into the mist—nothing else was visible.

Should we go back? None of us was happy about advancing into a nor'-wester with no clear idea where the route lay. Nor were we will-ing to waste a morning's hard work by returning. Squatting in the shelter of a crevasse we brought out some food and waited for a break in the clouds. Briefly the mists divided and there was the view we needed: the snow slope led into an ice-fall, heavily crevassed in parts, but with a route through it; and above the icefall was a smooth slope which, we knew, was Ngapunatoru Pass. Up there we would build our snow-cave.

We roped up and headed into the ice-fall. We knew the general direction of our route but not the details. Blindly we wound amongst the crevasses, sometimes finding a good lead, sometimes ending in a slot-bound cul de sac from which we would retreat, using fleeting breaks in the cloud to find a better route. Late in the afternoon we were above the crevassed area climbing steadily up a featureless snow slope. We were tired and moving slowly. One of us would take the lead, kicking steps methodically with what energy he could muster, then step aside to allow the next to take his turn. The wind blew at our backs; there was nothing to be seen but mist and snow merging into an amorphous grey-whiteness. It had a dream-like quality, for we seemed to be leaving behind us that more substantial world of rivers and forest, to enter another where there was only a great snow plateau enveloped in mist. With the cold, a numbness came over our senses: eyes refused to focus on the blur of greyness all around us, sounds became curiously muffled and our speech came out hesitant and slurred—it was as I imagine the world must seem to a man dying of exposure.

Once the clouds broke apart and we saw clearly into the oncoming storm. There, below us, were the snow slopes and crevasses we had toiled through, and beyond them, far below, the upper reaches of a valley with two grey lakes amongst the rock and tussock; across the valley was a snow-covered peak, and beyond it a glimpse of a leaden sea. But these were dwarfed by the swelling storm clouds ponderously rolling in; above those few insignificant folds on the surface of the earth they rose, tier upon tier, grey and black, vast, billowing, like ships under full sail driving before the wind. In a few minutes the clouds had closed round us and we turned again to the snow slope before us. It rose more gently now and at length we were on to the plateau. We had reached Ngapunatoru Pass—now for the snow-cave. We trudged on, interminably it seemed, and then abruptly the snow dropped away steeply at our feet—the situation on a lee slope was ideal and with barely a word, a glance at the time (now 6 o'clock), we started digging.

On a fine day with time to spare, snow-caving is a satisfying occupation, akin to bivvy-building. One lazes in the sun watching the digger disappearing slowly into the snow slope and lending a hand as one's conscience bids. In bad weather, however, it is a miserable business, and doubly so in the dark. We took turns at digging, one man at the face cutting out blocks of snow with the shovel, another behind him disposing of the debris, and the other two shivering in the background. First came the entrance tunnel, six feet of it, but even that was not finished before the last of the daylight faded. Stru dug a niche beside the working-face and placed in it a candle, its flame burning straight and clear in the sheltered air, and glowing out into the night from the depths of the tunnel. Then we started on the sleeping chamber by levelling out a platform at waist height. After three hours we'd had enough: the sleeping bench was still too small, the roof too low and not domed as it should be to run water to the side, but we were past caring. We laid out air mattresses, brewed soup, hot jelly and cocoa, and dropped into the sleep of exhaustion.

Once I woke during the night and noted that snow caves are not as warm as they are said to be. The others were breathing heavily with a rhythmical waxing and waning known medically as "Cheyne-Stokeing". I knew of this, for it is common enough at high altitude, but we were a long way short of Himalayan altitudes and it sounded sinister. I listened to Bob: first a slow increase in the depth of his breathing, then a falling away, and then, for a few seconds, nothing at all—it was as if he had just died; but soon he was away again, repeating the rhythm. I struck a match to see if there was anything blocking the entrance but after flaring momentarily it went out. Obviously there was no surplus of oxygen in the cave—but I took comfort from assurances I had read that nobody in snow caves dies of suffocation.

When I woke next morning the cave was light. Our bags were wet from the condensation of our breath, from rubbing against the walls and from water dripping off the roof. I crawled out of my bag, put on a pair of sandshoes and looked down the entrance tunnel: at the end of it was a pile of fresh snow—no wonder we were short of air! Through it I pushed an ice-axe so as to see what was happening outside. There was three feet of it, and at the end of the long oval peep-hole left by the shaft was only a misty whiteness barely distinguishable from the snow itself; and when I had cleared the entrance I emerged into a soft, still world of falling snow, white and featureless.

A rest day would do us no harm anyway: there was the reshaping of the cave to be done, enlarging the sleeping bench, doming the roof, and digging out a cooking bench. When that was completed there was little else to do but climb into a sleeping-bag and fill in the time as best we could, reading, talking or eating. Snow-caves have their advantages—they never blow away, for instance, as a tent can—but in the course of nine days on Ngapunatoru Pass I developed a distaste for them which I have never quite overcome. There is a clamminess about them that cannot be dispelled, and the cold seems to penetrate every bone; my toes went numb and though they were never close to freezing, it was months before normal sensation came back to them. Some enthusiasts claim that a snow-cave warms up with a few people inside, but ours remained exactly two degrees above freezing (we had a thermometer) except when the primus was burning, when it might temporarily creep up a few degrees. One virtue they have—there is always plenty of light. By day the entrance tunnel lets in all the light one needs and at night a couple of candles will light a whole cave; the snow walls reflect and diffuse the light, coldly white during the day, but at night, by candlelight, a warm glowing yellow.

The day passed slowly in talking, reading, trying to warm our feet. We all had the same sleeping-bags, a brand known as "Twenty Below" —and Paul, after a cold night, announced the reason: "because that's what they feel like". Stru told us a dream of the previous night; that he had been climbing the north face of the Eiger with a piton in each hand as a claw, but when asked to repeat the climb he had lost his way in a town. The conversation drifted from mountains, to yachting in the Hauraki Gulf, to sunny memories of tramping down Waitakere creek-beds with the sound of surf in the distance.

The second and third days in the cave were like the first, with snow falling steadily and by then there was four feet of new snow outside. on the fourth morning, when I repeated the ritual of pushing the ice-axe through the snow drift across the entrance, I saw a small oval of brilliant blue sky. With a whoop of delight I seized the shovel and in half a minute was standing outside in the sun. It was like seeing a film abruptly switch from black and white to colour, a miraculous world of brilliant blues and greens and dazzling white. The bivvy faced north; at our feet was the apex of the Darrans triangle, a net-work of dark-green forested hills and valleys, bounded east by Lake McKerrow and the Hollyford, and west by the sea. To the north-east were more distant ranges, a pattern of mountains stretching to the horizon. And now I could see what sort of a site we had chosen for our cave. The crest of our slope, as we knew already, was thirty feet above, but we hadn't realised that the foot of it was only twenty feet below. The slope ran down to a foot-wide ledge of rock—and then nothing. I walked down and peered over the edge with growing astonishment, for we had camped on the brink of the sheerest rock wall in the Darrans, 2,000 feet of vertical granite, grey and mossless and seamed with fine cracks.

And there was yet another surprise, for when I turned and climbed up to the plateau I saw to the south-east a great peak whose appear-ance was utterly strange to me. Rising from a big névé it presented a rock face buttressed by four ribs sweeping to a summit tower which projected upwards like a thumb. It could only be Tutoko, but I had seen no photo from this side and there was a startling contrast between this elegant face of rock and the hoary ice-face I had seen from Turner's Bivvy.

We spent most of the morning outside the cave, drying clothes and sleeping-bags. Then we climbed up to the plateau, which is bounded by three small peaks, scarcely higher than the surrounding snow. The nearest, which was unnamed and unclimbed, was barely fifty yards from the cave; having disposed of this we ambled south across the plateau—a ski-plane could land there with ease—to Paranui. The pros-pect was not perfect, for towards the sea a bank of cloud was building up and there was a light breeze coming in from the west. As we returned cloud was gathering and by evening it was raining.

Throughout the following day, our fifth in the cave, we were con-fined by the weather; but on the morning of the sixth the clouds melted away. Again we spent the morning thawing out in the sun. And then we looked about us for a climb. There was only one possibility so late in the day, a 5,000 foot virgin peak to the north-west on the divide between the Kaipo and Harrison Valleys. With a rope and a few pitons, we climbed down 2,000 feet from the plateau and set off along the broken rock ridge on which our route lay. We ran along the easy stretches, leaping from boulder to boulder and slithering down small gullies. The rock was dry, warm in the sun and so rough that our rubber soles gripped as though riveted to it— two hours of sheer delight! After building a cairn on the summit we returned to the cave. Before leaving the plateau I took a last look around. Out west the sea had a metallic gleam, and the snow about me, patterned by the wind, was gilded by the setting sun. Tutoko glowed warmly brown, the fresh snow already melted from its rocks. But over its summit a hump of storm cloud was forming, and as I turned back to the cave I felt a breeze blowing softly on my face from the north-west. The omens were bad.

There was no snow in the entrance next morning: it was wider than it had been and the tunnel shorter, for a warm insistent rain was blowing in from the north-west dissolving the new snow. The rock ledge below was widening and awash with water draining off the plateau; I could imagine how the rivers would come up after a few hours of this. I shrugged my shoulders—there was nothing we could do about it anyway.

By midday we had to do something. The snow was being washed away at an unbelievable rate; a few more hours and we'd have no roof over our heads. Retreat to the Grave Couloir was hardly to be thought of in a nor'-wester, and the only alternative was more digging. We set to work heaping more snow over the vulnerable part of the roof till we felt confident it would last through the night. But by morning it was nearly all gone so that only a foot of sodden snow separated us from the storm outside. Morale was ebbing fast. Water seeping through the roof soaked our sleeping-bags and there was only a day's supply of food and fuel left. We sat in silence, hunched in our sleeping-bags, and brooded on the alternatives. There was no easy way out, that was clear to all of us, and at the back of our minds was the uneasy feeling that a wrong move might lead to disaster.

"I reckon we can find our way across to Grave Couloir," said Paul.

"What if we lose the route? Get lost among those slots? We might end up down the Harrison and we'd be worse off there than we are here."

"Nothing's worse than this place," said Stru with conviction. "We won't have a cave soon anyway. May as well sit on a rock in the Harrison as sit on the snow up here. You never know, we might find the route. And once we're in the couloir we're as good as home."

"I don't know. At least we're in the lee of the wind here. We can survive the rain and the cold, I'm not so sure we could survive a night in this wind."

"I'm pretty sure we won't get lost," said Bob. "Why not have a shot anyway? And if we can't make it—well, we can always come back here."

We decided to move. Subdued, we stuffed the sodden gear into our packs. Outside, though the rain had eased off, the wind was blowing harder than ever with strong gusts flinging the rain in our faces. We put on the rope and trudged up the slope to the plateau. Till then we had been in the lee of the wind, but on top the storm blew directly off the sea with no ridge or mountain between and there we felt its full force. We had not realised the terrifying power of these storms. Leaning into the wind, grey mist and rain driving at us, we began forcing our way forwards. And then a gust of wind hit us, a howling squall of flung rain that bit like hail. Involuntarily we spun away—no one could face into that—and crouched over our axes till it had passed. We turned warily and began again down the slope. But another squall hit us, and a few minutes later another, and each time we reeled away.

Could we really take this for another hour or maybe two? Would the wind have beaten us into submission before we reached the couloir? And what if we lost the route? As if in reply, out of the greyness came hurtling a gust that lifted us like leaves and hurled us against the slope.

"Let's get out of this!" I shouted—the words were lost on the wind, but there was no need of them—we turned around, frightened, and pushed on by the wind at our backs, scuttled to the shelter of the cave. There was a gaping hole in the roof. We dug farther into the slope through the back wall of the cave, and blocked in the roof with the snow we had dug. Then we piled on top more snow from outside—it might last till next day and then we could rebuild if we still had to. Cold and wet we settled back to withstand the siege. I was too disturbed even to read, nor did I sleep that night.

It was the eighth day in our cave and the last. In the grey light of dawn next morning we saw that the rain had stopped and the surrounding hills were again visible. We knew we could get out. Across the plateau we sped, down through the ice-fall to the top of the couloir; we moved as if Lucifer himself were at our heels and in forty-five minutes the 4,000 feet of the Grave Couloir were behind us.

Back at Pawnbroker's we felt like men reprieved from death. There was no wind, no driving rain or snow; how warm the air was, how green the valley, and more than anything I remember the thick smell of the earth. The only reminder of the bleak world above was a great gush of turbid water pouring from the ice-fall above the cirque, and the thunder of the river in flood. For an hour the sun shone through a break in the clouds. Stru photographed some flowers, we unpacked, cooked a meal and spread our wet clothes in the sun to dry.

I recalled how extravagant my praise of the Darrans had been. I had said that the ill-repute of Fiordland weather was a myth, I had talked of the incomparable variety of ridge, lake and valley, of warm camps in the tussock. And then I had tried to explain how there is an atmosphere about the Darrans one doesn't easily forget . . .

Well, that part of it was true, anyway.

6

SABRE AND THE CENTRAL DARRANS

seeking before all things the honesty of substance,
touch of soil and wind and rock,

A. R. D. Fairburn

THE HARVEST year was 1959. That February Phil and I traversed the Darrans from the Milford road in the south to Ngapunatoru Pass in the north. We climbed the Te Wera virgin and Tutoko, we reached Lake Turner, and on the unclimbed west ridge of Sabre we found better rock than we had ever dreamt of. Partly our success was due to fine weather. But there were other reasons too. By then we knew our mountains, the routes to them from the valleys, the passes, the bivvies. We understood the pattern of icefall, névé and rock, and found routes where two years ago we had seen none. Speed is of the essence in climbing; we travelled fast over easy country, and where the going was rough, we climbed more safely and with greater confidence.

And we learned the virtue of travelling light. Load-carrying is a penalty of New Zealand climbing, or one of its glories, according to your point of view. Often enough you have no option but to throw eighty pounds on your back and tramp doggedly into the hills carrying everything with you, but in the Darrans this is unnecessary. A camp is never more than a long day's walk from the road, provided you know the country and travel light, and we took advantage of this. We set off with a week's supplies; when we ran short, or the weather was indifferent, we walked out for more. The spells of fine weather we seized for climbing, even if the distances were long, for with sleeping-bags, billy and primus we could sleep out if the need arose. It was the difference, you might say, between trench and guerrilla warfare.

Our base depot, loaded with food, fuel, spare pitons and rope was at the Homer Huts beside the Milford road. The shore of Lake Adelaide was to be our first camp. We set off on an overcast afternoon towards the end of January, over Barrier Knob on the divide that separated us from the lake.

"Where do we camp?" I said, when we got there. We were on the edge of a tussock amphitheatre, the lake below forming the stage, a sheet of smooth, black water dammed back at its farther end by an old moraine; around us rose the walls of the cirque down which we had just climbed. Grave had been one of the first to enter the valley and on thirteen of fourteen days there had been rain or snow. "But the snow came on in earnest," he wrote of one day, "and we took shelter under a rock about 450 feet above the lake." Only three hundred yards ahead of us was a fine pair of boulders, each with a big overhang towards the lake.

"Let's have a look at them," suggested Phil, and we ambled across. The space below the lower and larger of the two had been used by deer; there were piles of droppings, a few cast antlers and a strong smell. The upper rock, however, was perfect, dry and roomy with a long view across the lake to the Central Darrans. We improved the living space, levelled the floor, constructed a fire-place with an antler as a billy-hook, built a wall across the north-western corner; with an abundance of dry wood from patches of scrub, a stream nearby and a thick mattress of dry tussock to sleep on we had all we could wish for.

We were interested in one peak only and that was Sabre. On one of our flying weekend visits to Homer Huts from Dunedin the previous year we had found ourselves in the company of a group of Invercargill climbers from the Southland section of the Alpine Club. Late on Saturday night, the party was in full swing and leaning against the mantelpiece over the fire, mug of beer in hand, was a big bluff individual whose name, we discovered, was Gerry Hall-Jones. "By God! You should have a crack at Sabre if you want something tough. There's a peak for you!"

Sabre was first climbed in 1955. After Lindsay Stewart's activities in the 1930s the Darrans were relatively quiet, but in the early 1950s the Southland Section became suddenly active. One by one, as the standard of rock-climbing was pushed higher, the few remaining virgin summits of the area fell, until of the major peaks only Sabre was left. It stands between Lakes Marian and Adelaide, in shape like a bishop's mitre, with two almost vertical faces meeting in two ridges, east and west, both formidably steep at the bottom but easing towards the summit. The west ridge appears at first glance to be the easier, but the second of two vertical steps guarding its foot had turned back an attempt on it. Then Bill Gordon led the east ridge, adding Sabre to his already impressive list of new climbs. Now Phil and I hoped to climb the west ridge.

Early one morning, we packed rope and pitons and set off through the wet tussock to the cirque below Sabre. Easy ledges led up to the shelf above where a ring of snow and ice skirted the cliffs of Sabre. On crampons we climbed steadily, glancing up as our

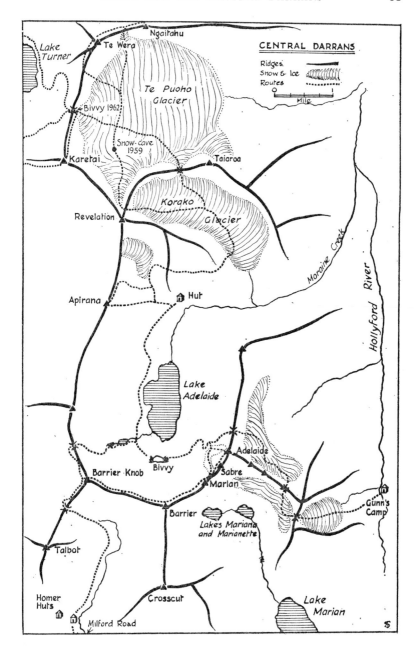

position shifted, reassessing those two guardian steps at the foot of the ridge; vertical, they looked, from any angle. Then suddenly a loud report rang out across the cirque. Somewhere close the ice was breaking. Frightened for a moment that we were on it, we both spun round to where a slab of ice was breaking off the edge. Ponderously it dipped downwards, skittered across the steepening slabs and disappeared over the edge of the cliff. A roll of thunder echoed back and forth across the valley, a cloud of snow dust billowed up, the silence returned.

We reached the col at the foot of the ridge and to see better the pattern of the rock, climbed a hundred feet up the ridge towards Marian. For a long time we looked in silence, uneasily aware that the two steps were a few grades more difficult than anything we'd attempted before. The first step was sixty feet high and split by a substantial crack with an overhang a third of the way up; on top was a roomy platform. It was the second step that worried us. Two hundred feet of it, smooth slabs and blocks of granite seamed by a network of fine cracks. Easy for the first forty feet but above that of a standard of difficulty which looked completely beyond us; and for artificial climbing our eight pitons would give us no more than a short start. It was 10.30. a.m. We could try anyway.

Down at the col we roped up: four favourite pitons easily accessible in a shirt pocket, hammer in hip pocket and a collection of karabiners clipped in to a waist loop. Phil settled himself in to a comfortable position: "On belay." "Climbing," I replied, to complete the ritual, and moved easily up to beneath the overhang. Crouched beneath it I hammered in a piton for a running belay. The rock angled sharply out for two feet and above it, unseen, the three-inch wide crack rose vertically. Awkwardly I wandered a hand around the overhang and leant out, my whole weight hanging on one arm. Now I could see into the crack above and explore it for holds. It was wide and smooth with no jug-handle holds to swing on, and I retreated back under the overhang for a rest. Then with the hammer slung by its wrist-strap, I leaned out into the same awkward stance, hanging from one clenched fist jammed into the crack. Two feet up was a crevice. I pushed in a piton and knocked it home, the hammer blows dull at first, but changing to a taut, rising "ping" as the rock moulded the soft iron. With the rope secured through it I swung out into space, hauled up, and jammed a boot in the crack. Now I was away on good holds clambering up to a good belay on the platform above.

"On belay," I shouted. "Climbing," came the reply, and with a grunting and muttering Phil was up to join me.

Pleased with ourselves we turned to the second step now directly above us. It seemed to have changed remarkably. Foreshortening had compressed the long slabs, apparently to half their length, the hair-line cracks seemed wider now and the angle easier. And what lovely rock it was! Rough, hard, with not a loose fragment on it. Moving together we climbed up to a good stance, forty feet out to the right. With Phil yoked up in the sort of belay that would hold a falling ox, I set to work on the problem of finding a lead.

For a start I climbed a flake of rock giving access to a ledge on the right, but this ended blindly sending me back to try a delicate traverse to the left. Treading carefully, safeguarded by a runner, I moved twenty feet to the foot of what proved to be the crux of the climb. It was a big slab rising sharply with a finger-tip crack on one side and a smooth corner on the other, like the edge of a steep slate roof. The first secure foothold was six feet up. Keyed up now I put all my strength into clinging to the rock between a finger-tip on one side and pressure through the palm of my hand on the other while feet sought desperately for friction on the slab. Four feet up I could go no farther. Was there a place for a piton? Yes, there was. A thin slip of a thing high to the right taking only half an inch of the blade, but with that, bending as I put weight on it, I had the holds I needed. A hand on it, a foot, and I was up at that tiny roughness above where I could stand in balance. And then another slab, but easier this time. Another runner, one more slab and unexpectedly, forty feet up, I found a good stance. It was a wide cleft in the rock under an overhang with room to stand. Protruding from it was the perfect anchor, a tusk of rock sticking up like the horn of a rhinoceros. From a solid belay I watched the top of Phil's head come closer as he climbed up towards me.

Now it was my turn again. A hand searching above the overhang, a solid knob of rock, and I was swinging out and up. The sun on the ridge above was much closer now. All this time we had been in shadow on the southerly aspect of the step which must be sunless most of the year. There was even vegetation in the damp crevices, little black clumps of moss and crumbly grey-green lichens. More cracks, more slabs, and fifteen minutes later I was on top of the second step, relaxing on flat and exquisitely warm rock.

The rest was going to be easy. Or so we thought. We basked in the sun and then, with the rope stowed in the rucksack, began a leisurely scramble up the big tumbled blocks that formed the ridge. By 1 o'clock the angle was easing off as we approached the summit. The ridge narrowed to a thin crest of rock—and then we saw that it wasn't all easy. Barring the way was a twenty-foot notch, easy on the summit side but smooth and overhanging on ours. I took another piton, dangled a length of spare rope from it and climbed down into the notch. It was an airy sort of place, with a shallow gully opening on to an im-mense precipice on the Marian side. Between my feet I looked down

4,000 feet into a barren cirque with a pair of turquoise lakes nestling amongst the scree. A minute later we stepped on to the summit. The air was still. Before us rose the Darrans, a cluster of peaks on whose familiar outlines we gazed lovingly. We were not weary, we had no cares about the descent; soothed by the warm air we were free to relax in the peace of that fine February afternoon.

We climbed down quickly, gathering up the fixed rope from the notch as we went and descending the two steps by double-roping in long gliding runs. From the col we chose the long way home over Marian to Barrier. Turning towards the sea we climbed over Barrier Knob and down the Gifford Crack. By nightfall we were back in the bivvy.

Before moving into the Central Darrans we needed food fuel and snow-caving gear from the depot. Back via Gifford Crack? We knew it too well already. I remembered reading of Gerry Hall-Jones' gallant attempts to short-cut the Moraine Creek track by traversing Gifford. Perhaps we might try something in that direction ourselves. East of Mt Adelaide, forming the divide between the Marian and Caples Valleys, was a string of stunted virgins, hardly worth a day's climbing by themselves, but they might provide an interesting route to the road. And besides, sorting out the topography of these forgotten corners has a fascination all of its own. Next morning, with sleeping-bags and a day's food, we set off towards yesterday's route up the cirque.

"I think I can hear voices," said Phil.

"Don't be daft," I said, and then I saw them, three figures on the scree. One doesn't expect to meet others in the Darrans and we approached these three with some curiosity. They were younger than us. The leader was Dick Stewart, just returned from a pilgrimage to worship at the shrines of the Central Darrans where his father had climbed twenty years earlier. They had even used the same tent.

Where had they been?—The Te Puoho Glacier. This was disturbing news indeed. Had they snatched our climbs only a fortnight before we got there? What had they climbed? The north ridge of Te Wera, a second ascent. High peak of Taiaroa, the first ascent. Tuhawaiki. And the east ridge of Te Wera, the south ridge, Lake Turner, the Te Wera virgin? No, those precious pieces of territory were still untouched.

Where had we been? The west ridge of Sabre, we said, trying to sound as if we did climbs like that every day. A few more words and we moved in the direction of the cirque ledges. As conquerors of the west ridge a turn of speed seemed obligatory and we scuttled up the ledge at twice our usual speed, so fast that we lost the route.

"We briefly exchanged notes," said Dick's article in the *Alpine*

An artist's view of the Darran country: Mitre Peak and Milford Sound as seen by John Buchanan in 1863

Eighty-pound loads on the Tutoko track

In the lower Hollyford Valley

Darrans Country – Leader Creek and the Age Glacier. On the left are the cliffs of Tutoko, and on the right, the bluffs leading to Turner's Bivvy

Tutoko Valley wit
snow filled Grav
Couloir behind

The great ice-face
Tutoko

In Tutoko Valley, 1958: Stru Ensor (left), Paul Bieleski, Mike Gill, Bob
Barrack

"Back at the bivvy we spent an indolent afternoon" – Phil Houghton and
Mike Gill outside Turner's Bivvy

The edge of the Ngapunatoru Plateau. Site of the snow-cave can be seen as two black dots on the extreme right

Snow-cave

Tutoko from Nga-
punatoru Pass

"You look to me as
though you're going
to fall off" – Phil
Houghton on Tutoko

Martin's Bay. The
Hollyford River runs
into the sea on the
left. Lake McKerrow
lies in front of the
main line of hills

Mountain daisy

Lake Adelaide. Sabre is the dominant peak with its west ridge on the right.
The bivvy rock is on the grass slopes beyond the lake

Lake Adelaide and the Central Darrans from the rock bivvy. Karetai (left),
Revelation, Taiaroa and Tuhawaiki are the peaks on the skyline

Above left:
Sabre – rappelling down
 the first step

Above:
 Sabre – the second step

Sabre – the notch

Te Wera (left), Ngaitahu and the Te Puoho Glacier – from Revelation

The top of the snow couloir on Ngaitahu

Madeline and Lake Turner

The Hooker Face of
Cook – Don Cowie on
front claw crampons

Bob Barrack on La
Perouse

Mt Tasman and the Grand Plateau. Syme Ridge is the right-hand ridge of the two leading up from the Plateau

Journal, "then attempted to follow them up the snow-grass bluffs to the cirque below Adelaide, but were soon left behind in a cloud of dust."

We reached the col north of Adelaide and from there for the next few hours we were in a strip of virgin country. A well-placed ledge led us quickly down a steep wall to the Caples snow-field. Above us on our right were the Caples virgins. Should we try them? No time we decided and they were easy anyway; little virtue in easy victory. And the Darrans had a secret or two to show us, for farther on we found an unmapped glacier, forming a broad easy highway down to the belt of tussock above the bush. Late in the afternoon we arrived at the collection of rough corrugated iron huts that form Hollyford Camp. Murray Gunn, in solitary residence, was just setting off to collect mail and gave us a lift to the Milford Road junction. There, under a clear sky we laid our sleeping-bags on the grass verge and soon were asleep.

The Te Puoho Glacier is the sanctuary of the Central Darrans. It faces east, a névé the shape of the new moon dropping sharply to an ice-fall poised above the Hollyford. Around the arc of the névé stands a ring of peaks: Taiaroa, Revelation, Karetai, Te Wera, and its virgin eastern outlier to which we later gave the name Ngaitahu. To see the Te Puoho one must climb close to it, for from other quarters of the Darrans it is hidden by the attendant peaks. And to reach it is a feat of climbing in itself. There is a bush-crasher's route in from the floor of the Hollyford, but the more elegant approach, a devious one discovered by Lindsay Stewart in 1936, starts from Moraine Creek. Steep bluffs lead to a slabby ledge which gives access to the Korako Glacier and from its névé a high col allows one to drop down to the Te Puoho.

Phil and I, after sleeping and reading through a nor'-wester at Homer Huts, returned to our Lake Adelaide bivvy. Already we were fitter than we had been a week ago and next day, we knew, we would need all the stamina we had. In the morning, with big loads, we set off to the foot of the Korako bluffs by way of the tussock ledges above Lake Adelaide. Sabre stood above us, its ridges etched against the sky and its superb unclimbed north buttress highlighted by the rising sun—the finest rock route in the Darrans. The bluffs were steep, the slabby ledge required great care in parts and our loads were heavy with pitons, snow-shovel and the extra fuel for melting snow: no streams, no bivvy rocks on the Te Puoho.

It was one of the hardest morning's packing I can remember; and then at midday we realised we had no idea where to move next.

"Where's the map?" I asked.

"Map?" said Phil. We emptied one pack, then the other. No map.

E

It was back at Homer Huts. Late in the day, exhausted to the point where we could barely lift our packs from the ground, we stood on a high mountain looking down into the Te Puoho, the nearest snow-cave site still a thousand feet below us. To reach it, we began climbing down a rock-enclosed snow couloir, its lower part a maze of crevasses. It was the familiar glacier game of snakes and ladders—cross three tricky snow bridges to nowhere, go back two rope lengths and start again; and I was forced to abandon a theory developed earlier that all Darrans crevasses can be crossed.

At 6 p.m. we turned the first shovelful of snow to mark the foundation of the snow-cave. It was reminiscent of that first ill-fated cave back on Ngapunatoru Pass: the time of day was the same, the climb up had been exhausting, and over the ranges to the north drifted an array of bright hogs-backs announcing a nor'-wester. At 10 o'clock we called it a day. Phil contorted himself to the shape of the half-finished sleeping bench while I stretched out in the entrance. We woke next morning to the familiar sound of water dripping on damp sleeping-bags and outside grey rain slanted in from the north-west. We passed the day quietly, shaping the cave, drying out sleeping-bags over the primus, and patching with sticking-plaster the holes burnt in the fabric in the process.

The nor'-wester turned out to be a half-hearted affair and next morning, like hibernating animals in the spring, we stumbled out of the stupefying atmosphere of the cave. Lying in the sun, thawing, we looked at the Te Puoho and its peaks, the dome of Te Wera, Ngaitahu to the east, and behind us, Karetai. There was no feeling of isolation, cut off though we were, but rather of intimacy; the peaks, small yet perfect in form, rose cleanly from an immaculate snow-field. Well, where should we start? The east face of Te Wera and its unclimbed ridges were tempting—but first Ngaitahu.

There was a couloir running up between the two peaks, rock below, snow above, steep but direct. Gathering together some climbing gear, we walked across to it. The lower part was an unhealthy sort of place, an avalanche fan pock-marked by stone-fall leading to glazed rock on which ice clung precariously. The central part of the couloir was out of the question but there was a route on the rock beside it. I stepped uneasily across the yawning gap between peak and névé, then I was clinging to the rock on fingers and toes. Cold and apprehensive I was awkward at first, but then I had the feel of it and moved more easily. Higher, above the broken ice, we were on snow and the sun was slanting down the couloir, lighting the patterned surface. We climbed to the col and from there, on easy rock, to the summit.

With whetted appetites we turned to Ngaitahu's big brother, Te Wera, on the other side of the col. The east ridge looked like a day's work but we knew by now that the face-on view of a climb is the most dramatic and that only by laying hands on the rock do you know its difficulties. Nevertheless time was running short—it was 3 o'clock—and the way home was long. Back at the col we picked up the ruck-sacks we had left there and started along the toothed crest of the ridge. A delectable little move up a six-foot step added interest but there-after we moved together on shattered rock with an abundance of holds. At 5 o'clock we were on the summit of Te Wera. A moment of in-decision while we looked at the choice of return routes. The virgin south ridge was the shortest and most direct. It was the most difficult too but our blood was up and we set off. Smooth unbroken rock curved steeply down, delightfully exposed, and with just enough holds for steady, rhythmic climbing. A final long rappell dropped us on to the névé as the last of the light was fading on the hills to the east.

There were hogs-backs on the hills too and for two days a nor'-wester kept us in the cave. As always after those cheerless days of rain and wind, the first fine day came like a miraculous rebirth. We packed up and crossed the névé to the col between Karetai and Te Wera. Two thousand feet below was Lake Turner, set about by cliffs except to the north where the outlet tumbled 1,200 feet into Cleft Creek. The rock face below us was almost vertical but slanting diagonally down to the right was a remarkable ledge first used by Lindsay Stewart on his climb of Te Wera in 1937. We followed this to a point a thousand feet above the lake feeling elated, for no one had been to it before. I looked more closely into a tiny secluded valley on the eastern shore of the lake: it was snug down there, a green-gold flat with tussock, and under the grey cliffs were a few big boulders. What a place for a bivvy rock! With the zeal of a prospector after gold, I climbed down the bluffs.

Even for the Darrans that valley was remote. I found no bivvy rock, but that hardly mattered. I stood on the edge of the lake, inexpressibly glad to be there; a breeze rippled the water and beyond it, through fine-weather mist, the ice-face of Madeline shone. There was no hurry either, for we knew the route to Turner's Bivvy well enough. I ambled over low cliffs separating the valley from the lake outlet where Phil was sun-bathing and there we had lunch beside the stream which a hundred feet farther down formed the Turner Falls. I found a piece of pink quartz as a souvenir, we lay in the sun for an hour and then it was time to move. Traversing north we climbed Tarewai and by evening were glissading down snow-slopes to Turner's Bivvy.

At Turner's after being assaulted by yet another nor'-wester, we went out to the road for more food. We were walking across the

Tutoko flats, enjoying the sun and thrashing at sandflies when out of
the scrub half a mile ahead appeared two figures. Just as we were
muttering darkly about the Darrans being swarming with people that
year, Phil recognised them: Ian Cave had been at school with Phil
and John Nicholls had worked in the Freezing Works with him. Ian
had a lean, restless look, and obviously meant business wherever he
was going. He had the build of a rock-climber, I thought, and as I
discovered later, could travel like the wind over any sort of mountain
country—three weeks earlier he had completed a solo traverse of
Malte Brun in four hours, a remarkable time by any standards. John
was on his first trip in the hills and seemed uncertain as to what was
going to happen to him. As he said later, if he'd known he might not
have been there.

"Where are you off to?" asked Phil.

"Tutoko," replied Ian, "up Grave Couloir."

"But where are you going to camp?" I asked.

"Pawnbroker's," he replied.

"But you can't climb Tutoko like that," I said. "It takes two days
from there and Grave Couloir's got so much ice in it now, you won't
get up!"

"I was up there a month ago," said Ian. "We'll make it."

I doubted it, but I was impressed. "Good luck," we said. "See
you later."

"That's a pretty crazy sort of idea," I remarked to Phil after we'd
left them.

"No crazier than some of ours," he replied, and we left it at that.
In two hours we reached the Milford Road and from the Tutoko
bridge hitched a ride back to Homer Huts. Loaded with supplies, we
drove back next morning in Doodle, and by evening were back at
Turner's.

The next climb was Tutoko, the south-east ridge, the one that had
alarmed us from a distance two years earlier. What a difference those
two years had made. Now we examined the three buttresses with an
almost professional eye and knew we could climb them. A strong
party had made the first ascent in 1956: Gerry Hall-Jones and Lloyd
Warburton from Invercargill and two Americans, Irvin and Robinson.
I had met Irvin and Robinson on the Aspiring trip, a week or two
after they had left the Darrans. Irvin responded well to an audience
and I listened, fascinated, to his tales of extraordinary cliff-hanging
feats in the Rockies. It was the sort of climbing I aspired to myself.
Nor was it simply idle talk for in the course of a season Irvin, Robinson and Hamish McInnes, between them picked the eyes of the best
unclimbed rock routes in the Southern Alps. Their opinions had a
ring of truth about them. Pitons, not entirely respectable in New

Zealand climbing circles then, were as fundamental to climbing equipment as an ice-axe; the rope was an impediment on easy rock if not an
instrument of suicide. The argument lost some of its force when
Robinson nearly fell to a lonely death while climbing unroped on the
Cook ice-cape, but there is truth in it nevertheless. On New Zealand
rock-climbers Irvin commented dryly, "You boys have got a lot to
learn!" and of the rock itself, "Rotten—except for the Darrans."

In the *Alpine Journal* Robinson wrote of Tutoko "this was among
the finest mountains any of us had been privileged to climb on," so
we knew that a climb of the south-east ridge would be a good one.
To reach the foot of it is a problem in itself for the two alternative
routes are both steep: either along the broken rock ridge from Turner
Pass or across a steep snow traverse below it. That season, when Phil
and I set out on our climb of Tutoko, we had no alternative for the
snow traverse was split open by crevasses. As we climbed along the
approach ridge we were brought to a halt by a fifty-foot drop, beyond
which rose the first buttress of the south-east ridge.

"We'll have to double-rope down this one by the look of it," I said.

"And do the Indian rope-trick when we come back?" replied Phil.
"Let's see if we can climb down it."

And so we started on the most difficult pitch of the day, climbing
separately, unroped. I found myself squatting on a small ledge, unable to move, looking across at Phil who was balanced on three small
holds searching desperately for a few more. "You look to me as
though you're going to fall off," I remarked. But we reached the col
in safety, roped up, and set to work on the ridge proper. The lower
part consists of three steep rock buttresses linked by snow; above this
a snow ridge continues, eventually running in to a big snow-face
below the summit. We found the first buttress steep but not difficult
with a variety of routes to choose from, ours being a broad crack with
ample room for jamming fists and feet. The second buttress was
easy—with "bomb-proof belays" wrote Robinson. And the third
gave us the sweetest climb of all. Then we were on crampons, making
fast time up steep snow. By midday we were on top.

Mist blew over while we ate lunch, and we decided to return to
Turner Pass by way of the north-west ridge and Donne Glacier—the
route used by Turner on his first ascent. Suddenly Phil said, "There
are some more people on this mountain. Over there on that shoulder."

More people! But of course. Cave and Nicholls. "About this
time the cloud rushed in and we heard voices discussing the state of the
Grave Couloir," wrote Cave later. Nicholls, who was in a rapidly
advancing state of exhaustion, claimed that this was a sign from heaven
that they should turn back, but a few minutes later, through a gap in
the cloud, they caught sight of Phil and me on the ridge opposite.

"Where did you camp last night?" asked Phil.

"Pawnbroker's." Pawnbroker's! Trying not to sound surprised I asked which was their route down.

"South-east ridge," said Ian.

"It's steep, you know."

"We've got plenty of rope."

"Think you'll make it tonight?"

"No. But we've got sleeping-bags. Do you think you will?"

"Should do. See you tomorrow at Turner's."

Late in the afternoon we were off the rock and wandering happily down the great névé of the Donne. A big crevasse splitting the glacier from side to side gave us a lively half hour but other than this I remember only an unreal green light glowing through cloud on the distant peaks of the Olivines. At 9 o'clock, after stumbling in the dark over the avalanche fans under the hanging seracs of the Madeline ice, we crawled in to the bivvy. Before going to sleep we looked up at the shadowy bulk of Tutoko—where were the other two?

The weather stayed fine. Outside the bivvy next morning, we lay in the grass, reading or dozing in the sun. Midday. Still no sign of Cave and Nicholls. Unwillingly we began to face the possibility that something unpleasant might have happened: an easy ridge for two exhausted climbers to fall off; or had they lost the route and now were wandering through the bluffs and ice-falls of the Age? At 2 o'clock there was a shout, and there they were, coming around the last bluff only fifty yards away. While we brewed tea they gave us an account of the climb—1 a.m. start, hard ice up the middle third of the Grave Couloir, a first ascent of the south ridge of Paranui in passing. And then Ngapunatoru Pass with cloud blowing in from the west, the long traverse to the foot of Tutoko, the climb of the peak itself, and their encounter with us. After roping down the first buttress they had hollowed out a sleeping-bench between snow and rock. And finally, the long trek back to Turner Pass that morning, with our tracks to lead them to the bivvy.

Turner's is a good place to relax. John washed in the stream and tried to forget the less pleasant hours of the climb, or those which he could still remember; we sat back, watching the sun sink towards the horizon and talking about our plans. Where were we going next? We pointed west across Tutoko's south ridge to where the black north wall of Grave was silhouetted. That was it, the grand finale to the season's climbing.

Another 5 a.m. start and this time we carried sleeping-bags, primus and two days' food. We had fifteen miles of climbing ahead of us: over Turner's Pass again to the Donne Glacier, across Ngapunatoru Pass, up Grave, and finally a traverse of Barren Peak to Milford

Hotel. It was an ambitious plan but never before had we been so fit and we prided ourselves on having mastered the art of fast travelling on this sort of country.

Ten minutes after leaving the bivvy we were nearly knocked into the Age. To save time, we were using a route across a fan of avalanche debris beneath the Madeline plateau, bluffs below and hanging ice above. It was still half dark but we could see the fan immediately ahead. Then from above, came the terrifying sound of ice breaking loose. Frozen in our tracks we peered through the gloom at huge blocks of ice bounding past like wool bales and leaping over the bluff. As the dust settled we were running across, stumbling amongst the broken ice.

Two hours later we were on the Donne Glacier in bright sunlight— we were making good time. "There's a deer up there," said Phil— "No it's not, it's a chamois!" Crossing the névé, close to the route we had used two days ago, a chamois was bounding over the snow as if intent on climbing Tutoko. Apart from keas and rock wrens, it was the first wild life we had seen since leaving Moraine Creek.

At 11 o'clock we were approaching Ngapunatoru Pass, but now a fresh wind was blowing in our faces and the pass was disappearing into thickening mist. A crevasse forced us far to the right until, in the mist, we had lost our bearings completely. But suddenly we found ourselves on the brink of a great rock wall—the precipice above which a year ago we had built a snow-cave. At midday on Paranui the rain began, driven by a cold wind—no storm yet but it must surely be the beginnings of a nor'-wester.

"I think it's time we went home," I said.

"I think you're right," replied Phil. In forty minutes we had left 4,000 feet of Grave Couloir behind us; we were on our way home. It was a case of ending not with a bang but a whimper. But Grave was not essential—Sabre, Tutoko, Te Wera, Lake Turner. It had been a good season.

7

THE COAST

the sea snores on the shingle, boils lazily among the rocks.
A. R. D. Fairburn

NOT ALL our trips were devoted so exclusively to mountaineering.
There was the coastline too, and for three years we used our August
vacations to tramp down the Hollyford to the sea. August is the end
of winter and too cold for climbing; there is too much snow in the
hills and the days are short. But August is also the beginning of
spring with sharp clear days and few storms.

Martin's Bay, where the Hollyford joins the sea, is a bewitching
place. We saw it from the summit of Madeline on that first Christmas
trip in the Darrans in 1957. There was the Hollyford, twisting from
side to side of its bush-floored valley, with the Pyke River joining it
lower down. The river runs into Lake McKerrow, twenty miles long,
its dark waters caught between the mountain walls. Swamp and
sand-dunes separate the lake from the sea. The outlet river coils
sluggishly for a mile or two through swamp, runs north behind the
sand-dunes of Martin's Bay, and where it strikes the rocky northern
headland it turns out to sea over a perilous sand-bar. North of
Martin's Bay is Big Bay.

One of New Zealand's mad pioneering ventures was an attempt in
the 1870s to establish the settlement of Jamestown on Lake McKerrow,
using the lake as a harbour. "Town" sections were sold and fifty-acre
"country" blocks for farming. From the beginning the project was a
failure. The first boat with settlers and supplies ran aground in the
outlet; later, boats were lost at sea, men were drowned in the great
floods that sweep down the valley or were lost in the bush. The
promised road to Queenstown was never started and the mail and
boat services were slowly withdrawn. Within ten years only a few
of the original settlers remained, and soon only the MacKenzie family
was left. The remnants of their homestead at Martin's Bay and some
grass flats grazed by wild cattle and deer are all that are left of those
early times.

We first discovered the delights of the coastal area in August 1957.

There were three of us, John Kent, a fisherman, Bob McKegg, a climber, and me. We began with a short but arduous trip into the triangle between Lake McKerrow on one side and Lake Alabaster and the Pyke River on the other. This was the Skippers Range, some tussock-topped hills which appeared on the map as a blank marked "unexplored". From Lake Alabaster we had forced a route up through thick bush and scrub to the open tops, where we found a small lake and mobs of tame deer. It was no great feat of exploration—no doubt deer-stalkers and prospectors in search of gold had been there before us—but we were pleased with what were, for us, discoveries.

We returned to Lake Alabaster with the idea of tramping out to the coast, by walking to the head of the Pyke, and from there carrying on to Big Bay. This was the round trip used by Davy Gunn with his tourist parties. There was a well-formed track then but by 1957 it was overgrown in parts. Shortly after leaving the Pyke we lost our way and when darkness closed in we were in the depths of a tangle of bush-lawyer and supple-jack with swamp on either side and no idea what lay before us. Laying our sleeping-bags on a bank of dry mud we fell asleep with the sound of the distant sea in our ears.

Next morning, as we struggled deeper into the swamp, the supple-jack gave way to flax and rushes. Pools and channels of stagnant black water separated islands and floating rafts of rotting vegetation.; around them glided big eels, vanishing in a puff of mud as we splashed past. We could still see no farther than twenty feet ahead and when at length we came to an isolated tree I scrambled up for the view. It was an extraordinary scene. There was water all around us—except behind where a tongue of vegetation had led us out into the centre of the lagoon which now surrounded us. The map had shown none of this! What a place for eels to breed, or ducks, or whitebait.

We might have been worried at landing ourselves in such a place but the day was too fine for that. Swamp water it was, maybe, but the blue sky glittered back from its surface and the water plants glowed green as an emerald. We set off across the lagoon, with mud to our knees and water to our thighs. Fortunately it was nowhere deeper than this and in twenty minutes we were emerging on the far side. As we were wading across John looked critically at my long thin white legs protruding from the mud: "You'd better not let the white-baiters see those, Mike," he said. For at Big Bay, we knew, there were fishermen. Once out of the swamp we were in beech forest. Winding through it was a slow shallow river which we followed and an hour later we rounded a corner to find two men ahead of us, bending over as they worked at fish-traps in the river. Steadily we splashed on till one of them heard us and turned round.

They were well set up. Just behind the dunes overlooking Big Bay they had a comfortable hut, and in the near-by river they were netting huge quantities of whitebait. The adult fish live in swamps and lagoons such as the one we had crossed, and in autumn run down to the sea where they lay their eggs close to the water's edge. With the next spring tide the larvae emerge and are carried out to sea where they grow into a small transparent fish. These are the whitebait which run back up the river in the spring, shoals and shoals of them wriggling against the current until they reach the still waters of the lagoon. In the old days, the west coast rivers were so full of them that farmers netted them on to their fields as fertiliser. Now their status has risen and those who fish good rivers such as that at Big Bay can live for a year on the profits of a three-month season.

Very likely the white-baiters are the only people who have made money out of Big Bay. About 1870, and again in 1886, there was a gold rush at the bay but the strikes had not been substantial enough to keep men there though there was one old hermit, Maori Bill, who lived at Big Bay for forty years. The receding tides of the Maori Wars and the Otago goldrush left behind them a residue of adventurers and social misfits, a few of whom lived in isolation along parts of the West Coast. Sutherland at Milford Sound was one of them. Charlie (Mr Explorer) Douglas, most entertaining of mountain writers, was another. And Maori Bill at Big Bay belonged to the same vanished breed. Rumour said that he had killed an officer in the Maori Wars, but whatever the reason, he spent the last half of his life by himself, subsisting on eels, fish, and birds caught by his dogs, until at the age of ninety he was taken away to die in an old men's home in Hokitika.

Later Davy Gunn ran cattle down to the coast from his homestead in the upper part of the Hollyford. And then, as if cattle were not trouble enough, he built a string of huts to take tourist parties down to Martin's Bay and Big Bay. Davy met the seemingly inevitable end of the Hollyford pioneers: in 1955 while crossing the river which was in flood his horse stumbled and he was drowned. An attempt was made to muster Gunn's cattle, then running wild in the bush, but that too ended in a drowning tragedy near the Hollyford bar.

Now there is fresh activity. Davy's son Murray runs his father's homestead and its surrounding huts as a sort of bush motel, known as Hollyford Camp. The Fiordland National Park Board has taken over much of the area, building huts and clearing tracks. A new tourist venture, a "luxury" tramp from Martin's Bay to Hollyford Camp has been started. And meat-hunters with their jet-boats, helicopters and aeroplanes have invaded the valleys. A few more years no doubt will see a road through to the coast, with water-skiers on Lake McKerrow and motels at Martin's Bay.

But in 1957 we found the coast almost deserted. At Big Bay, after sleeping out on the sand dunes, we called on the white-baiters, partly to say goodbye, partly because our own attempts at white-baiting had been a failure. Generously they offered us eggs, fresh vegetables—but no fish. A few hints having passed unnoticed, John put it to them bluntly: "Can you spare us a few whitebait?"

"Whitebait!" said one of them, as if surprised that anyone should eat them, and he dipped out a billyful from a holding pot.

By midday we had rounded the headland separating Martin's from Big Bay. Paua shells and crimson heaps of crayfish skeletons showed where others had been drawing on the sea-life that abounds there. Martin's Bay looked superb, an open sweep of white sand with a big surf rolling in from the Tasman Sea and behind it rose foothills hiding the hinterland of the Darrans.

The rest of the trip was uneventful, but we were back the following year, Phil, John and I, with three girls, none of whom had been on a serious tramping trip before—nor since probably. There was a snow storm in the upper Hollyford and a long day along the shores of Lake McKerrow when somehow we lost each other—while I was camped beside Hokuri Creek, John was battling through the McKerrow bush a couple of miles back. Phil, meanwhile, lost in the Martin's Bay swamp, was camped on a small dry island grimly filling a hot water bottle for his companion.

Anchored in the river that year was a crayfish boat come in for shelter from the open sea. The skipper was a genial Maori, by name Billy Bragg, who was generous to a fault. I doubt whether it was Phil or John who inspired this, certainly it was not me—I suppose in all his August visits to Martin's Bay, Billy Bragg had never before seen three girls standing on the banks of the Hollyford, and his sense of chivalry prompted him to open his larder to us. There were crayfish of course, flounder, trout, eels, whitebait from the river, blue-cod from the sea, swans eggs from a nesting colony on the sand-dunes, venison from the hills, and wild beef.

Phil was impressed by Martin's Bay and later he set about acquiring land there. Almost the whole of Fiordland is owned by the State but a few properties from the original Jamestown settlement are still freehold. One by one, over a period of years, Phil tracked down owners till at length he found a piece of unwanted land, a fifty-acre block on the shores of McKerrow. The praises of this property did not go unsung—kowhais hanging over the lake, trout rising on a still autumn morning—and finally, one May, I saw the place. After a long day's trek down the Hollyford we reached the head of the lake just before dark. From there we travelled by canoe. The lake was quite still, receding towards the fading evening light in the west. Inconspicuous headlands pushed out at intervals between rocky beaches. One by one they fell astern until at length we stepped ashore to a small sandy beach. This was it.

I saw it next morning just as it had been described—the lace-like kowhais along the shore, the water smooth as silk, and the outlet much closer now. We paddled down to it to find the current, which is tidal there, running against us, but not strongly. The banks rise steeply for a short distance and the bush is thick and full of vines, with an almost tropical luxuriance. In the shallows were a few trout lazily flicking their tails and showing no interest in the lures we cast towards them. Nor did a flounder seem worried by our attempts to stun him with a paddle. Farther on, round one of the wide bends of the river, a narrow channel led off to the right. We followed down assisted by the current and found ourselves in a lagoon half over-grown by raupo and bullrushes. There was cleared land at the end of it, for it was part of the MacKenzie property, with old stumps dotted across it and rabbits running everywhere. Pulling the canoe ashore we set off towards the beach. It was not far. And just short of it, under some huge gums, were the derelict remains of the old MacKenzie homestead, still offering some sort of shelter but no longer weather-proof. Inside were a few old newspapers on the wall, a rusted cray-fish-pot, rat droppings and dry leaves. Finally we wandered down to the beach itself and along to its more sheltered southern end, the so-called boat harbour. A few miles farther on, around the headland, the Kaipo River runs down a broad valley of beech forest and tussock flats, its head-waters arising from the foot of the great wall beside Ngapunatoru Pass where we had dug our snow-cave years earlier.

But we walked no farther than Martin's Bay. Some other year perhaps.

8

INVITATION ABROAD

*Sir Edmund Hillary is looking for two young New Zealand climbers
to accompany him on his forthcoming Himalayan expedition—and
he is willing to receive applications from anyone interested.*
                              The Auckland Star, 23rd Dec. 1959.

SANTA CLAUS, I thought to myself, you are just two days early.
I dropped the newspaper, took up pen and paper and spent two hours
drafting as persuasive a letter as I could write. The age limits were
25–35. I was 22, too young, and after some consideration I decided to
give myself an extra year. Climbing qualifications: I could muster a
reasonable record of climbs new and old. "I have an ape-like build
peculiarly suited to climbing," I added. And then my trump card:
the expedition was concerned not only with mountaineering but with
physiology and I had a Bachelor of Medical Science degree in
physiology. I sealed the letter, walked the mile and a half to Sir
Edmund's home and dropped the envelope in his mail box. The
following afternoon I was called to the phone. A voice barked out
of the ear-piece at me, "Is that Michael Gill? Ed Hillary speaking. I got your letter today. What about coming up and having a
yarn."
   "Yes," I said. "Yes. Certainly. When?"
   "Well, why not come up now if you can spare the time."
   What does one wear to such an interview I wondered. Climbing
gear (yellow shirt and a pair of patched saddle tweed trousers)? Best
suit (double-breasted and five years out of date)? Within an hour I
was knocking nervously on the door. I was warmly welcomed by an
attractive and vivacious Lady Hillary who looked at me with some
curiosity as she invited me in. "We've been just dying to know what
this ape-like person looked like," she explained. It was not a very
formal sort of interview, no searching questions, no taking of notes
or requests to climb a pole as a demonstration. It was, as Ed had
said, a yarn between two mountaineers, one very unimportant, the
other famous from one end of the earth to the other. Ed explained
his objectives.

"The whole expedition's going to take about nine months but not everyone will be there for the whole of that time. For the first part we'll be sitting about at 20,000 feet with binoculars looking for yetis— I've got a few ideas about how we might find one if there is such an animal—and I reckon there must be something behind all the stories you hear. Those tracks that Eric Shipton and Mike Ward found, some sort of animal made them. That'll be in the autumn. You'll hear people getting all starry-eyed about the rhododendrons in spring but I've always found the autumn colours just as spectacular. Then we'll build a hut at 20,000 feet—I've got a good place up the Mingbo sorted out for that—and leave Griff Pugh and the physiologists to spend the winter there. I'll be coming in again in spring with a few more climbers and we'll have a crack at climbing Makalu without oxygen. I've got a theory that the blokes who winter over at 20,000 might be so well acclimatised that they'll get up without too much trouble... Sounds a pretty good sort of expedition don't you think?" and his face lit up with an infectious grin.

"Sounds fantastic," I said.

"What are you doing in the hills this season anyway?" I outlined some plans: two new climbs from the La Perouse, the north-west face of Cook, a look at the east face, and a few odds and ends.

"Don't be too disappointed if you can't manage all that lot will you. I'll let you know in a couple of months' time whether there's a place for you on the expedition. I was talking to a doctor friend and he said this B.Med Science degree is a pretty good one. Your chances should be fairly high. Anyway drop us a line how you get on down south when you're finished."

From that point on the season's climbing became a qualifying round for selection. For the first time I had to hunt around for a climbing partner. Bob and Stru were both newly married. Paul had left Auckland. Phil had elected to spend his whole vacation working in a hospital, a decision strikingly at variance with his attitude to his medical career both before and since that time. The problem was partly solved through John Nicholls, who had spent a year in Dunedin doing medicine before switching to psychology. It was John and Ian Cave whom we had met on Tutoko. "Mike's the sort of guy to climb with. He's a mad bastard," Ian had commented as Phil and I took off towards Grave. John had repeated the remark to me: I wrote away to Ian asking if he'd like to join me in an attempt on the East Face of Cook. The reply was, "Yes, but not till February."

There was still January to consider. And then one evening while I was explaining the problem to Bob Barrack in Auckland he began to warm up to the idea of one more season's climbing, a grand finale before he finally screwed his ice-axe to the wall. Soon we were drawing up food lists, examining photos of Mt La Perouse and Cook from the Hooker side, reading about ways of climbing into the La Perouse Glacier to put ourselves into a position for attempting one of the two superb virgin rock buttresses on David's Dome.

By mid-January we were at Unwin Hut, the Alpine Club's base near the Hermitage Hotel. Our route up the Hooker Glacier to Gardiner Hut was said to be badly crevassed as the result of a dry season. Underlining the difficulties was the story we heard from two climbers returning in disarray from the foot of Pudding Rock, the site of Gardiner Hut. One of them had a familiar face.

"My name's Earle Riddiford," he said and I recognised him at once; Riddiford, Hillary, Lowe and Cotter were the first New Zealand expedition to the Himalayas in 1951, and Earle was well known in mountaineering circles.

"You'll find you can't get on to the normal route up Pudding Rock because of the crevasses," he said. "We were up there the day before yesterday. Tried using the avalanche fan just south of the rock—there are bits of ice breaking off all the time but most of them get only half way down—then just as we were starting, the biggest one of the day came down. The only thing we could do was leap into the nearest slot and there were chunks of ice the size of a grand piano jumping over our heads. Well, we were a bit demoralised and decided to toss it in for the time being. Then we went back again yesterday. And exactly the same thing happened. I reckon you can't push your luck too far. Where are you two going anyway?"

"Pudding Rock," I replied, "and Gardiner Hut."

"What are you going to climb?"

"We're hoping to try the south ridge of La Perouse." There was a pause.

"Damn!" said one of them quietly. "That's what we were after, too. You should make it this season if it's possible at all. I've never seen the ice so far back from the top of the rock step so there should be less danger from falling ice. Good luck anyway." And with that we parted. Farther on we worked our way through an intricate maze of crevasses to get a foothold on Pudding Rock without coming too close to the line of fire from the ice-fall that was causing all the trouble. A piton or two and three hours' hard work brought us to the hut totally exhausted after a long day which had included the most difficult rock climbing I did all season.

A morning packing food up to Empress Hut at the head of the Hooker, a leisurely return to Gardiner and we were ready to start for La Perouse the next day. The South Ridge had achieved some notoriety over a period of years. Various parties had climbed to the foot of it but turned back because of bombardments of falling rock, or worse, of ice. The major problem was a big rock step, steep at the bottom and menaced from above by an overhanging lip of ice. But that season the ice, as Riddiford had said, was well back compared with other years and from the hut in the evening light we saw a shallow gully leading up the steep lower section.

The weather was fine when we started next morning. To reach the foot of the rock we had first to climb some steep snow. Zealously I carved a row of steps up most of it rather than rely on crampons. "We won't be doing much high-falutin' rock climbing in the Himalayas," Ed had said, "but you have to cut a lot of big steps if you've got Sherps coming up behind."

"I'll get all the practice I can," I'd promised.

Early in the morning we stood face to face with the rock. "Doesn't look too bad to me," I said. "No stone fall either for that matter." As if in reply, out of the blue came the whine and whirr of a fusillade of falling rocks. We leapt to one side under an overhang as the rocks viciously clattered around us shattering themselves to fragments. In a more sober frame of mind we roped up. "We're going to need some good belays if someone gets hit by one of them," said Bob. Anchored securely and sheltered by the overhang he wished me luck as I led off up the gully. The rock was surprisingly solid with plenty of good holds and here and there a protruding knob over which I could loop a runner; where the lead was unprotected for too great a distance, I used pitons. It was pleasant climbing, but at intervals the familiar whine came from above, rising in pitch, and a small fast-moving black speck would appear on the sky-line. But we were lucky and none of them hit us. Two rope-lengths up the angle eased off and we traversed on to a broad sloping ledge, scarred and pocked by the battering of centuries of falling rock and ice. Moving together we ran smartly across to the shelter of the second steep rise in the ridge. From that point on we were out of danger for we were to the left of the main line of fall. More relaxed now we worked our way up in leisurely fashion choosing a satisfying route from the host of cracks, ledges and gullies offering. In an hour we were strapping on crampons before starting on the winding snow crest leading to the summit; by midday we were on top. Like a big yellow fly drifting in the summer heat, a tourist plane circled lazily overhead. We had lunch and then began the descent down the well-used north ridge, a mixture of snow and rock, so crumbling, steep and unstable that by comparison the south ridge was like a buttress in the Darrans. Avalanches of rotten shale slipped away from beneath our feet, rumbling and echoing down gullies to the valleys below.

Late in the afternoon we struck down from the ridge through lines

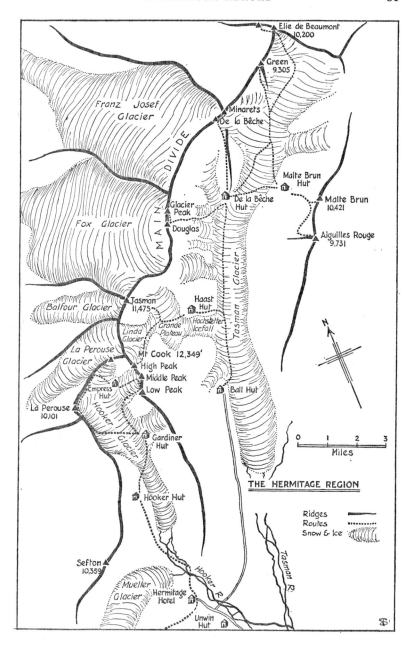

THE HERMITAGE REGION

Ridges
Routes
Snow & Ice

0 1 2 3
Miles

N

Elie de Beaumont
10,200

Green
9,305

Minarets
De la Bêche

Malte Brun
Hut

Malte Brun
10,421

De la Bêche
Hut

Glacier
Peak

Douglas

Aiguilles Rouge
9,731

Franz Josef
Glacier

Fox Glacier

MAIN   DIVIDE

Balfour Glacier

Tasman
11,475

Haast
Hut

Hochstetter
Icefall

Grande
Plateau

Linda
Glacier

La Perouse
Glacier

Mt Cook 12,349'

High Peak

Middle Peak

Empress
Hut

Low Peak

La Perouse
10,101

Hooker Glacier

Ball Hut

Gardiner
Hut

Tasman Glacier

Hooker Hut

Sefton
10,359

Mueller
Glacier

Hermitage
Hotel

Hooker R.

Tasman R.

Unwin
Hut

F

of crevasses, leaping eight feet down from the upper lip of the final schrund to reach the névé of the upper Hooker. Voices drifted down from David's Dome at the head of the valley but so distorted by echoes and muffled that we turned into the shelter of Empress Hut without discovering who or where they were. Sometime during the night there was a stumbling and clattering and the subdued voices of people coming into the hut, but we were too stupid with sleep to take any notice.

We met next morning. Leader of the party was Don Cowie, a taciturn Scot, and with him was Lyn Crawford who later did some fine climbs in the Southern Alps, Andes and Himalayas. The other two, more talkative than their Kiwi companions, were Australians. Originally Bob and I had planned an attempt on the unclimbed north-west face of Cook but the long day on La Perouse had blunted our drive. Instead we decided to join the other four on a traverse of Cook via Earle's Route. Plans changed in the early hours of next morning when the steep loose rock in the dark proved troublesome. Instead we moved farther south on to the smooth sweep of snow and ice of the west face. All went well up to the final steep ice leading to the Middle Peak, where a thin crust of snow lay over solid green ice. Here was step cutting practice with a vengeance, and I resigned myself to a few hours' hard labour. Then, surprisingly, Don Cowie appeared abreast of us, when a moment ago he had been fifty feet below. He was climbing on front claw crampons. The technique was a new one to me and leaning on my axe, fascinated, I watched a masterly demonstration: the rhythmic kick and bite of the protruding steel fangs, the swinging ice-hammer and the immaculate machine-like movement of arms and legs. Steadily he drew away from us. The sun in the east was now rising over the crest of the summit ridge, transforming the ice to a dazzling sheet of blue and pale gold. Showers of ice chips lit through like diamonds exploded into the cold air as Cowie hacked out a belay stance and placed an anchor piton.

I turned to Bob. "At this rate, they'll be back at the hut before we reach the top." Thoughtfully I looked at my well-used Grivel crampons, the points worn down to blunt stumps: ideal for rock climbing and glissading, but on ice . . . Tentatively I stepped out of the line of steps on to the untouched slope. Surprisingly the points gripped, if only just, and I began climbing upwards, cautiously at first but then more quickly. Bob enjoyed the precariousness of this technique even less than I but we were moving fast even if the safety margin was slimmer. Soon the angle eased and we moved together on to the Middle Peak.

I looked down the other side of the mountain with some interest for we had a good view of the two big unclimbed faces of Cook, the

East, and the south-east Caroline Face. In the 1950s the East Face was the Everest of the New Zealand mountaineering world, the most looked-at and talked-about climb in the Southern Alps. Speculation was finally brought to an end in November 1961 when a strong team made the first ascent: Pete Farrell, Don Cowie, Lyn Crawford and Vic Walsh. The Caroline Face is bigger and more dangerous—two people have been killed on it and Farrell and Crawford have turned back though they were then more than half way up. From the top of the Middle Peak I peered down the steep ice of the two faces and listened to the knock of rocks bouncing down—not really my sort of country I thought, even if I had arranged with Cave to try the East Face in a fortnight's time . . .

We turned south along the summit ridge, traversed the Low Peak and descended to Gardiner Hut. There, sitting outside the hut drinking mugs of tea in the last of the afternoon sun, we discussed plans for the next ten days. We looked up at the South Ridge of La Perouse, the face of Cook, at the head of the valley our route over to the La Perouse Glacier.

"It's not really a married man's country, is it?" said Bob choosing his words carefully. I looked at the big wild schrund below Harper Saddle and thought of what probably lay over the other side. "No," I said thoughtfully. "No. It's not married man's country at all."

"We've had a couple of good climbs already," Bob went on. "I think maybe I should quit while I'm still winning." There was too much good sense in this for me to disagree. And with the crevasses as open as they were, it seemed unlikely we would get in to the La Perouse anyway.

"Let's go back to the Hermitage," I said, "and think about something easier." A day later the weather changed for the worse, and I did no more climbing with Bob that season.

One evening while filling in time in the Hermitage bar I came across Barry Hayes, one of the Aussies we had met up at Empress. "I'm looking for a partner to join me on Tasman," he said. "You wouldn't be interested would you?"

I was. Tasman and Cook are the two peaks every climber feels he ought to climb, just as I imagine any European might want to climb Mont Blanc and the Matterhorn at some stage of his career. I could think of no better way of filling in a few days than a quick trip to Haast Hut and a climb of Tasman. The staff bar of the Hermitage, filled with hotel employees and the odd climber who slips in unnoticed, is a congenial place and we chatted for a long time about climbs we had done and climbing in general. Australians are coming to the Southern Alps in increasing numbers. They are keen—they have to be to travel 1,200 miles. Some are highly skilled on rock but the newcomer faces unfamiliar problems when he tackles the big ice-peaks, and the mortality rate amongst visitors at that time was high. Barry, more than most, knew of the dangers for the previous year while coming off Malte Brun, his companion, who had insisted on climbing unroped, had lost the route and fallen to his death. And that season another friend had lost his axe while glissading and been killed in a fall down some bluffs. We parted with an agreement to go together to Haast Hut.

Two days later we moved into an already crowded hut. Our route on Tasman was Syme Ridge, one of the classic ice climbs of the New Zealand Alps. It was a gift of a climb, for the day before a two-man party had been up, leaving behind them a staircase to the summit. By daybreak we were across the Grand Plateau, across the avalanche debris of the Mad Mile, and had a foothold on the ridge. It was a simple routine: up a rope length to a well cut belay-stance, pop the axe into a ready-made shaft-hole, a cry of "On belay!", and the other man was climbing up and through to the next stance. There was time to look around and appreciate the warmth of the sun. On the summit we paused to look again at the magnificent Westland valleys and névés. Of the two who had been before us the previous day there was no sign, though we knew they were along the divide somewhere, bound for Cook. For us the only route was back the way we had come awkwardly astride the steep ridge.

It was a good climb but not a memorable one. Snow is cold unfriendly stuff with none of the warmth and texture of rock, its subtlety and variety of holds. Compared with the short rock climbs and cross-country travel of the Darrans I found the long snow-routes a repetitive mechanical pastime, more akin to long distance running. Snow and ice give mountains much of their beauty, their grandeur—a peak without snow is like a clipper ship without sails—but for me snow is there simply as a convenient approach to rock.

Our climb of Tasman was the least important of the events of that week of January. The weather was fine throughout our stay and we had good company in the hut—hardly the setting for a tragedy, and yet before the week was out four of the climbers in the hut were dead. The death of two of them was not altogether a surprise, I suppose. Both of them, Tony Evans and Jim Board, were young and ambitious and they knew the difficulties of the climb they were attempting, a first traverse of the Main Divide from Tasman to Cook. Tony was from Canterbury with an impressive record of good climbs and he was strong and fit after a season as a student guide. Jim Board was a Canadian; he too was fit after a working holiday and he had the reputation of being a good rock-climber. They looked like a powerful combination but the climb they contemplated could hardly be more exacting, a long undulating snow and ice ridge which even under good conditions would have taken two days; and that season most of it was a sheet of polished ice, the result of warm weather with little snow. I remember them the night they left, lying silently in their bunks, apprehensive no doubt, while around them a dozen carefree climbers chattered happily. At 10 p.m. they left. It was their line of steps we followed on Tasman. They were seen the following day, well along the ridge, but never again.

Jim Glasgow and Harry Scott were in a different category altogether. Both were well out of their twenties. They had no hot-blooded ambitions to attempt the impossible, merely a yen to climb Cook before they finally gave up trips to the high peaks. Jim was editor of the *Alpine Journal* and widely known in mountaineering circles. Harry was known as a mountaineer too, but his reputation went further than this. He was then head of the Department of Psychology at Auckland University, and even in Dunedin I had heard of him, of his interest in student affairs, his enthusiasm and drive in building up his department and his wide interests in literature and the arts. My only memories of these two are trivial ones of Jim cutting sandwiches for his party on the night before a reconnaissance climb; and of Harry constructing a mousetrap to rid the hut of a plague of mice. Certainly the possibility of disaster ahead could not have occurred to anyone. To share the hut with them was a pleasure and when I left to meet Ian Cave down at the Hermitage it was almost with reluctance.

Ian and I began discussing plans immediately. He was fit from a trip farther south and the weather was fine—almost limitless possibilities lay before us. "Let's start with the South Ridge of Hopkins," I suggested. To get there involved a long trek south on the Mueller Glacier to the Three Johns Hut, and from there along the Main Divide several miles, until we reached Mt Hopkins at the head of the Hopkins Valley. We set off up the Mueller carrying bivouac equipment and five days' food. Throughout much of the day we heard the buzz of an aeroplane and now and again caught sight of it circling persistently around the area north of Cook—almost certainly a search for Evans and Board was starting. During the night a nor'-wester blew up and for four days it howled across the peaks and cols, a grey fury pounding and battering the corrugated iron walls of the hut, and we knew that if Evans and Board were still on the Main Divide they were doomed.

On the first fine day we raced along the warm rock of the Divide, big wild valleys on either side of us. A lunatic attempt to climb the Black Tower in passing left us slithering precariously on steepening schist slabs two-thirds of the way across the north face of Hopkins, and we returned to the Divide to continue on to a bivouac site at the foot of the South Ridge. But again the wind rose during the night and in the pale light of early morning we saw the sky flecked with high cloud and a hogs-back on the summit of Hopkins. It was no weather for starting a big climb, nor for returning the way we had come for that matter, and we resigned ourselves to a thirty-mile walk down the Hopkins Valley. From the road-head in the Lower Hopkins we hitch-hiked back to the Hermitage along dusty Canterbury back roads. Dozing amongst a heap of cameras on the back seat of the car of two American tourists, I suddenly remembered Evans and Board.

"Have you heard anything about two climbers missing on Mt Cook?"

"Yeah, yeah, I think there was something about two guys killed up there somewhere. Take a look through that newspaper behind you."

There it was on the front page: "Climbers killed on Mount Cook". And then I looked again. The names of the climbers were Harry Scott and Jim Glasgow. While forcing a route up the ice-cap of Cook in strong winds with the weather closing around them the leader had slipped; the second man on the rope, unable to throw on a belay in the icy conditions, had been plucked off and the two had vanished down the East Face.

It was the first time a climbing fatality had meant anything to me. I sat there, stunned and sickened, looking at the two names. And for the first time I became aware of another side of climbing, of its folly when it can lead to a tragedy such as this. There was I, the most casual of passing acquaintances, profoundly affected by what had happened. How many others were there I wondered caught up in the consequences of that one rash attempt to climb Cook.

And Evans and Board? They too were dead. To any better purpose, I wondered? Not really. But there was a difference, for they had known they were setting out on a difficult and dangerous climb. For them, as it was then for me, climbing was a passion more substantial than any other part of their lives. They had played for high stakes and lost. And as with Mallory and Irvine on Everest, there is romance as well as tragedy lingering over those who vanish without trace on a great mountain. It is not easy, on a climb, to draw the line between courage and folly. The weather changes, the river is high, there is a risk of avalanche, the climb is long—to turn back, is it wisdom or cowardice? There can be other pressures too. The success of an expedition may seem to depend on reaching the summit. And on a rescue operation, how much do you risk your life for another? In the mountains there is always risk, sometimes negligible, sometimes so great that the chances of survival are slim; and part of the business of learning to climb is acquiring an understanding of the dangers inherent in any situation so that each person can decide for himself how far to push his luck.

When Ian Cave and I arrived back at the Hermitage after our abortive attempt on Hopkins the search was over. Two bodies had been seen at the foot of the East Face of Cook; the other two had vanished completely. I was shaken by these events more than I would have believed possible, so much so that I contemplated abandoning climbing for the season altogether. The weather was still unsettled and even when there was sunshine around the Hermitage, up in the mountains cloud was down low on the summits, driven across the Divide by strong west winds. In such conditions there seemed little point in trying to climb so temporarily we joined the hotel staff as gardeners.

After a day weeding flower beds we were transferred to the less skilled job of maintaining the track from Ball Hut down on to the white ice of the Tasman Glacier. Each day at 8 a.m. we were driven from our quarters at the hotel up to the hut. Each morning and afternoon, lines of tourists stumbled down the track slanting across the crumbling moraine wall on which we were working. On the first day we worked hard. On the second we were joined by Hans (or was it Fritz) a handsome Austrian who had been working for the Hermitage for some time. He watched us muscling into the shovelling and boulder-rolling. "You work too hard," he said. "Do they pay you any more if you work hard? Only a bloody fool works when he doesn't have to." He pointed a thumb disdainfully back in the direction of the Hermitage. "I will show you how to work for them."

Until the morning bus-load of tourists arrived we worked quietly. Faintly in the distance we would hear the whine of the bus dragging up the hill. "Now we work," said Hans—dust rose around us and we gleamed with sweat. The tourists filed past, out on to the ice, the fat ones who puffed, the over-dressed who gave up half-way, the small boys who wandered off the track and had to be rescued before they met a terrible death down one of the sump-holes in the ice. Bringing up the rear was the massive figure of Chief Guide Mick Bowie, smiling benignly and grunting "Good morning", as he lumbered past; or some other guide looking down the slowly moving line of tourists. "Look at the peasants!" and he moved wearily after them.

When the buses had left we dropped tools and moved up to the hut for lunch and a three-hour siesta. The bus came again in the afternoon. On with our boots, a quick run down to the track, a burst of shovelling and we were ready to nod "Good afternoon" to Mick as he walked solemnly past with a slow knowing grin. The departure of the afternoon tourists marked the end of the day's work and from then till 5 o'clock we read or slept. At 6 o'clock (one hour's overtime) we were back at the Hermitage.

Confident that we could stand a week of this, we settled down to enjoy some comfortable living at the Government's expense. It was odd I reflected how we would happily drive ourselves to exhaustion each day while tramping or climbing for no financial reward at all, yet as soon as we had a paid job we devoted all our energies to avoiding work. And what a delightful place the Hermitage was to live in. The tussock flats in front of the hotel, Foliage Hill and White Horse Hill, were at their most beautiful: thick dry tussock, with fields of giant white ranunculi, and raspberry canes loaded with fruit. At the hotel we satisfied our swollen appetites with huge meals of good food and in the evenings there was the company of the staff bar.

Then one day we had a telegram from John Nicholls announcing his intention of joining us, closely followed by John himself. We collected our pay, packed food and climbing gear and set off up the Tasman Glacier for Malte Brun Hut. Despite my declared aversion to the Tasman there were some new routes worth investigating, and their virgin status was enough to overcome any scruples I might have had. There is a world of difference between a first ascent and those that follow. With repetition a climb always seems easier, for as in breaking four minutes for the mile, the first person to do it demolishes some sort of psychological barrier. But as well as the difficulties, there is an element of uncertainty, of curiosity, sometimes of fear, just as there is in exploring unknown country. A first ascent, even of a minor peak, is immeasurably more satisfying than any other.

We had no sooner reached the hut than a nor'-wester closed in and for two days we lay in our bunks being entertained at intervals by John's readings from Rabelais. When the weather turned fine we set out to attempt the virgin South-East Buttress of Mt Green. I must have been still stupefied by hut-wallowing for I remember stumbling absent-mindedly up the first rock pitch with some difficulty.

"Don't seem to be going very well today," I muttered apologetically.

"You do realise, do you," said John, "that you've still got your crampons on?"

I looked down. So I had. Higher up Ian was embracing a large boulder with a look of determination and it dawned on us that he was not trying to climb up it but simply stop it falling and annihilating us. Hastily we shifted aside while the rock went crashing down into the crevasses below. We began climbing with more care. Mid-way up the ridge was a bulge of smooth grey rock which from below we had wondered about and named variously the elephant's ear, the elephant's end, and finally the cod-piece. Even this was no real problem and by noon we were on top, idly planning new routes on to Elie de Beaumont from the Spencer.

We trudged happily back to the hut, ate well, read some more Rabelais, and finally as the sun was setting watched the hogs-backs forming in line over the Main Divide. Two days the nor'-wester blew and at the end there was a plastering of ice—the weather seemed to be establishing a pattern. We were hoping to climb the South Face of Malte Brun but after the storm there was too much ice around.

"What about a new route on Aiguilles Rouges?" suggested Ian. "I've never heard of anyone climbing that West Ridge."

We set about climbing it. There was only one incident worthy of note—the loss of yet another camera of mine. Glumly I watched the lens flashing in the sun as it spun down the mountainside and shattered into a thousand pieces. By good luck I had managed to insure it only two months earlier—my first policy since that unfortunate incident with the watch at Moraine Creek hut.

The next day we climbed our new route on the South Face of Malte and descended into the teeth of an oncoming nor'-wester. We had completed our training climbs—now for the East Face. The nor'-wester having spent itself, we moved up to Haast Hut for a close look at the face. None of us was enthusiastic. There was ice everywhere and a coating of fresh snow, there was rock-fall, gaping slots at the foot of the face . . . And then there were those two accidents to think over . . .

In the end we stayed clear of the face. The day after we arrived the weather closed in with an air of finality—or that was how we interpreted it—and three days later we retreated.

Back in Dunedin a month later an urgent telegram arrived for me.

"Appreciate you call me person to person at your earliest convenience."

Hillary.

The call came through:

"That you Mike? Thanks for your letter. Sounds like it was a good trip. Are you still interested in this expedition?"

"Yes I am."

"Well. I guess you may as well come along. And look, I don't know how tied up you are down there, but if you can get the time off I'd like you to go over to London for three months before the trip starts to get yourself *au fait* with the physiology side of things. How does that sound to you?"

"That—that sounds incredible. I think I can get the time off."

"Well I'll let you know a few more details later. Louise and I are going to Chicago in May and you could probably travel with us. How about dropping Griff Pugh a line in the meantime—here's the address . . ."

At the end of the conversation I put the phone down, stunned. A flat mate standing near by had picked up the gist of the conversation —Ed's voice carries well. He grinned enviously at me.

"You lucky bastard."

9

CHICAGO AND LONDON

To prosper in a strange land
taking cocktails at twilight behind the hotel curtains,
A. R. D. Fairburn

WE WERE called "The Himalayan Scientific and Mountaineering Expedition 1960–61", and seldom has there been in the Himalayas so varied an assortment of individuals pursuing so strange an array of objectives. Our sponsors were Field Enterprises of Chicago, publishers of *World Book Encyclopaedia*, and they financed the project in a staggeringly generous fashion, as they did later, in 1963, when they were financing the Sherpa school project. Because of the international flavour of the expedition—leader from New Zealand, money from the States, physiologists from England—we had a colourful collection of personalities, and for me, in the three months before reaching Nepal, meeting them was as much of an experience as coming face to face with the Himalayas themselves.

In New Zealand I had met only Ed and Peter Mulgrew. Ed of course was at the centre of everything, whether yeti-hunting, physiology or mountaineering. The concept of the expedition was his and he was leading and organising it. The area for the yeti-hunt had been chosen by him and he was the only one of us with the ability and experience to direct the climb of Makalu. It was his name which would sell the newspaper articles and film, and he would be writing the expedition book.

I had met Peter Mulgrew in Auckland while packing equipment. He was the sort of person one liked immediately: an abundance of energy and ability, a strong streak of optimism and determination and a sparkling sense of humour; with Pete around the conversation seldom flagged and between him and Ed there passed a continuing stream of banter. He was in charge of our radio communications, a job in which he had distinguished himself on Ed's expedition to the South Pole. "There were these two naval types sent along to me," said Ed, "when I was looking for a radio man. One of them saluted, and called me Sir, and said he'd make a good job of the communications.

The other one showed no inclination either to salute or call me Sir and said he'd have a go at anything at all. So I chose him. That was Mulgrew."

I left Auckland, with the Hillaries, on May 29th, 1960. For them it was no more than another tedious journey; for me it was the beginning of everything. Not only was I going to satisfy an inborn urge to travel abroad, but I was bound for the Himalayas. There were the names on my air ticket: Nandi, Honolulu, San Francisco, Chicago, New York, London, Zurich, Cairo, Bahrein, Delhi, Katmandu— names that seemed then more evocative than those of the mountains on which we would climb.

It was 10 p.m. when we left and there had been rain. Alone after the bustle of the air terminal building, the three of us walked through the fresh wet air to the Electra, gleaming against the black backdrop of the night. A steward met us at the economy class entrance—expedition finances fell short of first-class travel—"The Captain would be most grateful, Sir Edmund, if you would accept seats in the first-class cabin." He looked at me dubiously as I followed; who was I? Brother, son? The plane taxied to the end of the runway, steadied for a moment, then unleashed itself; blue marker lights flashed past and fell away below; the lights of Auckland, misty through the rain, dropped behind and we were into the clouds.

We landed in San Francisco at sunset that evening; at a quiet cocktail party I met two more of the expedition, Leigh Ortenburger and Larry Swan. Leigh belonged solely to the climbing contingent, one of the group to come in for the last phase of the expedition, the attempt on Makalu. He was a mathematician, but his record of climbs in the American mountains and in the Andes seemed to indicate that his interest in mathematics, like mine in medicine, had its limitations. He had the compact build and weather-beaten complexion that one might imagine a climber should have. And he had read his mountain literature too, something which made me warm to him at once—we were talking earnestly of the scientific programme: "What would Tilman say?" commented Leigh. What indeed! During the dark days on Makalu when the situation seemed almost hopeless Leigh showed the tenacity and courage that more than anything else were responsible for saving Peter Mulgrew's life.

Larry Swan was our zoologist, a scientist, with a foot in the Publicity camp, for he had an affable articulate manner which came across well on television. When we had captured our yeti, Larry would be the man to examine him professionally, determine his genealogy and give him a proper scientific name—though James Morris, *Times* correspondent on the Everest expedition, had already suggested the admirable title, *Homo niveus disgustans*. But we had trouble finding our yeti, or for that matter any large animal to grow excited over, and Larry spent much of his time directing the movements of an enthusiastic Sherpa with a butterfly net.

After a night in San Francisco we flew on to Chicago, home of *World Book Encyclopaedia*. We were met by John Dienhart, the ebullient crew-cut Public Relations Director of the organisation. Originally he had planned to direct publicity from Chicago, but later he decided that if information of the right sort was to flow smoothly from the Himalayas to the world, then he would need to be on the spot. "I think every man should spend a year of his life in the Himalayas," he had said, and he went—though soon it became clear that less than a year would be enough.

Without John there might never have been an expedition. He had met Ed the previous year during the recording of a series of television programmes for World Books. He had asked Ed where and when he planned to lead his next expedition and Ed had described his idea of combining a research and acclimatisation programme with an attempt on a high mountain without oxygen. "But of course there's not much chance of finding money of that sort."

"Hold it," said John. "I've got an idea. Just give me time to work on this one." The result was that World Books agreed to supply $200,000 dollars, to be used by the leader as he thought fit. It was sponsorship on a scale one could find only in the United States.

I remember John describing the interview between Ed and the executives of World Books when finance was discussed. "Here was this guy Hillary who'd climbed Everest, got a knighthood for it, the lot. We didn't know Ed too well at that stage—he was a nice guy, sure, but we knew he wouldn't be working in with an outfit like us for nothing. Probably he'd have a bunch of lawyers and accountants with him—but we reckoned we could handle them. Then in comes this big tall guy, by himself, with his hair all over the place, and carrying an old brief-case held together with string. Well that threw us right from the start. And then we came to the bit where we asked how much would he like for himself and he says, 'Well, on an expedition we don't usually take any money for ourselves.' We didn't know whether he meant it. For a bit we thought he might be just the coolest cat we'd ever met. Then we began to feel sorry for him. We felt we had to help the guy—force him to take the money. Up till then I'd never been able to understand why he hadn't made a million bucks out of Everest." John paused. "I think Ed's the most honest guy I've ever met," and he thought for a moment. "I'm not sure he's not the only honest guy I've ever met."

While in Chicago we stayed in a hotel suite kept by World Books for their guests. Being unused to such luxury I prowled around examining the various rooms with interest. In the back of a large wardrobe I found an old leather brief-case, its handle and catch held together by nylon cord. Ed laughed. "That's mine. After about the third time they'd seen me with that someone tactfully presented me with a new one." I looked at the case with its year's accumulation of dust. Maybe it was battered, but it was functional. Just what I needed for air travel. I still use it.

The expedition business was completed in the course of the week against a background of sumptuous luncheons and nocturnal tours of expensive night clubs, John being something of a connoisseur and blessed with a liberal expense account. Much of the time was spent at the Merchandise Mart, the huge office block where World Books had their headquarters. I remember at a luncheon there when Ed was guest speaker, my admiration for the ease with which he was able to entertain a large assembly with his tales of past expeditions and talk of the future, for there was something about Ed that Americans loved.

The major event of the week was a television preview of the expedition. It was held on the roof of the Mart, a place as windy as the South Col of Everest but with Chicago on the skyline, not Tibet. Along one side tables were laid for a luncheon, along another was a multi-coloured assortment of tents, ropes, down-jackets and other equipment; in the centre was a battery of cameras. There were Martinis and Manhattans in disposable plastic packs (not, I was told, part of the expedition supplies); there was freeze-dried shrimp and freeze-dried steak which, despite the protestations of the manufacturers who were supplying us liberally, had a familiar dehydrated flavour. After lunch the filming and interviewing began. Besides Ed, there was Marlin Perkins to talk on the yeti, and Barry Bishop on glaciology. Marlin, who was Director of the Lincoln Park Zoo in Chicago, was an old hand on television and his programmes on animals were known throughout the States. Travelling with Marlin one would step into a plane or bar to find half the Americans nudging one another and whispering, "There's Marlin Perkins!" And indeed he was easy to recognise: Slimly built, with a quietly distinguished look and a head of well-groomed white hair, he looked less than his fifty years. I too had white hair and for a while on the expedition there was debate amongst the Sherpas as to which of the two of us was the older.

The television business started with a practice run. There was a preamble from Ed, then Marlin began on the yeti. Standing behind him on a big placard was an artist's impression of a yeti, seven feet high, a massive, hairy, barrel-chested yeti, far removed from the docile creature I had imagined. I wondered how I'd handle such an animal if I bumped into him on a dark night. Run downhill say the

Sherpas, for the yeti has long hair which will fall into his eyes. They said that the female of the species has pendulous breasts reaching to the ground (a typical Sherpa embellishment) and for a moment I had a nightmarish vision of myself being pursued downhill by a lusty female yeti, brushing the hair from her eyes with one hand and flinging her breasts over her shoulders with the other.

"Tell me, Marlin," said the interviewer, "what makes you think there is such a thing as a yeti?"

"Well Dave, everyone who goes to the Himalayas hears about them and after a while you begin to think that, well, where there's smoke there's fire. But I think the best evidence is these photos of yeti tracks I've got here. Eric Shipton took these in 1951 right in the place where we're going hunting. All I know is that something must have made these tracks."

"And you hope to catch him do you?"

"Yes we do. We've got powerful spotting telescopes, we've got cameras set off by trip-wires and we've got tape-recorders for picking up the noise he makes."

"But how are you actually going to catch him, Marlin?"

"Well, I'll show you Dave. You see this gun I've got here? This is a Capchur gun which shoots a needle loaded with tranquilliser. All you have to do is estimate the size of the yeti, adjust the dose and let the critter have it. Like this." And raising the gun, with great deliberation he plunked a dart into a padded area on the animal's belly. "If you make the dose too big, of course, you might kill him."

"And I guess if you make it too small he might kill you."

"Yes Dave, I guess that's so."

"Just one more question, Marlin. What are you going to do with the yeti once you've got him?"

"Dave, I couldn't think of a better place for him than the Lincoln Park Zoo in Chicago." Then someone was draping a microphone around my neck and I was placed in what was meant to be a nonchalant pose sitting on top of a packing case. I felt very lonely.

"Can you tell us, Dr Gill, what are the aims of the physiological programme." By the tone of the interviewer's voice I gathered that he, as well as I, was expecting this part of the programme to be uphill work. Nervously I squinted down into the tiny microphone protruding upwards on a sort of stalk, and began talking confidentially into it. There was a pause and from near the camera someone walked wearily towards me.

"Listen bud, this here thing round your neck is the microphone. You don't look into that, you look at the camera, which is that big one-eyed thing out front, on the stand. Now let's do that bit again." I gave an account of the physiology programme based largely on guesswork for at that stage I knew remarkably little. "Don't let that worry you, bud," someone had said earlier when I mentioned my ignorance. "Never let yourself be limited by the facts. All you have to do is put together something that sounds good. I don't think there'll be any physiologists watching this programme anyway."

Barry Bishop carried on with an imaginative account of the glaciology programme. Barry was a jack-of-all-trades even more than most of us: photographer, glaciologist, surveyor, climber, he was one of the members of the wintering party. At that time he was employed by *National Geographic* and it was largely through him that they put $10,000 into the expedition. In 1963 Barry was one of the members of the American Everest Expedition who reached the summit.

After a week in Chicago we moved on through New York to London. Standing expectantly around the steps leading from the first-class entrance was a group of reporters. As we filed out from the rear of the plane Ed looked at them with a cheerful grin: "They always expect me to travel first-class," and then they spotted him and rushed over. We were met at the airport by the scientific leader of the expedition, Dr Griffith Pugh, who I knew already by reputation. He had had an interesting career. After studying law he had switched to medicine and in 1936 was a member of the British Olympic Ski Team; during the war he had trained ski-troops in the Lebanon. Then he had joined the Division of Human Physiology of the British Medical Research Council, doing research into a variety of topics, most of them concerned with adaptation to extreme conditions: heat, cold and high altitude. In 1952 he was invited on the Cho Oyu Expedition, the British preliminary to Everest. His observations were simple—in such conditions they had to be—but his insistence on large quantities of oxygen, a lengthy acclimatisation period and ample fluid at high altitudes were of importance in the success of the 1953 expedition. In 1957–8 he was in the Antarctic for the summer when Ed was there as leader of the New Zealand party supporting the British Trans-Antarctic Expedition. Ed had mentioned his ambitions to lead a party to climb Everest without oxygen and Griff had explained a scheme for improving acclimatisation by spending six months at 20,000 feet— preferably with a well-equipped laboratory to study the process. Obviously the two plans were complementary. All they needed was money . . . and that was where World Books had come in.

As we moved through the airport building I saw coming towards us a tall, slightly stooped figure with a splendid head of thick orange hair. "There's Griff," said Ed and we joined him. Griff's greeting struck a reassuringly British note after the effusive American welcome in Chicago.

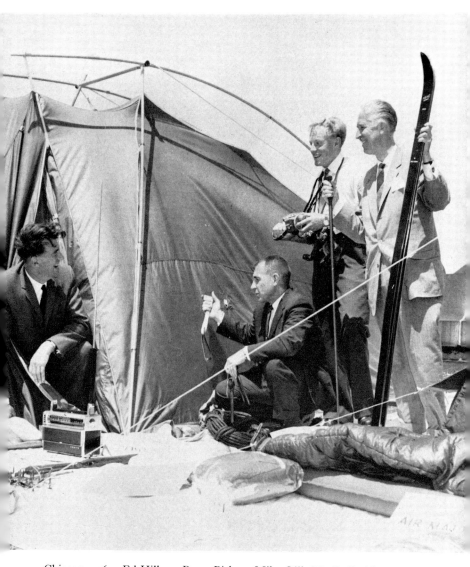

Chicago, 1960: Ed Hillary, Barry Bishop, Mike Gill, Marlin Perkins

The tracks and terraced fields of Nepal. Beneath the trees is a group of porters

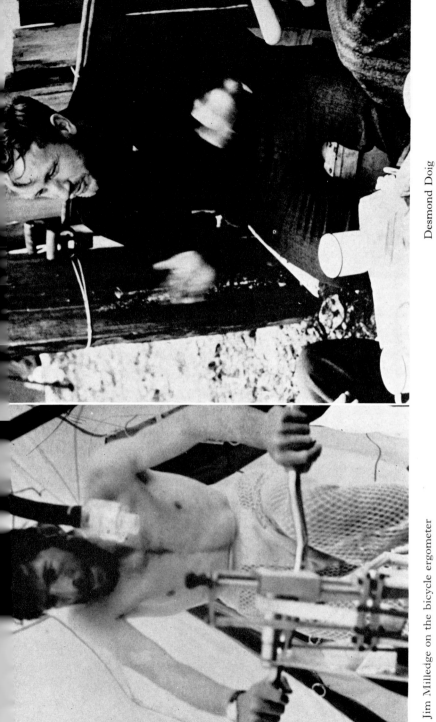

Desmond Doig

Jim Milledge on the bicycle ergometer

Kumjung and Ama Dablam. Tengboche monastery stands on a spur on the far side of the valley. Our route on the mountain leads from the right-hand rock ridge up the central snow-face

Ama Dablam: Barry Bishop on the upper face

The summit of Ama Dablam: Mike Gill, Wally Romanes, Mike Ward,
Barry Bishop

Makalu – Wind!

Makalu: Camp V on the col. Camps VI, VI½ and VII are on the glacier behind

The cover photo of John Pascoe's *Unclimbed New Zealand* – the Ramsay
Face of Whitcombe from Kinkel Ridge. Our route lies on the buttress leading
to the low peak

The summit of Taweche – "More a matter of luck than skill"

"Hello Ed. Nice to see you. Where's your luggage—I've got a car outside." It was a new silver-grey two-seater Austin Healey. "Nice little car," said Griff with a gleam in his eye as he climbed into the driver's seat. We tied our luggage on the back as best we could. Ed took the front seat while Louise and I perched on top of the baggage in the space behind. As the car drew out and picked up speed we felt the force of the wind striking us at shoulder-level.

"Bit windy up here isn't it," shouted Louise to me.

"'Tis a bit. Hope he doesn't go too fast." We could just hear Griff talking to Ed:

"I'll take her down the M1 and show you what she can do . . ."

"That was a hundred and ten miles an hour," explained Griff when we had slowed down, wondering perhaps why Louise's hair was standing on end or why my jaw was twitching. It was the first of a series of car journeys with Griff that turned out to be the most exciting and dangerous moments of the expedition.

After staying a few days at Griff's delightful old house at Hatching Green, our ways parted, the Hillaries to a mews in South Kensington, I to a bed-sitter in Belsize Park, a move that led to a sharp drop in my standard of living. The bed-sitter, small and bare, was on the third floor of an old stone semi-detached house. There was a gas ring on the floor, a bed, a chair and a wardrobe, all for thirty shillings a week. The landlord, a large, unkempt man sprouting a ginger beard, was a writer—a fact I discovered later when I read in the *Observer* a review (scathing) of one of his books. He lived on the ground floor. The middle floor was shared by an out-of-work Irishman and an eighteen-year-old girl who painted and would alarm me by suddenly appearing in nothing but bra and panties. "You are too healthy," she told me with a trace of condescension. "Here, in London, we are all sick. . ."

Each morning I walked a mile up the tree-lined main street to Holly Hill, Hampstead, where the Medical Research Council laboratories were housed in a huge dingy building. I learned to manipulate the bags and tubes, analyse gas samples and ride the bicycle ergometer, a machine which was to dominate three months of our lives in the Himalayas. Working with Griff at the same time was Dr Jim Milledge, a physician with an interest in climbing, and like me, a new recruit to the physiology team. Jim introduced me to British climbing. One afternoon he took me to Harrison Rocks, a line of low sandy cliffs twenty or thirty feet high, half hidden by trees and dotted with climbers clawing their way up steep corners and overhangs. The surrounding countryside was old and mellow with hedgerows between the fields, big spreading trees and lovely old houses. How raw the New Zealand landscape was compared with this, how bare the fenced paddocks, the stump littered hills or the scrub country.

G

The climbing was difficult but limited. "Don't judge our rock-climbing by this," said Jim. "It just happens to be the only rock within easy distance of London. Wait till you get to Wales."

The chance came a fortnight later. There was a phone call from Ed: "Louise and I are going up to an Everest reunion at Pen Y Gwryd. Would you like to come along? Don't think I'll be doing any climbing myself but you might like to get out on the cliffs and try yourself out."

The Hillaries had the loan of a Triumph Herald coupé for their three months in London and with me crammed in behind the two front seats they set off on a circuitous route through the Cotswolds, reaching North Wales at dusk. All around were bare hills and in the valleys stood a few stone cottages, one of them Pen Y Gwryd Hotel, a climbing centre famous throughout the mountaineering world. Crowded around the bar were groups of climbers and amongst them some, though not all, of the 1953 Everest team.

Not obviously fitting in anywhere, I settled in to a corner with a pint of beer. A moment later through the smoke and hubbub I heard my name being shouted. It was Dave Herron across the other side of the room waving a tankard at me. Dave was from Dunedin where he had been lecturing in history and completing a doctorate. Everyone in the New Zealand climbing world knew Dave, his sociable habits, his genius as a raconteur and his enthusiasm for climbing in the Hermitage region. Students had a high regard for him as a lecturer and he was a gifted historian, but this Dave dismissed as being unimportant compared with his climbing—or that was the impression he gave. He was unhappy in the dustily academic atmosphere of St Andrews where he was working then but an invitation from Ed to fill a vacant place in the yeti-hunting team had changed his outlook. "We're going climbing on Cloggy tomorrow. Come along. Let's see how 'the white hope of the Darrans' performs on the English cliffs."

We set off next morning in sunny weather. "Make the most of it," said Dave. "Fine days are as rare in North Wales as they are in the Southern Alps."

From the hotel a strip of sealed road ran across the barren countryside to a low pass just north of Mt Snowdon, the highest of the surrounding hills. Cloggy was on the west side of Snowdon, but before we reached it Dave began pointing out rock outcrops. Up on the right was a fine-looking cliff, perhaps a hundred and fifty feet high, with a big open corner running vertically up it. "The cliff's Dinas Cromlech and the route up the centre is Cenotaph Corner. One of Joe Brown's routes."

"Joe Brown? Who's he?"

"You're not quite with it yet are you?" said Dave. "You'll be asking who Winston Churchill is next." And he told me about Joe Brown, the Manchester plumber who had added two new grades to severity to English rock climbing and become a legend in his own time. Cenotaph Corner said Dave, had been declared impossible in the early days of climbing in North Wales. As standards rose it became a challenge and then one day in 1952 the word went about that Joe Brown had led it. The climbing of Cenotaph Corner and similar routes was the opening of a new era and the middle-class of British society who had dominated climbing for a century found themselves trailing behind the groups from Liverpool and Manchester.

Some of the biggest of the new routes were on Clogwyn du'r Arddu, commonly known as Cloggy. Having parked the car Dave and I set off up Snowdon on the track to the top. Half-way up we swung off to the right and there was Cloggy, the fiercest and most famous cliff in the British Isles. It was broad and black, perhaps 600 feet high, a band of sheer rock outcropping from the side of the hill; below it, scree slopes lead down to a small black lake. I looked at the guide-book with its criss-cross of routes marked on the photo, like some complicated game of cats'-cradle. Already a few climbers were up there, clinging like coloured flies to impossible positions on the big wall. On the scree and grass ledges below, others were roping up or changing into P.A.s, snug-fitting canvas shoes with stiffened rubber-soles which improved one's climbing miraculously.

Our climb was an easy VS (very severe) on the west buttress. Two ropes of climbers were queuing up there already while the first party of the day worked its way up. A notably articulate individual wearing a red jersey, one of the "hard men", someone said, was entertaining the assembled throng. He was pointing out an improbable crack high on the cliff.

"Yes, I'd traversed across that slab, almost up the crack, then I fell off—Ah! That was a good fall that was. One of the best falls I've done I should say." He looked up reflectively. "Yes, I wouldn't mind going back and doing that fall again some time." As a raconteur he had a good style, and our two hours of waiting in the shadow of the cliff, cold though they were, passed easily. He talked about the party of Russian climbers who had been in England recently. "They were in London for a while and every morning they'd be up early, run round Hyde Park, no smoking. No wonder they were out of condition. But it didn't last long once they'd got to Pen Y Gwryd. First morning they were out there doing pull-ups; the day after, half of them stayed in bed; and next morning one of them was hiding in his sleeping-bag with cigarette smoke drifting out the top."

When we finally began to climb it was something of an anticlimax.

There was a short, greasy central pitch but otherwise it seemed easy enough, particularly from my position on the bottom end of the rope. From the top of the last pitch we ambled upwards to reach the summit of Snowdon early in the afternoon.

Hillary, Hunt, Lowe and Gregory, the four who had carried in the high camp to 27,000 feet on Everest had been there before us. They were out of condition and on the way up there had been a certain amount of sweating and panting. Near the top three athletic young men and a girl had gone steaming past. George turned wearily to the last of them: "You do realise do you," he said, "that you have just passed the spearhead of the attack on Everest?"

There was no more climbing that weekend but my curiosity was aroused: just how high was our standard of climbing in the Darrans?

A fortnight later I returned with Dave and an English friend of his, Ted Johnson. We climbed a few Severes, then a VS—I began to like this sort of climbing more and more. The grading system added enormously to the interest of the climbs for it brought in a competitive element. The Easy grades, I found, were sheep-tracks; Difficult and Very Difficult were the sort of country Phil and I had carried packs over in the Darrans; on Severes, the holds were shrinking but still easily found. Then came the VS, and beyond these the Joe Brown grades, Extremely Severe (XS) and Excessively Severe. The grade where I climbed most happily was VS: each was a neat little problem, never easy, never impossibly difficult. The placing of runners became an art in itself, hunting out projecting knobs and flakes, looping a sling from a convenient holly tree or threading it behind a stone jammed in a crack. And there was always company—as often as not someone else would be grappling with a problem only twenty feet away. I was on Dinas Cromlech with Dave that weekend when we noticed a couple of climbers approaching the foot of the cliff. "That's Snow Williams," said Dave and he shouted down to them: "Hey, you rough bloody colonial. What the hell are you doing up here?"

An African climbing on the next route along turned with flashing eyes. "We are not a bloody colony. Now we are independent."

Dave apologised. "Thought we might try a V.Diff," Snow was saying and he moved to the foot of Cenotaph Corner. For the next half hour we were busy on our own route and by then Snow was half-way up the Corner. An hour later he climbed out the top and we were chatting together in the sun, watching cars stream past on the road below. "It's partly a matter of practice," said Snow. "A couple of months ago I could hardly lead a VS. Ten years ago, I'm told, VS was the top bracket but nowadays if you don't lead one of them on your first weekend, you're a failure . . . Makes you realise that back in the

Southern Alps we do hardly anything that could be classified as rock-climbing . . . I doubt whether I ever got past a V.Diff."

"What's the easiest of the XSs around here?" I asked. "Anything I might have a crack at?"

"No harm in trying—well, usually you don't come to any harm anyway. Got plenty of runners? Try Spectre. It's labelled XS, though I have my doubts. I suspect it's only a hard VS. It's certainly your best bet anyway."

Spectre was on another of the Snowdon cliffs close to Dinas Cromlech. Ted was happy to follow my lead and we set off after lunch. All along the cliffs there was intense activity with climbers strung everywhere and a couple of hundred feet below, spectators were lined up beside their cars with binoculars. I hadn't realised before that climbing could be a spectator sport.

The climb was tough, technically the most difficult I'd done. The crux was a ten-foot traverse to the left on the most tenuous of holds. Even a marginal loss of friction would have dropped me fifteen feet to the first runner, and for ten minutes I was stretched across the rock working out a line of holds. The final pitch was a wide overhanging crack, but by then I had learnt the elements of hand-jamming, a technique unknown to me in New Zealand, and the strong-arm type of climbing came easily to me anyway. Elated, we strode back down to Ted's car.

"Eh lad, but I thought you were going to come off that lot," said one of the spectators. "What a stretch of legs you've got there! Y' looked like a big bird strung up there."

But I'd had enough of XS for one day. We returned later to Brant and Slape (what marvellous names the climbs had!) but before we were half-way up the first, rain set in; from a sling draped over the nearest belay point I rappelled back to ground level. I'd got what I wanted anyway. It was the end of the climbing I did on British cliffs.

There was a tragic sequel to that weekend with Dave and Snow. Early in August, back in London, I was travelling on the Underground. Idly, to fill in time, I read the inverted newspaper of a bowler-hatted gentleman opposite. Two . . . ? . . . Killed in . . . ? . . . read the headline. By leaning forwards I picked up the rest. "Two Britons Killed in Avalanche". Wonder if I know them I thought and after leaving the train I bought a paper. I did know them. The two Britons were Dave Herron and Snow Williams. It was like the tragic affair of Harry Scott and Jim Glasgow all over again. A massive soft snow avalanche had picked up several ropes of climbers on the Aiguille d'Argentière; five of them had been carried over an ice-cliff and buried while the others escaped. A party had been on the same

slope the day before and to none of them had an avalanche seemed
at all likely. It was as near to unavoidable as a mountain accident
can be.

In July, Ed and Louise took me with them to Chamonix. Ed drives
with dash and determination and we shot across France as if we were
the Triumph Herald entry in the Monte Carlo road race. Porsche,
Citroën, Jaguar—if they were doing two miles an hour less than our
maximum speed we passed them. We would draw in close to some
sleek limousine and hang on grimly like a terrier chasing a racehorse.
On the first clear straight Ed, with set jaw, would put his foot down
and with a shaking and whining the car would inch ahead, Ed gripping the wheel, Louise watching tensely while I leaned forward from
my cramped position behind. I was the navigator. Travelling at
speed this was no easy job. At each town we would end up *centre
ville* circling the central roundabout, Ed passing pungent New Zealand
comments on the driving habits of the French, while I tried frantically
to sort out from the map which of the available exits we should take.

Ed's interest in France centred around four topics, wine, food,
mountains and cathedrals, roughly in that order of importance. For
myself, I had some theoretical knowledge of wines but not a great
deal of experience; Ed had little theory but a lot of experience. We
took it in turns to order the wine at the various restaurants where we
ate and many and vigorous were the discussions on the merits of our
wines. A 1938 Château Margaux turned out to be a minor success
on my part; a mould-encrusted bottle of Clos de Vougeot was a major
failure, for it was sour and I had neither the knowledge of French nor
the courage to tell the waiter to take it back. The final victory however
was Ed's. On the way home as he began pouring me a glass my
stomach involuntarily turned over. By then, after a week of wine with
every meal, I was saturated. "No . . ." I said hesitantly. "I don't
think I'll have any this time." Ed shrugged his shoulders in the best
French fashion and there was a gleam of triumph in his eye as he
filled his glass. Comment would have been superfluous.

Chamonix is the climbing centre of the French Alps. Mont Blanc
is close by with a host of other famous peaks, and from the township,
railway, track and *téléphérique* lead into the mountains. Though it
was still early in the season there were holiday-makers enough to give
the streets a festive air. The tourist with a telescope can watch a
group of climbers on a peak as easily as in North Wales—though
the scale is vastly bigger. I had the impression that it would be
difficult to feel lonely in these mountains, whereas at home in the
Darrans one had the feeling of living in a lost world.

We were booked into an expensive hotel which in four days would have left me bankrupt. "I'll have a word to Jean Franco," promised Ed. "He runs the school for mountaineering and ski-ing here—bound to have some young bloke there who'll be only too keen to go off up to one of the mountain huts and do a climb with you." Monsieur Franco was willing to oblige and that afternoon a dashing young man in climbing costume presented himself at the desk. Ed had already given me some idea of what to expect. "We all have some sort of image of ourselves. The New Zealander wears his oldest clothes and prides himself on being able to carry a seventy-pound pack over three mountain passes in a day. The Englishman apologises for starting on something so ridiculously easy then skims up the fiercest looking bit of rock you ever saw in your life. The Frenchman is *très formidable*." And he posed dramatically, stuck out his jaw and looked upwards through narrowed eyes to show what he meant. My companion fitted the description perfectly. He was short, slim, with clean-cut handsome features, moved neatly and confidently and talked volubly; by my standards his climbing garb was elegant in the extreme.

"Jean Cabri," he said with a dazzling smile as he shook hands.

"Pleased to meet you," I said. "I'm Mike Gill. Do you speak English?" A blank look. "Je parle français," I added—Cabri's face lit up and he broke into a flood of incomprehensible French. "Un peu," I added. Obviously communication was going to be a problem, but at this point the hotel receptionist came forward to act as interpreter.

At length we came to the question of where to go to. Mont Blanc was clearly out of the question, for lack of time if nothing else; and besides, I longed to set foot on the granite of the famed Chamonix Aiguilles. We would have to use the Montenvers Hut as our base. At Cabri's suggestion we walked down to the climbing school where there was a model of the Chamonix peaks; fascinated I pored over the layout of miniature rock needles and glacier-covered peaks. There was the Grepon, of course: the Mummery Crack was one of the classic climbs but Snow Williams had dismissed this—"a one-pitch climb. May as well do a VS on Dinas Cromlech for all the climbing you'll get. The Mer de Glace face is the only route on the Grepon." But that was too inaccessible. Next to the Grepon was the Charmoz. Hopefully I pointed to a long pinnacled ridge leading to it. "Très longue," said Cabri shaking his head, and I looked again. On the other side of the Grepon was a peak with a big unbroken ridge leading directly to it from the direction of Chamonix. Again I pointed. "Ah! Le nord-ouest de Blaitière. C'est bon." And then more doubtfully, "C'est difficile." But we agreed to attempt the Blaitière. The standard of climbing on the north-west ridge? Grade 4 with two pitches of Grade 5—which by English standards should be easy VS at the most.

Crampons and boots had to be hired and food bought: Cabri took me to a small grocery store and collected together bread, cheese, butter, sausage and oranges. Breakfast and evening meals we would get at Montenvers. Cabri handed me the grocery bill. "Well," I said, "back home we share the cost of this sort of thing, but I suppose there's not much point in having an argument over it; even if you could understand English." There was an agreeable sense of freedom in being able to say exactly what I wanted to with no chance of being understood. I paid the bill.

Late in the afternoon we took the train to Montenvers. Cabri and I practised communication. If we were going to spend a long day on a difficult climb a few words would be indispensable. I held up the rope. "La corde," said Cabri. Crampon was a French word anyway, and piton. The translation of "On Belay" took ten minutes of pantomime with rope and axe: *l'assurance* was the word. By the time we had sorted out "Hold!" and "I'm falling" we had reached the top of the railway. The view was exciting. We looked down on a huge glacier, peaks rising all around. Many I recognised for I had seen photos of them in a dozen books. Tales of the ascents of the great faces of the Alps, the Eiger, the Grande Jorasses, the Dru, had always fascinated me, and from Montenvers I could see at least one of them: the west face of the Dru rose from across the other side of the valley, a superlative sweep of sheer granite.

The hut was a huge structure by New Zealand standards. An evening meal of thick soup, bread and a bottle of wine was served in a dining-room set with long tables and forms and we slept on straw mattresses laid on the ground in a communal bedroom. The place seemed strangely empty considering that this was summer and the weather fine, but the season had not properly started. Besides ourselves there were three Spaniards, Pablo, Pancho and Sancho, who were training for an attempt on the North face of the Dru. Before darkness closed in the five of us strolled up to a big boulder a short distance above the hut. One face, about fifteen feet high, was scarred by the nail-scratches of innumerable mountaineers' boots. We began climbing. Partly this was for the fun of it, partly to give Cabri some idea of whether I was likely to get up the Grade 5s on the Blaitière. We took our turn one by one. An easy pitch to start with and then progressively harder. The toughest route began on small holds and ended with a haul up a narrow crack. Cabri was half-way up the small holds when he came unstuck. He landed lightly on the grass below, on all fours, like a cat. With a Gallic oath he sprang up, glared at the boulder, then seizing a flake of glass which he had in his pocket he began shaving the edge of the rubber sole of one boot. It was the first time I had seen someone sharpening his boots. The next time Cabri was triumphantly successful. The rest of us followed. By then he was happy enough about embarking on the Blaitière and we returned to the hut. The three Spaniards decided they would come with us next day.

At 2 o'clock next morning, after a cup of coffee, we set out towards the foot of our peak, which rises close above the hut. Strange how fickle is one's memory, for though I remember every foot of the Darrans, of the route between Montenvers and the foot of the northwest ridge I have no recollection. Except that it was a great distance to travel before breakfast, and that I seemed to have lost fitness through living in London. Our breakfast halt was beside the first patch of snow and how welcome it was—bread, cheese, sausage and a flaskful of coffee.

We began to prepare for climbing, sorting out the rope and strapping on crampons. Cabri emptied all our gear into one rucksack which, to my consternation, he gave to me indicating that leading would consume all his energies. I felt fairly sure that carrying the pack would consume all of mine—it was heavy. You're lucky to be here at all, I told myself—stop complaining, and we set off. After a trudge up a snow slope we struck the ridge proper and there we roped up. With Cabri in a particularly photogenic position I pulled out my camera: "Photo?" I said, and obligingly he struck a pose, *très formidable*. Then the climb began. The rock was truly magnificent, as good as the Darrans at their best; indeed anyone less loyal than I might have said better. It was all clean granite, huge blocks of it, rough and solid, so that even the smallest hold felt like a platform. I could hardly fail to enjoy myself on such rock. Cabri led effortlessly. After I had muscled my way up the first of the Grade 5s, a wide crack with little in the way of footholds, Sancho, who was following close behind, encouraged me with the comment, "Vous êtes très fort," and he flexed a biceps to show what he meant. "Je suis très fatigué," I replied with some heat for by then I was growing weary. "You couldn't persuade my good friend Cabri to take a turn with the pack could you?" But alas! He understood no English either.

By the time we reached the top the view had been blotted out by cloud except in the direction of the Charmoz. I was admiring what looked like innumerable little rock needles dotted along its flat summit when I realised with a start that they were people, twenty or thirty of them in a long line. As we started down they too disappeared in the drifting mist, and light snow began to fall. The route down was a steep snow couloir and here Cabri decided to link up with the three Spaniards. Around me there developed a tangle of belays and ropes.

There was always Pancho or Pablo or Sancho tugging on my rope and pointing up, down or sideways, or giving me a loose end to tie myself to, or shouting, "L'assurance! L'assurance!" Or Cabri would come hurtling out of the mist as if falling and brake to a dramatic halt in front of me, and above all there was a continuous chatter of instructions and comment in Spanish and French.

Despite the confusion we completed the descent safely. Early next day, after I had paid the bill at Montenvers, we returned to Chamonix. In the foyer of the hotel we farewelled each other effusively. Cabri seemed to be trying to say something else as well. After the third "Au revoir," he explained something to the receptionist.

"He wants you to pay him now," she said.

"Pay! Pay for what?"

"For the climb. The north-west ridge of the Blaitière is two hundred and eighty francs."

Two hundred and eighty francs. There was a thirty-second delay, while I translated this into pounds. Mon Dieu! Eighteen pounds! The cost of a couple of months in the Darrans!

Cabri, noticing my alarm, spoke again to the receptionist. "He has decided," she said, "for the sake of international friendship, to reduce this to two hundred and forty francs."

After emptying my pockets I hunted down Ed to raise a loan. "Just let me know if you come across any young Frenchman in New Zealand wanting a climb in the Southern Alps. I'll take him. I've got a bit of international friendship I'd like to pay back." Next day we left, after Monsieur Simond, maker of mountaineering equipment, had entertained Ed and Louise to a mid-morning bottle of champagne. And then we were away, across France like a rocket—or as much like a rocket as a Triumph Herald ever will be.

By the last week of August the loose ends of the expedition had been tidied up. The last of the sea-level physiology tests had been completed and the innumerable pieces of equipment for a laboratory at 19,000 feet had been packed: the bicycle ergometer, boxes of electronic gadgetry, glass flasks, rubber bags, fire extinguishers—the list lengthened daily. We had spent one weekend practising the assembly of the insulated prefabricated hut we would live in at 19,000 feet. Jim had been in Oxford for a month developing techniques for the work he was interested in, while I had spent a short time in both Cambridge and Oxford, ostensibly on expedition business. Between times I had been consumed by Colonial Fever, the hectic scramble to the theatres, opera houses, art galleries, concert halls and historic monuments of the great city of London.

On September 4th I left by plane for Katmandu.

10

THE HUNTING OF THE YETI

"It's a Snark!" was the sound that first came to their ears,
And seemed almost too good to be true.
Then followed a torrent of laughter and cheers:
Then the ominous words "It's a Boo ——"

Lewis Carroll

I HAVE heard it said that you either love the East or loathe it: there is
no room for lukewarm appreciation or mild dislike. In New Delhi I
met a middle-aged couple just come back from Nepal. "Katmandu!
Why! It's just the filthiest place you ever saw!" said one with a
shudder. "Those dirty streets . . . All those people . . . I don't think
you'll like Katmandu one bit."

Happily they were wrong—I was fascinated by Katmandu, indeed
by the whole of Nepal. From Delhi we had flown high over the
chequer-board plains of the Ganges. Then hills appeared on the
horizon, their steep sides clothed thinly with forest or patterned with
terraces. After crossing a pass, so close that we could see the chickens
and children outside the houses, we dropped down the other side into
a fertile green basin surrounded by hills. We were in the fabled Vale
of Nepal. Between the monsoon clouds were the great peaks of the
Himalayas and then we were banking steeply over the clustered brown
roofs of Katmandu and coming in to land.

The airport building, a small cream-painted concrete affair, was a
sleepy place with lizards darting across the walls and a ragged assortment of porters snoozing in the sun. We passed through the Customs
—no more troublesome on that occasion than their Western counter-
parts—and we were free to enter the city.

Parts of Katmandu are new, with airline offices, a few westernised
shops and cinema hoardings. But compared with the ancient temples
and the bazaar these are like a Coca-Cola machine in a cathedral,
decayed though the cathedral is. The streets teem with people of a
dozen races, for Nepal, and all the Himalayan regions, are the melting
pot of the mongoloid races of the north, the Aryans, and the small
dark-skinned men from the south. In appearance Katmandu is

medieval. The bazaar is a network of narrow lanes and open squares
flanked by leaning walls of weathered brick. Carved eaves support
tiled roofs tufted with grass; three stories up a girl leans over the rail
of a ramshackle balcony, and the back lanes are cobbled and muddy.
There is little rubbish, for the peelings and old jars we would throw
away are either food for a goat or useful utensils for a poor man and
his family. At ground level all the houses are shops, dark recesses
behind carved pillars where you will find anything from transistors to
betel nut, canned peaches to marijuana. A small boy who speaks
English will seize you by the hand—"Genuine Tibetan souvenirs,
sahib!"—and he leads you upstairs to a room crowded with dusty
bronze buddhas and richly carved temple goddesses. Outside again,
dazzled at first by the bright light, you move on to a square where the
steps of a temple are loaded with piles of handsome goat hair rugs
and homespun jackets, which for the moment are fashionable amongst
the European population of Katmandu. Food is piled everywhere:
tomatoes, cucumbers, mangoes, heaps of crimson chilis and mountains of rice. In one corner, beside the ornate façade of a Hindu shrine,
a few serious young men with red flags and loud-speakers are preaching Communism. And everywhere there are temples, Buddhist or
Hindu or an amalgam of both; in the temple complex known as
Hanuman Doka you will see a stone carving of the goddess Kali with
a sword in one hand and a fistful of severed heads in another. Beside
it is a series of erotic carvings ("resolutely and offensively coarse"
wrote one 19th century traveller) and if you examine them too closely,
you will find yourself surrounded by a swarm of small boys who wil-
fully misinterpret your interest in the art of the East. Move outside
the bazaar and abruptly you are amongst the paddyfields, which lap
against the old houses like the waters of an emerald lake. On the
outskirts you will find the squat concrete palaces of the Ranas, the
old ruling class of Nepal. One of them is the Hotel Royal.

The Hotel Royal was the headquarters of the expedition. We drove
into the grounds and emptied ourselves and our luggage out of the
jeep. Huge packing-cases, obviously ours, were strewn across a tennis
court and working amongst them was a cheerful group who I immediately recognised as Sherpas. Upstairs a dozen or so expedition
members were eating lunch. George Lowe of Everest fame was there,
resplendent in a beard grown on a preceding expedition to Greenland.
Wally Romanes and Pete Mulgrew were giving an account of the Push
to Patna, the truck convoy which had carried our gear from Calcutta.
Tom Nevison, U.S. Air Force physiologist, was there complete with
ten gallon hat. Pat Barcham, a climber from New Zealand, described
some outlandish flight during which the barefooted hostess had been
cleaning her toe-nails in the rear compartment. And then there was

Desmond Doig, journalist, interpreter, and yeti-hunter *par excellence*. As it turned out Desmond was two-thirds of the yeti-hunting expedition, for without him we would have found nothing but the tracks.

Desmond is an Irishman with all the genius of that unpredictable race; by education he is English, by inclination, Oriental. As a journalist on the staff of the Calcutta *Statesman* with a special interest in the Himalayan kingdoms of Nepal, Sikkim and Bhutan, he is known across India; he speaks Nepali as if born there and he writes and draws well. With these accomplishments there had been little hesitation in accepting him as journalist to accompany the expedition. Later, when I came to know Desmond better, my admiration increased. For though his professional accomplishments were considerable, it was in the gracious art of living that he excelled. He lived in a flat in Calcutta like a minor maharajah, surrounded by an entourage of displaced Tibetans and indigent Nepalis. On the walls were Tibetan scroll paintings and gilded buddhas, and on the floor fine carpets. His parties were like no others: in one corner a group of Nepali musicians singing the latest pop tunes from Katmandu, in another a prime minister and a maharajah, and outside, the sounds of an Indian summer night – for not all of Calcutta is a slum.

Travelling with Desmond in Nepal was never dull. Where the rest of us might walk through a Nepalese or Sherpa village and find nothing, Desmond would uncover a host of strange tales: the old crone over there was a witch, there were bandits in the area, the shifty-looking trio whispering near by were planning to rob us; last autumn a family of yetis had burst into the monastery, carried off a set of musical instruments and now, on stormy nights, could be heard playing to each other in the mountains. Desmond did not work entirely on his own but had as typist and general assistant Bhanu Bannerjee, an excitable and affectionate Bengali whose fluent Nepali gave him the position of second interpreter.

Before leaving Katmandu we had first to divide the expedition equipment and personnel into two lots: 180 loads and most of the sahibs for the yeti-hunt in the Rolwaling, and 320 loads for the hut-building party consisting of Norm Hardie, Barry Bishop, Jim Milledge and Wally Romanes. Norm, with good reason, called his team the work-party and the rest of us playboys: there was no doubt that escorting 320 loads 200 miles to a height of 19,000 feet was a much tougher proposition than ours: no frivolous detours up side-valleys for them, no indolent reclining at an observation camp with telescope and a book.

On September 14th, equipped with umbrellas and water bottles, we set off towards the east, our destination the Rolwaling Valley, a march of ten days. I know of no pleasanter occupation than walking through the foothills of Nepal. Someone has called the Milford Track the finest walk in the world: he's wrong. The finest walk in the world is from Katmandu to the foot of Mount Everest, and if one goes by way of the Rolwaling so much the better. The track winds over steep ridges which become wilder and higher as one approaches the mountains; there are neat villages, terraced hillsides of rice paddy and corn; bamboos sprout like huge ostrich feathers beside the spreading banyan tree and the pipul. There is always a sense of discovery, as if one is exploring, yet no discomforts to speak of. Shelter, whether house, rock or tent is easily found, food can always be bought and for those whose thirst outweighs their fear of dysentery, there is the solace of chang shops. Chang is the local beer, made variously from rice, corn or millet, and though the flavour and texture may at first seem muddy, one can soon become addicted: some time before I die I would like to do a pub crawl from one end of Nepal to the other – I can think of no pleasanter way of dying.

Mid-September in the Himalayas is early autumn, the tail-end of the rainy season. There was the cool of the last of the monsoon thunder-shows but for most of the time we walked in tropical heat. When we found a pool we bathed. A line of porters would come down to the floor of a valley to find, to their delight and astonishment, a group of lily-white sahibs, splashing about like a herd of water buffaloes. The porters would line up to watch, their loads resting on sticks, and loud was the laughter greeting the sallies of lewd wit that passed between them.

The low-land porter's lot was not an easy one, for as well as his sixty-pound expedition load he carried his own food, cooking utensils and blankets. For an average day's walk of twelve miles he was paid five shillings. Our Sherpas on the other hand, who enjoyed a status somewhere between that of a sahib and a porter, carried little else but their personal belongings and even these were often piled on to the load of some suitably intimidated porter. Their pay was eight shillings a day, and on top of this the expedition fed them – no small item, for a Sherpa eats like a camel preparing to cross the Sahara. In return they cooked, pitched tents, blew up air-beds, laid out sleeping-bags and kept an eye on the porters that none absconded or fell by the way at a chang shop.

The term 'sahib' sounds like an undesirable relic of the British Raj. In effect it simply means any foreign member of an expedition as distinct from Nepalis or Sherpas or Tibetans. Sherpas use it all the time with no underlying suggestion of class distinction and the word is too convenient to be discarded. Attached to each sahib was a Sherpa to act as personal assistant and interpreter, for most have a

smattering of English and some speak it well. One might criticise this
undemocratic relationship as being demoralising to sahib or Sherpa or
both; in practice it had the effect of establishing a strong bond of
affection and loyalty between the two and to criticise someone's
personal Sherpa was like pointing out the defects of his wife. Though
a Sherpa is paid to serve he is never servile. He has an uncanny
instinct for sorting out the good from the bad in his employers and
adjusting his level of service accordingly. Hypocrisy, bombast,
laziness, selfishness, are recognised for what they are; so too are
courage, generosity and strength of personality. Warmth of affection
is returned in ample measure. Win the respect of a Sherpa and he will
risk his life for you: fall short of his standards and he will work well,
and usually with courtesy, but no more.

With me, was Dawa Tensing II, a powerfully-built but rather shy
Sherpa. As a mountaineer he was less than perfection—we discovered
this to our cost on Makalu but he had a huge, infectious grin which
brightened many a weary mile on the more torrid days of the march-
in. Like most Sherpas he had a sharp eye for things I would otherwise
have missed: a snake escaping into the scrub, or langur monkeys on
the cliffs climbing overhangs with enviable ease. There were birds of
all sorts, the whirring, crimson pheasants that one could hardly miss,
or huge Himalayan eagles; there were little pink finches, humming
birds, birds with trailing tails or curving crests. He showed me a
Nepalese village post-office, a wooden bench in the market-place,
whose begrimed letters would bear the thumb-prints of a hundred
passers-by.

We left behind us the last of the fertile terraced hill-sides of the
lower foothills. The Rolwaling is a high hanging valley, a tributary of
the Bhote-Kosi River, which has carved a great canyon through the
main range of the Himalayas from Tibet. From the bridge which
crosses this torrent we followed the track up cliffs and through forest
to a pass at 15,000 feet. It was the tenth day, the last of our march-in.
Early that morning we stood on the threshold of the mountains themselves. Till then we had not seen them. Gauri Shankar, 23,400 feet
high and now directly above us, had been hidden by the monsoon.
Rain had fallen during the night but now sun broke through the
melting cloud and warmed us. And then, as if a curtain had been
pulled aside, the mists parted and we saw the ice-cliffs and rock walls
that beset the summit of Gauri Shankar. There is no more dramatic
way of seeing a mountain. The rock and forest which seem to tether
it to earth were hidden by cloud. There was the summit, floating
infinitely high, an ice-clad island in a remote region of dazzling white
light. Little wonder that those who live at the foot of the Himalayas
should see them as dwelling places of the gods.

Gauri Shankar is the most prominent of the peaks visible from Katmandu and was once thought to be the highest mountain of all: ". . . the highest peak on the surface of the earth, the Gaourichnakar of Nepal, at the foot of which the Brahmin pilgrims who are seeking Nirvana come to die; one may say that no human being ever could drag himself to this height following uneven terrestrial surface . . ." There are many since that was written more than a century ago, who have dragged themselves higher, but none have approached even remotely near to the summit of Gauri Shankar: it is one of the greatest of the challenging climbs with which the Himalayas are still strewn.

We ate breakfast that morning just beyond the pass. From there we had only half a day's march before we reached the site of our base camp, the Sherpa village of Beding. Ed was out in front, as usual, and at his heels George Lowe, Tom Nevison, Pat Barcham and I; invariably the pace would quicken until we came to the end of the day's walk almost at a run. Beding is at 12,000 feet and I was beginning to notice the altitude; at a speed which would have been comfortable lower down I was blowing heavily, and my discomfort seemed to be greater than that of the others. Anyone going to the Himalayas for the first time is plagued by the thought that he will acclimatise poorly. It seems to be an unpredictable process and is said to be less successful in younger people—I began to grow alarmed that I would be a failure from the very beginning.

Beding was a typical Sherpa village. Rows of low stone houses faced south into the sun, and in their centre was the gompa or monastery, a larger building, plastered with mud and painted red ochre. In front of the village the river wound its way across a shingle flat on which stood a chorten, burial mound of the Buddha and symbol of Buddhism wherever it is found. We camped on the flat. Ed and Tom paid off the Nepali porters who were glad to leave those cold and inhospitable upper regions. From now on we would rely only on Sherpas for transport. To add comfort to the base-camp, a mess hut was constructed from stone, timber and a roof of clear plastic sheeting. Near it was a similar structure where the Sherpas could cook and congregate, and beside this, a dump of kitbags and boxes of food; finally there were the tents, red, blue, green and yellow, two of us in each. The floor of the valley was narrow and for the most part covered in low scrub while cliffs and grass-covered hillsides rose steeply to the mountains on each side.

Next morning we set off in pairs for a brief reconnaisance of the slopes above in the hope that we might find a hanging valley suitable for yeti-hunting. I was with Tom, Da Tensing, and another Sherpa, Sonam. To my dismay I found myself being left behind. I was forced to adopt such well-known stratagems as taking photographs, or calling a halt to discuss the topography, but even so, at the end of our three-hour jaunt, I trailed in a quarter of a mile behind. After lunch I retired to bed slightly breathless. At the back of my brain an ache began to throb and that night I could not sleep; in desperation I swallowed two codeines and a sleeping pill, and when they had no effect, another lot. I woke in the morning to find Larry, who shared the tent, gazing intently at me: "Man, you look like a corpse."

"I don't feel too good." I tried to explain and rambled off on to something quite unconnected.

"You don't seem to be functioning too well" said Larry. "What's 37 times 456?"

"For God's sake don't give me an IQ test now," I muttered, and drifted off again. Vaguely I remember being assisted along to the mess-hut . . . Tom was bending over me with a stethoscope . . . and then he was connecting me to an oxygen set. When I tried to eat breakfast I vomited; and in the background I heard voices trying to decide what colour I was. "Black as your hat," said one. "Navy blue," said another. After a day on oxygen, the blue had turned to pink again and I was able to drink a cup of tea and talk a little. I slept well and next morning, convinced that I was cured, stood up, only to find my legs buckle beneath me. So short an illness, and yet for ten days I was too weak to walk more than a short distance at a time and it was three weeks before I was fully fit again.

I have little doubt now that I was suffering from high altitude pulmonary oedema, though at the time we called it 'pneumonia'. The story was classical: a young person becoming blue and breathless after over-exerting himself within a few days of arriving at altitude, and then a rapid improvement on oxygen. Men have undoubtedly been dying of this strange hazard of high altitude for centuries, yet only over the past ten years or less has it been generally recognised that this is not a pneumonia due to bacteria, but oedema – a leaking of fluid from the blood vessels of the lung into air-spaces, so that one literally drowns. The cause is lack of oxygen; the cure is to give it, either from an oxygen set, or by taking the victim down to a lower altitude. If I have little doubt that I had pulmonary oedema, I am equally sure that without the oxygen we carried with us, I could easily have ended up underneath a burial mound of my own alongside that of the Buddha on the shingle flats of Beding.

Meanwhile however the hunters were limbering up for the pursuit of the yeti. I was well out of action but living in the mess-hut gave me a box seat from which I could watch the saga unfold. The opening stages were at first unproductive because of the continuing rain. Desmond occupied himself by prowling about the village in search of tales of the yeti. Of these there were many; even the most mentally

H

defective of the inhabitants of Beding (there were many of them, for
because of lack of iodine in the water, cretins are common) could
see that the yeti business was a profitable one, and each was determined to find for himself a share of the market. As a result of
Desmond's talent for locating the more intelligent and imaginative
members of the community he soon had a network of investigators
abroad. The most promising was a slim youth with one blind eye
who looked more like a Japanese than a Sherpa. Eye-to-heaven Ang
Temba he was called, to distinguish him from one of our high altitude
Sherpas of the same name.

John Dienhart was recording tapes for the American public in
difficult circumstances and with limited success. After about a week
he decided to return to Katmandu. Urkien, sirdar in charge of our
Sherpas, organised a party of villagers to carry John's loads. And that
led to the episode of blood on the gompa steps. Departure had been
delayed, chang had been circulating freely and by the time John was
ready to leave not one of his porters, nor any of the rest of the Sherpas
for that matter, was sober. One villager, who at the time was sitting
on the gompa steps, was no longer capable even of lifting his load off
the ground. Urkien took this as a direct affront to his authority. He
was the strongest of all our Sherpas and though a gentle likeable
person when sober, when drunk he was apt to become violent.
Seizing the nearest weapon, which happened to be a six-foot length
of timber, he struck the unwilling coolie a great blow on the head.
And a pool of blood began to collect on the gompa steps.

The first we knew of all this was the noise of a group of agitated
Sherpas approaching the hut. In the centre, supported by two friends,
was our porter, who appeared to be dying; his small son, walking in
front, was lamenting just that. The man was covered in blood, his
head lolled to one side and some well-wisher had thrown a few hand-
fuls of flour on to the wound in his scalp which was still bleeding
freely. Desmond began the interrogation—in Nepali, but we understood well enough even without the translation.

"What has happened?" said Desmond.

"Nothing," replied Urkien with a contemptuous wave of his hand.
"This man, who was meant to carry a load for John Sahib, has got
drunk and fallen over." There was a buzz of angry conversation in
Sherpa from the villagers, but no explanation in Nepali.

"Why then are these men angry?" Urkien brushed the questions
aside. So did the other expedition Sherpas though less brashly. At
length Desmond turned to the man's son. "Who has struck your
father?" and with trembling finger, the small, terrified little boy
pointed to Urkien.

The story was told in full. Then began the business of appeasing the villagers, sewing up the wound and chastising an increasingly contrite Urkien. For him it was a disaster. He was never trusted completely from that time on, and despite his outstanding abilities as a mountaineer, he was never again accepted as sirdar on a major mountaineering expedition.

Shortly after John had left, Ed announced during lunch that the moment had come to tell us about an important purchase that Desmond was hoping to negotiate: there was said to be a yeti skin in the possession of an old nun in the village. At the time this was an exciting piece of news, for none of us had yet acquired the cynicism which characterised the later stages of our interest in the yeti. Negotiations were carried out in secrecy, for it was thought that should the less scrupulous of the local lamas hear of the deal, they too would be delving their hands into the expedition money-bags. Little eye-to-heaven Ang Temba was dispatched to arrange a clandestine meeting and that afternoon Desmond walked across to the village, trying to look as inconspicuous as a fourteen-stone European can amongst a group of Sherpas. Those of us who were in camp crouched behind loop-holes in the mess-hut and watched through telescopes. There was a long wait. And then Desmond emerged from a house carrying a bulky sack. The Sherpas gathered around. The potatoes filling the upper part of the sack, as camouflage, were tossed aside and the skin hauled out. It was a bear skin. "Yeti! Sahib," said the Sherpas. "Blue bear," said Desmond.

Meanwhile George Lowe had spent a few days a couple of thousand feet higher at an observation camp. With him was Annulu, a delightful Sherpa, wise in the ways of mountains and sahibs. George, it seemed, had enjoyed the trip. He came back with an extensive knowledge of the breeding habits of yaks—but of yetis, not a sign. Marlin had set up his trip-wire flash-cameras and produced some enigmatically blank photographs, presumably of the gusts of wind which had triggered them. Enterprising Nepali hunters from down valley appeared in camp with a langur monkey and several lesser pandas, beautiful little creatures with shining red fur, broad faces, short fox-like snouts and round white ears. "Yeti! Sahib! Only 500 rupees," and we bought them as pets for 50.

We shifted camp to 14,000 feet, the site of a summer yak-grazing and potato-growing village called Nangaon. Parties scoured the surrounding hillsides, unsuccessfully, and a week later we moved again, this time to a grassy flat at 16,000 feet beside the moraine of the Ripimu Glacier. Just beyond the pass at the head of the glacier was the névé where Eric Shipton had discovered the only convincing evidence for the existence of the yeti: the large, well-formed, five-toed tracks which he had photographed. Most of us by now were pessimistic about our chances of finding the animal in the flesh, but we still had hopes of seeing some tracks.

A few days after our arrival at Ripimu there was a sudden commotion in the camp. Da Thondu, Pete's personal Sherpa, came flying down the ridge as if bringing the good news from Ghent to Aix. "Yeti! Sahib." The old cry rang through the camp. We gathered around the wildly excited Da Thondu, his breath coming in gasps and his face shining with sweat. There was a lot of shouting and gesticulating and then, kneeling on the ground, he drew an outline of a yeti-track. He and some other Sherpas had been carrying loads up to an observation camp when they came on these strange tracks circling around a sardine tin tossed there by some sahib. The smell of sardines had lured a yeti from his lair—we had only to follow the tracks and he was ours.

Ed quickly organised a hunting party. Within an hour the lot of us, dressed in our bright orange windproofs, were milling around a lone sardine tin on a snow-covered ridge. Where were the tracks? Da Thondu pointed out some ill-defined depressions, which looked suspiciously like the footprints of the person who had dropped the tin there in the first place. There was no long line of freshly-formed prints that we could follow, and somewhat disgruntled, we took photographs and returned to camp.

Three days later Ed gave the order to shift camp to 17,000 feet at the head of the valley, a base from which we could explore slopes on our side of the Tibetan border. On the following day, while Ed led one party to explore the eastern slopes, Pat Barcham and I, with three Sherpas, set off on a four-day trip to explore a high névé to the west. Early on the morning of the second day we were struggling up a long snow slope at 19,000 feet when Pat's Sherpa, Gumi Dorje, stopped with an exclamation. Seizing Pat by the arm, he pointed dramatically to the top of the slope: "Yeti! Sahib." Had I known the Sherpa translation of "I've heard that one before mate," I would have said it. It was becoming clear that for ten rupees, Gumi, or any other Sherpa for that matter, would have sworn his wife was a yeti. But wait! There was an indistinct line crossing the snow high up. Faint hopes stirred within us as we toiled up towards an increasingly prominent line of tracks. An hour later we reached them, two parallel lines of animal tracks. Each print was roughly circular, six inches in diameter, and had toe-marks on the downhill side; they were twelve inches apart.

"Well," said Pat. "I don't know whether they're yeti tracks but they're the closest thing to them we've seen yet. Let's see where they lead to."

On one side they ran on to a scree slope. On the other they turned steeply downhill under a rock wall. And there, in the shadow, a remarkable change took place: each print separated itself into two small sharply delineated pug-marks. Our yeti prints were no more than fox tracks, fused and enlarged by the heat of the sun. There was no more to them than that. And unknown to us, Larry, Desmond, Bhanu and Marlin, had investigated an identical series of tracks lower down, on the same day, and come to exactly the same conclusion about their origin.

Three days later we retreated, all of us by now disillusioned about yetis. We felt an urge for pastures new: to be more precise, we felt the time had come to cross the Tesi Lapcha Pass to the Khumbu.

The Khumbu region forms the headwaters of the Dudh Kosi River. It is the home of most Sherpas who go on mountaineering expeditions (though some have lived for months or years in Darjeeling or Katmandu) and around it, on or close to the Tibetan border, stand Everest, Lhotse, Makalu and Cho Oyu, four of the six highest peaks in the world. Within this outer group of giants is an inner ring of spectacular summits: Ama Dablam, Kangtega, Thamserku and Taweche. There are five main Sherpa villages in the Khumbu—Namche Bazar, Kumjung-Kunde, Thami, Phorze and Pangboche—and a large and very beautifully-sited monastery, Tengboche. The villages are built on terraces at about 12,000 feet; above them stone-covered slopes, which grow grass in the monsoon, extend to a height of 17,000 feet before they become useless to man. Below the villages, steep pine-forested slopes plunge 2,000 feet into the gorge of the Dudh Kosi. There are two commonly-used routes into the Khumbu, the gorge of the Dudh Kosi giving access from the lower regions of Nepal, and to the north the 19,000 foot Nangpa La crossing the border from Tibet. The Rolwaling is an isolated pocket of Sherpa country west of the Khumbu, separated from it by a range of mountains whose lowest point is the Tesi Lapcha.

To cross this 19,000 foot pass, with 150 loads was going to be no easy matter, even if we could find enough porters. Urkien went forth on to the highways and byways of Beding and Nangaon, but even with the halt and the maimed included, we could muster only eighty. In the end Ed was forced to radio to Norm an urgent request for a battalion of Khumbu Sherpas to come to our aid. They arrived late one sunny afternoon. We were camped at the foot of an immense cliff which separated us from the snows of the pass 3,000 feet higher. Down the lower part there was a track of sorts, but for the most part it was fearsomely steep and rock-swept.

Suddenly, from the cliffs high above, came a chattering and laughing and the knock of falling stones. We looked up: there they were,

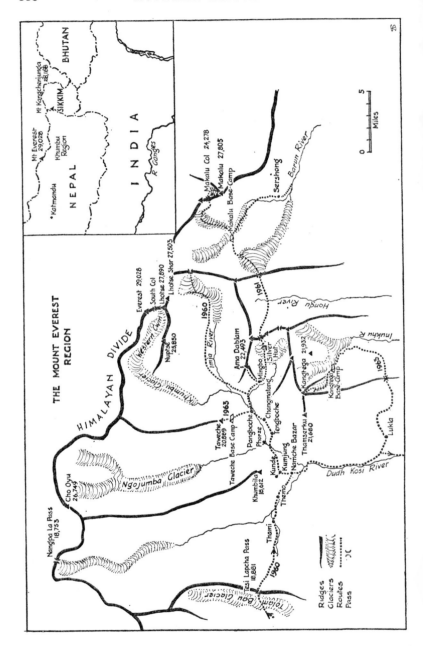

THE MOUNT EVEREST REGION

dozens of small dark figures swarming down the rocks like so many gnomes. Soon they were thronging noisily in to camp, greeting old friends and exchanging news. Though a few wore old expedition clothes, most were in Sherpa dress, the women in long robes of black homespun and striped aprons, the men in shirts and sheep-skin trousers, and on their feet were brightly-coloured felt boots with smooth leather soles. As the evening closed in and the temperature fell below freezing, they settled themselves in small groups around fires amongst the shelter of moraine boulders.

On October 28th we crossed the pass. The day was perfect, for though the Himalayan autumn is cold, usually it is fine. I left early with the idea of shooting film of the crossing, and by climbing a rock ridge found a small platform, sheltered from the wind, with an uninterrupted view of the broad sweep of snow crowning the pass. Sitting in the sun I looked east, across a deep valley, to the peaks of the Khumbu, a tangled array of white spires and fluted faces most of which, even to my optimistic eye, looked hopelessly inaccessible. Below me, on the Rolwaling side of the pass, the line of porters toiled upwards amongst the network of crevasses. For a moment it seemed as remote from human habitation as the wastes of the Antarctic. But then I saw that we were not alone on the Tesi Lapcha. Working their way up from the Khumbu side were a few Sherpas with a herd of yaks and a flock of thirty goats. They had no ice-axes, no crampons, no ropes. I thought for a moment they must be lost, but, no, the Sherpas had said that men quite often crossed the pass with animals. The goats looked unhappy, for though the snow was soft on the sunny Khumbu side, over the crest it was still ice. The leading animal dithered at the top of the slope until a sharp Sherpa kick from behind set him moving. There being no foothold, he simply sat back on his haunches, front feet thrust rigidly forwards, and slithered down to the gentler slopes below, closely followed by the rest of the flock. They could have been a school party tobogganing in the Alps.

In the vanguard of the expedition were Ed and George, with Desmond and Bhanu close behind. Desmond had by now fined down his figure considerably and could stride along with the carriage and speed of a Gurkha officer going into action. Bringing up the rear, at a gentler speed more in keeping with his years, was Marlin accompanied by his Sherpa. On top, where others had hurried on out of the wind, Marlin paused and began rummaging in his rucksack. What secret business was this? Ah, yes! The flag. If Americans have a weakness it is for flags. Tom for a while had flown the stars and stripes over his tent and now Marlin was securing a photograph of the Adventurers' Club flag at 19,000 feet. I hope the Club were aware of the level of such an achievement, for if anyone deserved merit for the crossing of the Tesi Lapcha, it was Marlin.

Twenty minutes later I joined him, in time to see rockfall in a couloir nearly hit a string of porters. Standing beside us at the time was a worried-looking little man, who was so frightened by the sight of a ton of rock roaring past that he dropped his load. The basket tumbled over a cliff, broke apart, and Ed and George, standing below, suddenly found two biscuit tins hurtling out of the sky, closely followed by a Zenith radio. By mid-afternoon, however, we were safely off the upper slopes and wandering down through yak pastures.

During the two days that followed we walked through the inhabited regions of the Sherpa country, through Thami, and Namche Bazar, and Kumjung. I thought the Khumbu was the most beautiful country I had ever seen. The monsoon was well past and the ground dry and dusty; it was warm in the sun and the trees and shrubs were still aglow with autumn colours. Thami was crowded with the black, domed tents of Tibetan refugees and the air full of the fragrance of burning juniper. From Thami the track ran south above the river through pine forests to Namche, the administrative and trading centre of the Khumbu. Having presented our passports at the Nepalese check-post we continued on to Kumjung. After a climb of five hundred feet the track eased off. There were long mani walls of carved stone slabs, and beyond them a pair of chortens on which were painted the all-seeing eyes of the Buddha. The surrounding country, with its stone walls, close-cropped grass and clumps of trees looked homely, as if it were kept as a garden.

I came over the hill and before me was Ama Dablam. I had had a surfeit of mountain scenery, yet I caught my breath at the sight of it. Ama in Sherpa means mother. Demons dwell on other peaks but Ama Dablam is too lovely a mountain to be the home of an evil spirit. As you walk through the village of Kumjung you see the summit serenely poised in the sky across the valley, the supporting ridges extended like arms. And so they call it Ama.

We came to Kumjung and there we camped. We had not yet finished with the yeti for there was still the business of the scalp to be cleared up. This was kept at the Kumjung gompa (there was another at Pangboche) and at a special ceremony, for a sum of money, we were invited to view it. It was a rather bizarre dome-shaped affair, patchily covered in coarse hair, dyed red, and one had the impression that for many years it had probably been used as a clown's hat in the more lively of the monastery's celebrations. Most of us agreed that it had a home-made look. Desmond was at the top of his form, making everyone laugh uproariously, extracting strange stories from the lamas, and taking the headman aside for secret talks. The result was a signed agreement allowing us to borrow the scalp for a month, on condition that we paid a suitably large sum and that one of the head-men, Kunjo Chumbi, should go along as escort.

On November 25th, Ed, Desmond, Kunjo Chumbi and the scalp set off around the world: Chicago, London, Paris. Though the scalp was duly found to be a fake, Kunjo was declared genuine and as an exponent of Tibetan dancing was asked to perform wherever he went, from the Merchandise Mart in Chicago to the night clubs of Paris.

A few days after his return I met Kunjo striding along the track below Kunjung. He was wearing a bowler hat, a pair of emerald-green cotton trousers and carrying a Pan Am bag. After a decent show of reluctance I accepted his invitation to drink chang at his house and see his gifts: a photograph album, aluminium watch, Eau de Cologne gentleman's spray, a string of artificial pearls, nail polish, a 3-dimensional French photo-viewer showing nudes, a blue jersey, suède shoes, a china bird, a tiny scented bouquet of artificial roses, and last but not least a Merchandise Mart lunch menu signed by the senior executives of World Books.

"And now," said Kunjo. "I have something for you. Yeti skin, Mike Sahib. Only five hundred rupees." And he dragged out the skin of an ancient dog which only two months ago had been limping around Kumjung.

"Kunjo," I said, "the West has not spoiled you."

What is the yeti? In Sherpa mythology, it seems, the yeti is an evil spirit. To the Sherpas, spirits are as real as atoms, or angels, are to us – though to prove they are there is not easy. But then, the few of us who believe in angels must trust in hearsay or faith, and though we accept atoms without question, there are not many of us who can prove our belief. So if a Sherpa finds unknown tracks in the snow, or catches a glimpse of a vague shape at dusk, or when by himself in a lonely hut on a stormy night hears strange noises—why then, it is a yeti. And if a sahib with a sackful of rupees comes hunting the yeti— Oh yes sahib! We have yetis! The trading instincts of the Sherpas are too sharp to allow doubts to intrude in such times of plenty.

11

WINTER AT 19,000 FEET

... most of the tourists whose narrations fill the Alpine journals have hardly any scientific interest in their ascents; they climb for the sake of climbing, or seeing, or often of telling that they have climbed and seen. It is generally this last feeling which dictates their accounts, and that is why one sees them every year seeking some horn, spitze, or joch, hitherto inaccessible or merely forgotten: a virginity often hard to conquer, the sterile conquest of which they will dispute.

Paul Bert: *La Pression Barométrique*

PAUL BERT, was the pioneer of high altitude physiology. The year was 1878, a time when the last of the virgin summits of the Alps were being trampled underfoot, and Bert's criticism, founded as it was on a perusal of the entire literature of mountain travel, sounds reasonable. In the second half of the twentieth century the situation has changed. The mountaineer who has wandered into the labyrinths of the literature of science is tempted to retaliate: to point out that many a scientist "writes for the sake of writing, or publishing, or often of telling that he has written and published . . . and that is why one sees them every year seeking some insect, enzyme or molecule, hitherto inaccessible or merely forgotten . . . the sterile investigation of which . . ." And there have been no shortage of disputes either.

Had Bert seen the Himalayan Scientific and Mountaineering Expedition he would, I hope, have admired the way we toiled in the cause of science throughout the winter. At the end of it all, papers were published, a few tiny ripples on the oceans of science. High altitude physiology is a field which has been worked over before: untouched areas for investigation are as hard to come by as forgotten jochs and horns in the Alps. Our claim to originality lay in the fact that we planned to carry our investigations higher than had been attempted before. We hoped to build a laboratory at 20,000 feet, work there through the winter and then do as much as we could at higher altitudes on Makalu, even on the 27,800 foot summit itself. The maximum height at which man could live for a long period, was unknown; miners in the Andes, though they had lived permanently at 17,500 feet, had found 19,000 feet too high. On Everest and other mountains, men had spent a month or two over 20,000 feet and climbed, without oxygen, to 28,000 feet, but they had shown, to use another of Bert's phrases, "hardly any scientific interest in their ascents".

When Bert began work on the problems of high altitude the nature of altitude sickness was unknown. In his monumental *La Pression Barométrique* he proved that reduced pressure of oxygen in the atmosphere is the cause. It is a fascinating book, "rich in outside observation" as one might expect from a man with a distinguished and varied career in times more spacious than our own. He began as an engineer, qualified in law and then medicine, and eventually took a Chair of Physiology in Paris. Not content with this he moved into politics, and at the time of his death was in Hanoi reorganising foreign policy in Vietnam, a task which was no bed of roses even then.

La Pression Barometrique opens with a survey of mountain sickness as described in the journals of mountain travellers. There is a glimpse of Marco Polo crossing the Tibetan Plateau in 1298: "Always one rides through mountains, and mounts so high that it is said that this is the highest spot in all the world. No flying fowl is there, because of height and cold. And I tell you that fire, through this great cold, is not so bright nor so warm as in other places, nor can it cook viands so well."

The most vivid accounts of mountain sickness came from the Andes where the Spanish conquerors were afraid of its mysterious power. The Jesuit priest Acosta, who crossed the Andes, wrote in 1596: "In certain parts of the Indies, the air and the wind blowing there dizzy men not less but more than at sea . . . In Peru there is a high mountain called Pariacaca, and having heard tell of the variation it caused, I went there . . . when I began to mount the stairs, as they call the highest part of the mountain, I was suddenly attacked and surprised by an illness so deadly and strange, that I was almost on the point of falling from my horse to the ground, and although there were several in our company, each hastened his step without waiting for his companion so that he might leave this evil spot quickly. Being left alone then with an Indian, whom I asked to help sit me on my horse, I was seized by such a spasm of panting and vomiting that I thought I should give up the ghost . . . I was told that in the past some men had lost their lives from this distress. I saw a man lying on the ground in a passion, crying out with the rage and pain caused him by this passage of the Pariacaca . . . And it is not only the pass of Mount Pariacaca that has this characteristic, but also this whole chain of mountains, which extends more than five hundred leagues . . ."

The accounts of a host of travellers, besides Acosta, gave a complete picture of mountain sickness: the vomiting and headaches, the panting and ease with which one is fatigued, the insomnia and distaste for food. Bert noted that "different constitutions seem unevenly affected" and that old age and ill-health aggravate the symptoms: "those of the peons who are old and addicted to bad habits suffer more from the puna than the others . . ." And of cold: "when the icy wind of high places rises it makes the symptoms unendurable, and may bring on death . . ." He realised, too, that those who live in high places are less prone to the sickness—that there is such a process as acclimatisation.

Bert went on to describe balloon ascents, a pastime then in its heyday. As in the mountains, fatalities were not uncommon. He refers in passing to "the unhappy Cocking who had made a parachute wrong side out, the absurdity of which no one could doubt . . . he fell like a stone." And Groof, the Flying Man, who was carried up in a balloon, "with his complicated apparatus suspended under the basket . . . at 1,000 feet Groof disengaged himself, and falling head first, was dashed upon the ground." There is a certain grim humour in the madness of these two, but there was none in the ascent of the balloon 'Zenith' which was sponsored by Bert himself. Three Frenchmen rose to the unprecedented height of 28,000 feet: at 26,000 feet all three were unconscious, and when the balloon drifted back to earth only one was alive. M. Tissandier, the survivor, wrote of their entry into the upper atmosphere: "I now come to the fateful moments when we were overcome by the terrible action of reduced pressure. At 22,900 feet . . . torpor had seized me. I wrote nevertheless . . . though I have no clear recollection of writing. We are rising. Crocé is panting. Sivel shuts his eyes. Crocé also shuts his eyes . . . At 24,600 feet the condition of torpor that overcomes one is extraordinary. Body and mind become feebler . . . There is no suffering. On the contrary, one feels an inward joy. There is no thought of the dangerous position; one rises and is glad to be rising. I soon felt myself so weak that I could not even turn my head to look at my companions . . . I wished to call out that we were now at 26,000 feet, but my tongue was paralysed. All at once I shut my eyes and fell down powerless and lost all further memory."

Shaken by this disastrous result of what was partly an experiment, Bert returned to his work with the decompression chamber. Before then a wide variety of theories, none of them well tested, had been put forward to explain mountain sickness. They included evil spirits, pestilential exhalations from the ground, fatigue, cold, lack of oxygen in the air, the mechanical effect of reduced atmospheric pressure, and excess of carbonic acid in the blood. Bert proved conclusively that the reduction in pressure of oxygen alone was the cause and in doing so paved the way for the rational investigation of acclimatisation.

We began work on the Wintering Party's hut at the beginning of November. The site Ed had chosen, only ten miles from the Sherpa village of Pangboche, was on a col at the head of the Mingbo Valley, one of the three major eastern tributaries of the Dudh Kosi, the other two being the Khumbu, which leads to Mt Everest, and the Imja, a broader valley running along the foot of the Lhotse–Nuptse wall to the 27,500 foot peak of Lhotse Shar. While we were yeti-hunting Norm's party had found and flagged an easy route up the Mingbo and carried the hut sections and supplies to a broad névé a few hundred feet below the col where the hut was to be built.

On November 4th, Ed, Norm and the rest of us, along with a crowd of Sherpas, arrived on the névé for the final carry to the col by way of a steep fluted snow-face. It was a dangerous route for Sherpas laden with awkward loads and Norm had already erected a winch, brought with us for use in such places. There was a steel pylon on the col, another on the névé, and stretched between them, a cable on which ran pulleys supporting the loads. Urkien and old Da Tensing, and those who were winding the winch, claimed that back-packing the loads up a good line of steps would be easier, but those of us who were there in a supervisory capacity were more willing to give the winch a trial. I was in charge of loading at the lower end of the cable.

We had been working about an hour when there were some agitated cries from the Sherpas on the col and from the way those around me were diving for cover I gathered that this was a warning. There was a high-pitched whining sound growing louder, the cable and pylon began vibrating urgently and a few seconds later a flying pulley smashed into the lower end of the cable. The pylon was groggy but still standing and we carried on. A trifle uneasy now, especially at the thought of what a load on the loose might do, I kept an eye on the slopes above. Sure enough, about ten minutes later, to the accompaniment of a whirring sound, a black object appeared on the skyline. With a great cry of warning I leapt into the shelter of the crevasse beside us—much to the delight of the Sherpas, for the black object was a chough, a bird which amuses itself by flying to a great height, placing its wings behind its back and descending with the sound and appearances of a flying bomb. But an hour later a second unattached pulley came down. This time it delivered a knock-out blow: the pylon was laid low and the winch used no more.

By now, anyway, those on the col were frozen to the marrow by the freshening gale blowing up there. Those who were below climbed to the col and into the shelter of our wildly flapping tents. The altitude seemed to be affecting most of us and I spent a restless night, lying awake much of the time with a headache listening to the Cheyne-Stokes breathing of those around me. Ed too slept poorly, giving him ample time to brood on the siting of the hut. The roar of the wind outside and the memory of the steepness of the slopes below were powerful arguments and in the morning he gave the order to retreat to the névé and begin the building there.

The site chosen was on one side of the upper end of the névé, at a point where it dropped away sharply over a line of rock bluffs. As a member of the Wintering Party I found myself looking at the site with a more critical eye than those who would be spending the winter elsewhere. None of us had much idea what the weather would be like but it seemed logical to expect heavy snowfalls—and avalanches. The site was protected on the uphill side by a shallow snow gully, but any sizable avalanche would fill this in a moment: a gentle push and our hut would be tumbling over the bluffs. As it turned out there were no snowfalls to speak of the whole time we were there; our only problem was the heat of the sun undermining the foundations. When we returned to the hut at the end of the climb on Makalu six months later it was an extraordinary sight, for the warm air of the oncoming monsoon had thawed twenty feet off the surface of the névé, leaving the hut perched on a stalk of rotting snow, like a monstrous mushroom.

Because of its colour we called it the Silver Hut. It was twenty-two feet long, ten feet wide and shaped like a tunnel, with windows at either end. The walls were panels of prefabricated plywood wired together, and the whole structure was anchored to buried kitbags of snow. Inside were eight bunks, a central kerosene stove, a dining table, and at one end, laboratory benches and a clear space for the bicycle ergometer. A snow-cave for storage of food and equipment was dug into the side of the snow gully, tents pitched for those who preferred to sleep outside and a big dome tent erected for the Sherpas. It was a long time before the interior was fully furnished, the wiring and electricity generators installed, laboratory equipment set up, but at the end of the third day's work, all of it in bright sunshine, the outer shell was complete and secure, the stove working, and the bunks ready for occupation.

The main tasks of the autumn parties were now complete. In a fortnight they would be gone, leaving behind them the physiologists, four of whom had not yet arrived, plus Barry Bishop and Wally Romanes. There were still some loose ends to be tied up. Ed had the unenviable responsibilities of leadership: establishing lines of communication for the Wintering Party, checking on food supplies and kerosene and storing surplus equipment till the spring. Desmond was fashioning a yeti scalp from a piece of goat skin hammered out on a wooden mould; Pete was on a holiday trip to the foot of Everest, and later, Taweche; Barry was boring scientific holes in the Mingbo Glacier. And while all this was going on, Norm, Wally and I were on a reconnaissance of Lhotse Shar from the Imja Valley. The leadership of this excursion had been handed to Norm as a reward for having completed so successfully the carry from Katmandu to the Mingbo. There are some who might regard attempting the lower slopes of a 27,500 foot mountain as more of a punishment than a reward but Norm was made of sterner stuff: we had fourteen good Sherpas and ten days' food, and he had every intention of reaching 24,000 feet. Nor was this mere idle talk for five years earlier Norm had been to the 28,900 foot summit of Kangchenjunga. I began to prepare myself for hard times ahead.

There was nothing hard about the first three days. We ambled up-valley at an easy pace, chatting to each other or to the Sherpas, using Norm's broken Hindi or their broken English. Norm had been on two previous expeditions; he had also lived six months in Kumjung and written a book about it. As a result he had a fund of expedition and Sherpa lore, parts of which a sympathetic listener, without too much difficulty, could extract. During those days in the Imja, Norm was our guru, Wally and I the disciples. Though he had just led in a huge and unwieldy train of porters from Katmandu, Norm was essentially a devotee of the small mobile expedition travelling with a few good Sherpas and living off the land, a tradition which I imagine had been partly absorbed from Charles Evans, who in turn had walked through the Himalayas with Shipton and Tilman; and Tilman was a self-confessed disciple of the great Mummery. The lineage was an ancient and honourable one.

The Imja, up which our route lay, was a much longer and more roomy valley than the Mingbo and was separated from it by the bastion of Ama Dablam. Urkien pointed out the route used by an English party in an attempt on Ama Dablam the previous year. His descriptions of the difficulties of the ridge seemed to us a statement of the obvious, and the sequel not surprising. The summit pair, Harris and Frazer, had eventually changed from the traditional fixed-rope and camp method of Himalayan climbing to the Alpine technique of carrying a bivouac. The Himalayas deal harshly with those who take risks—the success of such climbs as Hermann Buhl's fantastic solo ascent of Nanga Parbat, is the exception rather than the rule—and Harris and Frazer never returned.

Ama Dablam, however, was dwarfed by the immense Lhotse–Nuptse rock wall which rose on our left. We looked up there often, for the weather was deteriorating. The four-mile-long crest was more than 10,000 feet above us, yet even from so far below we could hear the wind blowing across it, like the bass notes of a vast celestial organ, and each day the snow plumes were flung farther into the sky from its pinnacles. Radio reports from the Silver Hut told us of heavy gusts of wind sweeping the névé and the Sherpas shook their heads knowingly.

After three days we established Base Camp at the foot of Lhotse Shar, which stands at the eastern end of the wall. Here the rock precipices give way to a steep but broad snow-face and up this we hoped to find a way. Camp I was placed at 20,000 feet. Early on the morning of the fifth day we set to work on the ice-face proper. Wally began with a lead up a ten-foot ice wall and above this we climbed steadily on steep snow towards some broken ice, moving at times over piles of avalanche debris. We reached our limit at about 21,500 feet, below a line of seracs. There was no easy lead anywhere. Ice walls bared their teeth at us across the width of the mountain and on the slopes above the wind was eddying back and forth, shifting the loose snow so that the whole face seemed to be moving, or rising into the air like the spouting of a huge fountain. And over all there was the earth-shaking roar of the wind, a torrent of sound fading and swelling so that at times it seemed half the ice-face had broken loose and was descending on us. There had been suggestions that we climb Lhotse Shar in the spring, rather than Makalu, but there was no route for an expedition as large as ours, equipped with the impedimenta of science as we were. No place there for a bicycle ergometer.

We retreated. Next day, at Base Camp, Norm produced a modified plan designed to extend our reconnaissance of the mountain. Annulu and I would climb Island Peak, a 20,000 foot knoll at the end of a spur which abutted on to the western edge of the ice-face; he and Wally, with Urkien and Ang Temba, would climb to a col on the ridge bounding the farther edge of the face. It seemed a good plan. But a few minutes later an avalanche swept Norm's route: a puff of white appeared on the slope below the col and then the familiar roar was swelling in our ears. Around the camp there was a heavy silence, broken at length by a gay laugh from Annulu. "Eh! Mike Sahib! Tomorrow we climb Island Peak!" In the morning we departed in opposite directions. There was no gay laughter from Norm and Wally as they set off towards the col, a climb which was accomplished at whirlwind speed. Nor for that matter was there much laughter from me by the time I had reached the last and highest of Island Peak's summits, a long and exhausting climb which I completed, in Annulu's tracks, almost on my hands and knees. The effort was worthwhile, however, for we could see a steep but avalanche-free route leading up the spur to a point high on the ice-face. Norm, too, from his col, could see a way up the ridge, but neither his route nor mine was the easy one we were looking for. We rejoined the rest of the expedition with the recommendation that we keep to our Makalu plan.

December was a slothful month. All except the Wintering Party had by then departed for Katmandu, but because the last of the physiology team had not yet arrived, we were unable to start on the main part of the programme. We did what work we could and between times wandered back and forth amongst our complex of Base Camps, for we were not by any means confined to the Silver Hut. Down at 13,000 feet, in a village called Changmatang buried in the woods near Tengboche Monastery, Ed had hired a house which formed our lowest base; at 15,000 feet we had a well-established tent-camp in the tiny grazing village of Mingbo; and at 17,500 feet Wally had built the canvas-and-timber Green Hut.

Changmatang, sited as it was in a clearing in the forest, was a delightful spot, but the interior, lacking a chimney, was too full of smoke for anyone to want to stay for any length of time. Throughout the winter a caretaker was in residence, a wrinkled Sherpa called Changju who had the happiest face in the Khumbu. He was one of the more widely travelled of the Sherpas for at the conclusion of the Kangchenjunga Expedition he had been invited to London with the sirdar Da Tensing. There was a story that someone had asked what they would like to take back to the Khumbu. Changju's interests ran to more frivolous objects, such as clothes and gadgets, but of such things old Da Tensing was scornful. As an affluent yak-owner, he had been impressed above all by the size of English cows and their milk yield. "I would like a good English cow!" he said with finality. It was Changju's turn to be scornful: "Don't be a fool, Da Tensing. What would the people on the plane say if you brought a cow with you?"

An hour's walk from Changmatang was Pangboche, farthest east of the main villages of the Khumbu. Here our route turned up the Mingbo Valley. In early winter the hill-sides were bare and brown except for patches of dwarf rhododendron or the low juniper scrub we used as fuel. At 15,000 feet was Mingbo, a small flat area with stone walls for holding yaks and three low stone houses. In the monsoon, there are flowers and the grass here is thick; Sherpa families live in the houses, yaks graze happily on the surrounding hills and there is an abundance of milk and curd. But in autumn the earth freezes and the houses are left empty. Griff chose Mingbo as the lower of our two laboratory camps. A big dome tent was equipped with benches, one of the houses was converted into a mess hut and

I

tents were used as living quarters. A helicopter could land on the flat and later, in a small valley near by, we constructed the highest and most dangerous air-strip in Nepal.

Above Mingbo there were no tracks other than those made by Norm's party in the course of ferrying loads to higher levels. At 16,500 feet the grass gave way to scree. A cairned trail led round the foot of the ridge of Ama Dablam—of which there is more to be said later—and on to the moraine of the Mingbo Glacier. In a trough close to the white ice of the glacier was the Green Hut, placed there as an intermediate laboratory but seldom used except as a staging post *en route* to the Silver Hut an hour and a half farther on.

The Silver Hut was by far the most comfortable of our four winter camps. There was heat from the stove, light from the electrical system, sponge rubber on the bunks and a ski slope at the door. Even the weather was finer at 19,000 feet, for there were times when snow was falling at Changmatang while we skiied in bright sunshine at the Silver Hut. Tom, who was not only a physiologist but a gadget man of rare ability, had added to our comfort by setting up the wind and petrol generators and wiring the hut so that eventually we even had bedside reading lamps. Above all we were acclimatised: we slept, ate and worked without any discomfort, even if not quite so heartily as at sea level, and we moved freely and easily down to Changmatang and back as the whim took us. When we heard of the big religious festival at Tengboche on December 4th there was no question of the trip being too much effort—we packed our sleeping-bags and went.

It was called the Mani Rimdu and so far as we could gather its importance was comparable with that of our Christmas. Like many Europeans I had grown up with a romantic interest in the remote peoples and religion of Tibet, and here, in the Mani Rimdu, was a chance to see Tibetan Buddhism in action. For the Sherpas are simply Tibetans who crossed the Himalayan Divide two or three hundred years ago and settled on the unoccupied high pastures they found there. They brought their religion with them and Tengboche, which was built half a century ago, is an offshoot of the famous Rongbuk Monastery on the north side of Everest. The Sherpa festival of Mani Rimdu is identical with that celebrated at the parent monastery on the other side of the mountain.

I made no great progress in understanding Buddhism, either through being with Sherpas or visiting their monasteries—I daresay a Sherpa who found himself at a celebration of the Mass would make equally little sense of it—but two things struck me. One was the apparent care with which monasteries are sited so as to be in view of the mountains for it seems that any amount of inconvenience is acceptable provided the splendour of the scene is not diminished. The setting of Tengboche is incomparable. It stands 2,000 feet above the river gorge, on the crest of a spur which juts out from the side-wall of the valley. Great mountains rise north, south, east and west: Everest, Lhotse, Nuptse, Ama Dablam, Kangtega, Taweche, Kwangde — Tengboche is at the centre of them all.

And the second thing that struck me was the obvious strength of the religious convictions of the Sherpas. The heartiest and apparently most westernised of our expedition group would stop silent and bare-headed on the track for the blessing of a respected lama who happened to be passing, and in the presence of the Head Lama he would behave as a Catholic might who suddenly found himself confronted by the Pope. Buddhism to the Sherpas is no empty formula but permeates, to their benefit, every part of their lives; without it I doubt whether they would have so stable and happy a society, or be so free from violence or any deep dissatisfaction. The monks are not all virtuous by any means, but most of them are, and one is left with the conviction that some of them are striving after the high ideals of their religion.

The Mani Rimdu began with an assembly outside the main temple on an open grassy space where the Head Lama, resplendent in crimson robes and gold brocade, sat under an awning flanked by an assembly of monks. The villagers filed past, hat in hand, each receiving a blessing and presenting an offering. The monks chanted in a deep monotone, the temple trumpets made strange noises in the background and the smell of burning incense hung in the hot afternoon air. In three hours the invocation and blessings were finished, and except for a mysterious concluding ceremony, the rest of the three days was taken up with dances performed by monks in the more sheltered surroundings of the temple courtyard. All the dances were colourful, some were graceful, many were pure slapstick.

In the evening by the light of an ancient kerosene lamp, the villagers took over. Sherpa dancing looks easy. You stand in a line, shoulder to shoulder, arms around each other's waists, men on one side of the courtyard, women on the other. And then, to the rhythm of a song, you begin stamping and shuffling backwards and forwards at an ever-increasing tempo. The rhythm is more intricate than appears at first sight. At the insistence of Dawa Tensing, who had fortified both of us with chang, I joined in. It was strange how seldom I made the correct move: as one hundred Sherpas in unison went forward, I went back; while each of them stamped with his right foot I stamped with my left; and once Dawa Tensing, through no fault of his, came down on my right foot like a stonemason's hammer. Time and chang happeneth to us all, and by midnight, though I was ready for bed, I was in no state to tackle the track to Changmatang. Dawa Tensing and his sister, a fine buxom wench, though they were in little better condition than I was, found a spare sleeping-bag and helped me into it—an incident that neither sahib nor Sherpa allowed me to forget in the months that followed.

Shortly after the Mani Rimdu I established my reputation as an obstetrician. We were working on the physiology programme one afternoon when a sweating Sherpa arrived from Pangboche with a request for a doctor. A Tibetan woman had been in labour for three days, a time they regarded as a death sentence. By now she was prepared to try anything. My week's experience in obstetrics as a student was only marginally better than nothing, but as the others were busy I went. I found the family crowded into the sort of low stone house that only the poorest of Sherpas would have considered living in. Acrid smoke from a yak dung fire filled the room. Mother and unborn child were both alive I discovered, and I saw no reason yet for calling for more expert help. After reassuring the mother I gave her a shot of morphine to settle her for the night, and took a sleeping tablet myself for the same reason. When I woke in the morning the baby had been born for over an hour, the cord having been cut with a kukri and tied with yak hair. And though the mother was eying me with distrust, the rest of the family gave me full credit for the miraculous delivery, proclaiming me a very great lama indeed.

When I called on my patients again three days later, mother, still surly, was feeding an apparently healthy infant from a well-filled breast. The other breast was missing; where it should have been there was only a scar, a mutilation which I could only assume was a part of some punishment she had received in Tibet. Dawa Tensing, who had no further information, merely gave me a playful jab in the ribs, a wink, and a comment to the effect that even if one was missing the other was good. When I called again two weeks later I was welcomed with a smile. How was the baby? The baby was dead. I seemed to be the only person present who was either surprised or upset by this information. How had it died? I learned nothing—except that such an outcome is so common as to be hardly worth remarking on.

My second delivery was less of a success. Late one afternoon I was called to the house of a lama who had grown tired of chastity and taken a wife. They were living in a tiny village called Nganga Dzong at 15,000 feet, the highest permanent settlement in the Khumbu. His claim to be eighty years old made him the oldest father in the region, as well as the highest. Things were not going well for his wife: the baby was dead and apparently stuck fast, and she herself was in great distress. Using my only therapeutic weapon, a massive injection of morphine, I sent off an urgent letter to Jim Milledge. When he arrived, the mother was not only sleeping peacefully, but had delivered the dead baby, an event neither she nor I had been aware of.

Before leaving we looked over the rest of the village, such as it was. The few houses were perched on steep slopes above the grass flats and moraines of the Imja. Nearby, a nun who had taken the vow of silence lived in a house cunningly constructed by walling in the front of a cave. Below her lived a nun who for twenty-six years had eaten neither salt nor meat, her diet consisting solely of roast barley flour and water. The old lama's house was the best of them all, small but well-made with a stone balcony in front. Ama Dablam reared up only a mile or two across the valley and to the east rose Lhotse Shar, crisply white against the blue of the sky. With the taste of buttered tea lingering on our palates, and a Tibetan blessing in our ears, we turned towards the Mingbo and began the journey home.

The last contingent of physiologists arrived just after the middle of December, a time when all of us except Griff were living at the Silver Hut. Two of them, Dr 'Larry' Lahiri and Captain Motwani, were Indians, adding further to the cosmopolitan character of the expedition. They had little in common except nationality. Larry was small, unassuming and an expert physiologist. The Captain was a huge, noisy, bushy-headed Army officer who spent most of the winter at Mingbo, making blistering curries and trying to instil discipline into our Sherpas, a project which met with little success. The other two were from London. Mike Ward, a surgeon, had had more experience in Himalayan climbing than anyone other than Ed; from the beginning he had been closely connected with the post-war interest in Everest; he had been a member of the reconnaissance parties, and the successful 1953 expedition; he was leader of our Ama Dablam party and of the Makalu assault when Ed fell ill. John West was our only Australian, though a few years in London as a respiratory physiologist had anglicised him to the point where his nationality was no longer recognisable. He carried out his work with that ease which marks the professional: there were never any re-runs with John, no anomalous results, no revisions, and the experiments were completed with the minimum of time and effort. And though he had done no climbing, when it came to trudging up a couple of thousand feet of steep snow or pedalling on the ergometer, he was as good, or better, than any of us.

The first meeting of the Wintering Party was held in the Silver Hut on Christmas Day when full dinner was served, with trimmings. Tom had organised a Christmas tree from the nearest pine forest. The inside of the hut was aglitter with improvised decorations: silver and crimson streamers, a varied array of Christmas cards, even a yak tail. Rakpa, our small orange dog was galloping in and out of the hut, delirious with excitement. At 10 o'clock the Sherpas announced the arrival of our guests. Lined up on the snow outside, we sang Christmas carols as a welcome. "God Rest Ye Merry Gentlemen" we sang as the leading group moved up the last slope with the staggering gait and pale faces of the unacclimatised. Below them, far down the gentle incline which stretched a mile or so before joining the crevasses of the ice-fall, we could see the others, sahibs and attendant Sherpas, a straggling, unpurposeful group looking like a wood-cut of an early ascent of Mont Blanc.

The presentation of gifts followed, mainly mail and whisky; Tom produced a soda syphon and we celebrated the reunion. After a short burst of social skiing we sat down to Christmas Dinner. It was a long and pleasant meal, particularly for those who were acclimatised. There was mushroom soup, freeze-dried shrimp with Sauce à la Milledge, roast Sherpa sheep, fried yak, Pangboche potatoes, green peas and corn, canned Christmas Pudding with Sauce à la Nevison, fresh oranges, coffee and cherry brandy. The combined effects of altitude, alcohol and food left us reclining in a stupefied silence which was broken eventually by the sound of an Indian raga, located by the Captain on the radio. Suddenly Griff stood up, announced his departure, and on the spur of the moment convened a meeting at the Green Hut next morning.

With the others gone we settled down to the serious business of drinking away the rest of the afternoon and the evening. Then someone remembered the Monitor tapes: on-the-spot recordings which we were posting to Chicago for the American radio network. We began with a sober account of the process of acclimatisation: "People have said that man cannot live permanently at 19,000 feet, that at this height there is irreversible brain damage . . . We can now categorically deny this . . ." We tried a tape on the Christmas Dinner. "This is the Himalayan Scientific and Mountaineering Expedition broadcasting to you from 19,000 feet. We have just finished eating . . ." Pleased with ourselves we became more ambitious. What about some Christmas carols! That should really get the spirit of the occasion for the folks back home—Baritone, B. Bishop and W. Romanes, Solo tenor, M. Gill. Descant specially composed and sung by J. Milledge. Your compère: Tom Nevison. The tapes were duly sent off. I hardly dare think what they must have sounded like back in Chicago. I imagine some hardened radio editor listening incredulously: "Just take a load of this Himalayan stuff will you, Sam. Poor guys. They've gone nuts now. And they think they're all right!"

There were no celebrations on New Year's Eve, for only Jim, Ang

Temba and I were in residence at the Silver Hut; Tom had left for London and the others were working at Mingbo. 1961 was ushered in by a storm. Till then the weather had been almost wholly clear, but on the last day of the year a layer of soft grey cloud closed off the sky and later the wind rose. It was our first storm of any violence. To begin with, like small boys, we enjoyed snuggling down into our sleeping-bags while the wind raged and the night grew blacker, but there came a point when we began to have misgivings about the security of our hut. Once I thought we had started the long fall down the bluffs. The background roar of the wind swelled to a crescendo as a gust caught us, the hut shook then slowly lurched forward as if the foundations had crumpled. "We must fix those fore and aft guy-wires," said Jim. By morning the wind had passed as quickly as it came. But the cloud remained, and snow fell, big silent flakes like a storm of white rhododendron petals.

At the end of the first week in January, Mike and John came up from Mingbo. They were followed a day or two later by Annulu, bearing a note to the effect that there had been 'serious drunkenness' down below and that Annulu was to be kept occupied at the Silver Hut. This sort of news was no surprise to those of us who had spent a week or two with idle Sherpas in the Rolwaling. The memory of 'blood on the gompa steps' was still fresh. But Annulu refused to give an account of his crime. At the mere mention of chang he looked shocked and reproachful, as if he were the Head Lama of Tengboche accused of visiting the local nunnery. All we could extract was a garbled account of a holy man from Katmandu, who, while making a pilgrimage to the mountains, had heard of the Silver Hut and decided to include it on his list of shrines to be visited.

The full story was more interesting than Annulu had led us to believe. The coolness of the winter weather had prevented our pilgrim from reaching as high as the Green Hut even, and he had settled into Mingbo. One afternoon the Captain was preparing blood films on glass slides when suddenly a small brown hand shot forward and removed one. Turning round the Captain found himself looking at a small, travel-stained Nepali, wearing a red turban, a black jacket and dirty cotton trousers. Sheepishly, he was chewing the glass slide into small pieces. Later a three-foot length of glass tubing was eaten with satisfaction, and while the sahibs drank afternoon tea, our holy man tossed off a handful of bent nails. That night he slept out under a boulder without so much as a blanket, even though there was snow on the ground.

The true scientist sees opportunity where others are not even curious, and next day Griff designed an experiment to investigate the temperature regulation of our holy man. Thermo-couples were attached to various parts of his body and connected to recording instruments. Shortly after the experiment had commenced, Annulu, who had been busy with a pot of chang, discovered these strange dials and pieces of wire and removed the lot. And that was why Annulu had been banished to the Silver Hut. Eventually the experiment was brought to a successful conclusion and a paper, concerning observations on a Nepalese Pilgrim at 16,000 feet, was published.

When Griff moved up to the Silver Hut, the physiological programme entered its most active phase. Each morning one of us would be sweating away on the bicycle ergometer, the others crowding around with bags for expired air, syringes for blood and leads for the electrocardiograph. The ergometer was a shiny yellow machine constructed along the lines of a bicycle; applied to the rim of the only wheel was a friction band whose tension could be varied and hence the amount of work done in pedalling. It might be thought that one could ease off simply by pedalling slower but a metronome was set clicking to fix the rate. Once on the machine there was no way out except by openly admitting defeat, and that we were reluctant to do. The results were interesting. Our work capacity, for instance, was about half that at sea-level, improving to about two-thirds towards the end of the winter; and our pulse rates during maximum work were only 120–130, when at sea-level they might be 180 or 200, though this too improved. We had noticed how blue we became with hard work and this was explained by finding that the efficiency of oxygen absorption from our lungs was reduced during exercise. Blood, made thick by an increase in red cells and blackened by the lack of oxygen, oozed into a syringe from a vein like purple treacle.

On some experiments we worked together but we had projects of our own as well. Most of these were too technical to be easily explained, but mine, which were designed by a Cambridge research unit, were simpler. They were an attempt to assess intellectual function, which is known to deteriorate if one goes high enough. None of these tests were popular but the worst of them was diabolic. The subject performed two tasks concurrently, one a visual recognition and marking of number sequences on a typed sheet, the other a memory test: in this, a woman's voice on a tape recorder read out ten letters of the alphabet one of which was repeated. At the end of each sequence of ten, the voice would ask, cynically, accusingly or jeeringly, according to one's mood, "Which letter was repeated twice?" Even the maximum rate of work on the ergometer was more popular than that experiment. Comparison of our performance at 19,000 feet with that at sea-level seemed to show a slight deterioration. Subjectively we were never convinced of this and in *our* estimation we were able to think and reason as well at the Silver Hut as in London. Subjective statements however, like the protestations of the drunken driver, carry no weight. A knowing smile demolishes the whole argument.

Our physical condition was not perfect. During the first month we all lost a stone or two in weight, and we were lean before we started. We slept less easily, ate less heartily and a long bout of hard work, such as a day's climbing, left us more exhausted than we would have been at lower altitudes. Even so, we seemed to reach a state of equilibrium, and some at least could have stayed in the Silver Hut for a long period. One of our youngest Sherpas found it was too high for him and had to go down permanently. And once I slipped into a phase of deterioration myself: after an exhausting day's climbing I began losing weight, sleeping poorly, and these continued till I went down to Changmatang for a rest. The height at which an individual can live comfortably varies from person to person—for some it is 16,000 feet, for others 19,000, and some of our Sherpas could probably have stayed happily at 20,000 feet.

How did the days pass? Very easily. We were roused each morning in the traditional Himalayan manner by a Sherpa bringing cups of tea. A leisurely breakfast at eight and by nine the day's work was starting. Before lunch we went skiing for half an hour on the steeper part of the névé just below the hut. We skiied with varying degrees of skill, Griff with an easy mastery that was the despair of the rest of us, Jim, Mike and John concentrating fiercely on their parallel turns, while Wally and I, who were beginners, were usually slower to reach the foot of the slope than the dog. The snow was firm, the weather fine, the setting incomparable—only the ski-tow was missing. And though the combined skills of half a dozen scientists were brought to bear on the problem, even to the extent of considering using Sherpa power in the absence of a sizable motor, we never found an easy way back up the hill.

After lunch there was more work till five when we again stepped out on skis, this time down the full mile of névé into the ice-fall. A flagged route led between crevasses and seracs, till a final swoop ran up to an ice-platform perched on top of the terminal ice-face. By then the shadows were lengthening across the snow and the harsh white of midday giving way to a softer light. Five hundred feet above us stood the hut, its silver panels shining against a backdrop of fluted snow. The orange tents made a splash of colour, anemometers whirred and turned on their masts and the heavy blade of the wind generator made a chopping sound like a small helicopter trying to take off. It was a good home and as the weeks went by our affection for it grew. One might have thought the routine would have become monotonous but it never did. Sometimes a climb or a ski-touring trip added variety but we would have been as happy without them. Our few links with civilisation became disproportionately precious: the arrival of a mail-runner with his pile of battered air-mail envelopes was a great occasion, friends in Katmandu sent in whisky which was savoured lovingly, and on rare occasions a piece of familiar music came crackling through the radio static to delight us. Thanks to the light hand of Griff's leadership, and perhaps an element of luck, there was never a trace of the personal friction which proverbially crops up in such isolated situations. In many ways the winter months were the best of the expedition.

What of the scientific harvest? Though the world of physiology was not set abuzz with excitement, there was an impressively large pile of data on a wide variety of topics. Corners of knowledge were explored, or re-explored, and written about. We proved we could live and work in comfort at 19,000 feet and that our acclimatisation improved steadily over this time. And later, on Makalu, we proved convincingly that the benefit of our long stay could be wiped out by a few days' deterioration at 24,000 feet. Some thought that the Wintering Party, though better at intermediate altitudes, had less stamina high on the mountain than those freshly arrived in the spring, but the statistical evidence for this was unconvincing. During those days of disaster on Makalu all were struck down in one way or another. But before I come to that woeful tale, there is the happier story of Ama Dablam.

12

AMA DABLAM

That sunny dome! those caves of ice!
And all who heard should see them there,
And all should cry, Beware! Beware!
Samuel Coleridge

BY HIMALAYAN standards Ama Dablam was a dream of a climb. Often enough the story of a climb in the Himalayas reads like Scott's return from the Pole—bad weather, atrocious snow conditions, sickness, exhaustion; the difficulties are piled one upon the other so that the perplexed reader wonders why anyone should voluntarily submit to such an ordeal. There were days on Ama Dablam when we had the same sort of doubts, days made miserable by the agony of trying to force exhausted bodies to an apparently unattainable altitude, but they were the exception rather than the rule. For the most part the weather stayed fine, the snow firm, and the route more feasible than we had ever suspected.

An attempt on Ama Dablam had never been one of the objectives of the expedition though some of us might have idly thought of the possibility. I remember one season in the Darrans talking of a trip to the Himalayas. "What about Ama Dablam?" someone had suggested, for we had seen photographs of the mountain. When I saw it, however, first from the Tesi Lapcha, then from Kumjung, I saw no route anywhere, or not from that side anyway. I was not alone in this. "Appears utterly inaccessible," wrote one visitor. "Easily the most formidable peak ever photographed." "Outrivalling even the most sensational aspects of the Matterhorn." The mountaineer is overwhelmed by the sheer spectacle of the mountain. The ill-fated English attempt of 1959 did nothing to diminish the peak's reputation; Harris and Frazer, who were last seen at 21,000 feet on the north ridge, never returned to tell the tale of that last desperate struggle.

In the Wintering Party, several of us had been looking for a route. At first we had hoped there might be an unseen easy way around the back but in this we were disappointed. Then one day it dawned on us that the obvious route was directly up the front of the mountain—

up the Mingbo Ridge and the fluted snow-face that we had been gazing at ever since we arrived in the Khumbu. All through January we nursed plans for a reconnaissance when time could be spared from the scientific programme. Towards the end of February, the last weeks of the winter, Griff suggested to Wally Romanes that he might like to have the first look.

Probably he was glad to escape from the clutches of the physiologists, or from the saddle of the bicycle ergometer anyway. From the time he had arrived in the Khumbu, Wally had been engaged in setting up our various camps, a task which had not prevented him being used as an experimental animal like the rest of us. Though I had never met Wally outside Nepal, I knew his name well enough because of his first ascent of the Black Tower, the most notorious of the virgin peaks of the Southern Alps in the 1950s. No one on the expedition worked or climbed harder or less selfishly than Wally.

He set out with Pemba Tensing on February the 18th. Below 19,000 feet the Mingbo Ridge is merely a few easy slabs showing through a broad sweep of scree. Above this height there is a dramatic change: the jagged blade of the ridge proper is abruptly upthrust from the surrounding slopes, to rise in a series of big steps to the foot of the fluted, upper snow-face. On this, two ice-bulges stood out prominently; the lower and smaller of the two was topped by a snow shelf which later formed the site of Camp IV; the upper, a huge bulge of glistening ice, is the dablang from which the mountain takes its name —dablang is the Sherpa name of a silver and turquoise locket worn around the neck. By the end of his second day on the mountain, Wally had established Camp I on the scree and climbed to the foot of the first big step. Up to there the rock was of a moderate standard of difficulty. And at the foot of the step was the perfect site for Camp II: nestling into a gully on the steep flank of the ridge, like a limpet, was an accretion of ice whose upper surface was a level platform, ten by thirty feet. It looked as though we had established a foothold.

Mike Ward, Barry Bishop and a group of Sherpas set off a few days later with tents for Camp II and ironware and ropes for the overhanging step above it. Through the telescope at the Silver Hut, those of us who were still working on the scientific programme watched the line of tiny figures climb slowly along the teeth of the ridge to the site of Camp II. On the ice platform tents went up, a red dot and a yellow dot, bright against the backdrop of brown rock. For two days Mike and Barry worked on the 200 feet of steep rock rising above the camp and almost overhanging it. The climbing required was of a high standard but the situation was ideal: the camp-site and the rock above were not only sheltered from the wind, but because they faced south the heat of the sun was focused there. Were it not for the altitude and the panorama of névé and mountain spread below, it might have seemed like a rock-problem on a Welsh cliff. At the end of the second day the pitons and fixed ropes were replaced by a wire ladder.

Wally had been down lower for a rest. He returned and the three of them set to work on the next big step, an exposed and wind-swept cliff of pale grey rock split by a big crack. It took two days of high-class climbing and at the end of them another ladder and rappelling line had been fixed in place. At this point I came up, my work at Silver Hut having been completed. Though I was disappointed at having missed the rock-climbing I was full of admiration for the work that had been done. And I was delighted by the pleasant and easy style of living on the mountain. Wally and I spent a day pushing the route another 400 feet higher on the mountain past a third big step; and then the others retreated to lower levels for a short rest, leaving me in solitary residence with two Sherpas. I read, wrote letters, ate well, and watched activities around the Silver Hut which was in full view below.

When the others returned, we established Camp III midway between the two ladders. This too was a sunny, indolent spot. The tents were pitched on three precarious platforms built out from the sloping ridge; and though we were only 300 feet higher than Camp II the ascent and descent of the ladder had been taking two precious hours out of each day. Camp IV, from which we would attempt the summit, was to be placed 1500 feet higher on the Snow Shelf at the foot of the upper face. On March the 8th, Wally and I set out in an attempt to reach the Shelf. Beyond the top of the second ladder we were on steep but fairly easy rock. By traversing left across a plunging gully of rotten rock insecurely embedded in ice we were able to sidle past the third step in the ridge and we regained the crest farther on. The performance of such manœuvres takes longer than the description of them and the day was well advanced by the time we stood on top of the ridge with a clear view of the final 400 feet leading to the Shelf. Steep, unstable-looking snow and ice were balanced precariously on the crest while access to the Shelf itself was guarded by a fifty-foot ice-wall. The route looked impossible; when we returned we told Mike and Barry that so far as we could see we had no option but to go back. Wisely refusing to take our word for it, they set out the following day to look for themselves; and they reached the Shelf. Looking back on it, our decision that we should abandon the climb was a curious one. On my part there was a lack of enthusiasm for forcing a route up steep rotten ice of any sort. But it was also a bad error of judgement: the ice-wall was ten feet high, not fifty, and the ridge leading up to it, though broken, was in no way dangerous.

The assault began. The first and most intractable problem, was that of carrying to the Shelf the climbing apparatus, food, cooking gear, sleeping-bags, air mattresses and tents that were necessary for Camp IV. With us at Camp III were Pemba Tensing and Gumi Dorje but already we had promised that they would be going no higher. Poor Pemba had found the ascent of the first ladder a shattering experience, and the whole of the route to the Shelf was of that order of difficulty. He pointed out to us that there are easier ways of earning eight shillings a day than by carrying forty-pound loads up the Mingbo Ridge of Ama Dablam. We were becoming increasingly despondent when Barry came up with the idea of using an igloo instead of tents: one had simply to dig out cubes of firm snow, deftly trim one edge and lay them spirally so as to form a neat and weather-proof dome. The drowning man clutches at a straw—privately we may have had reservations but the certain knowledge of the agony of carrying thirty pounds of tent to the Shelf suppressed our doubts. And there was the comforting knowledge that if the igloo failed we could dig a snow-cave.

We ended up with an irreducible minimum of six loads. Wally and I carried two of these to the Shelf one day and on the next, March 11th, all four of us set out to establish Camp IV. It was the grimmest day of the whole climb. Carrying forty pounds on steep rock is bad enough at sea-level, but at 20,000 feet it defies description. At three o'clock we hauled the last load up the ice-wall. The Shelf was a level area of firm snow a hundred yards long by thirty wide. Below, an ice-cliff dropped down to the rock walls of the Mingbo; above, the snow rapidly steepened before running up to the right-hand edge of the menacing dablang.

We began by unpacking to find food and warm clothing. My first move, after laying an air mattress on the ground, was to stumble and plant a ten point crampon squarely through the centre of it, a mishap which gave me three very cold nights at Camp IV. During the first night there was not much sleeping anyway, for the snow-cave was not completed till midnight. The attempt to build an igloo had been abandoned at an early stage for no amount of shaping and pressing had produced even a beginning; we foreswore our sunny pleasure-dome and began on the cave of ice.

There was a chill wind blowing across from the north but as blocks of snow were flung out from the entrance of the enlarging cave we built a sheltering wall. While one pair dug the other two stamped about outside. It was one of the loneliest places I have been in. Though the villages of the Khumbu, and the Silver Hut, were visible from the Shelf we were isolated from them by the precipices dropping away around us—except where that tenuous line of ropes, ladders

and ice steps that we had been fashioning for three weeks led downwards. As the evening light faded we watched the changes of colour
of the Himalayan sunset: the sky, bright blue at first, momentarily
flushing crimson, and then darkening to the inky blue of dusk; and
the snow changing through pale gold to lilac as the sun dropped below
the horizon. Within an hour there was no light but the tiny glow of a
candle inside the cave.

By midnight the sleeping-bench was large enough for the four of us
and we had eaten a meal of sorts. Without bothering to remove boots,
windproofs or down-jacket I crawled wearily into a sleeping-bag,
swallowed two sleeping-tablets (the new wonder-drug thalidomide, the
sleeping-pill without a hangover) and slept as though dead till 8
o'clock next morning. The weather remained fine, but it was clear
that we were in no fit state to make an attempt on the summit after
our labours of the previous day. While Barry and I improved the cave
and made what preparations we could for the following day, Wally
and Mike cut a line of steps up to the dablang. And they did more
than this for when they returned they brought the good news that
they had found a route around the right-hand edge of the ice cliffs of
the dablang—the way to the top was open.

The 13th of March was our summit day. Lack of an air mattress
made me the lightest sleeper and at 6 o'clock I staggered out of bed;
sleeping in one's boots simplified the procedure considerably. By
8.30 we were away, Mike and Wally in the lead. For the first 500 feet
they were climbing in the zig-zag line of steps they had cut the previous day. Then we were abreast of the dablang, sidling past its
shining walls of green ice on a rock ledge a foot wide. Without that
single narrow ledge we would have been forced to return. There was
no other route: nothing but sheer ice on one side and a rock wall on
the other.

Beyond the ledge we stepped out on to the relatively flat upper
surface of the dablang, a brief respite before we began on the final
thousand feet. Our route was up the most prominent of the big
flutings formed by the wind on the upper snow-face. A third of the
way up stood our only landmark, a prominent rock outcrop. Mike and
Wally, who were still in the lead, began cutting up to it, in snow at
first but then as the angle steepened, in ice. It was steep. There is
no relaxation in such places: if you stumble, if you catch a crampon
point in your trousers, you fall. To the tension induced by exposure
was added concern at the passing of time.

At 12.30 we reached the rock outcrop. We paused a while, ate food
for which we had little appetite, and then anxiously returned to the
snow-face. It was my turn to lead. The other two between them had
already led two-thirds of the day's climbing: Mike had been working

hard for three days without a rest and Wally for four, a sterling performance at that altitude. I was almost afraid to cut the first step for fear of what I might find. If it was ice we had several hours of work ahead of us and probably a night out. But the first blow of the axe bit easily into crisp firm snow: a couple of scrapes, a kick, and I had a neat pigeon-hole of a step. The conditions were perfect. The weather too was perfect, though as we left the outcrop I saw mist agthering on the outlying ranges. For two hours we climbed steadily, seemingly making little progress towards the snow horizon above which was the summit. Then suddenly it was close. The angle eased, step-cutting became unnecessary, and then, elated, we quickened our pace as we stepped on to the summit. It was not the narrow crest we had imagined but a plateau the size of a football field, split by a single narrow crevasse.

How spacious it was after those last six hours clinging to the face. And what mountains we now saw before us. Ama Dablam it seemed was little more than a footstool from which we could see the great peaks in their true proportions. Cloud was closing in but through gaps we saw the leonine outline of Makalu to the west; across the Imja the crest of the Lhotse–Nuptse wall rose 3,000 feet higher than where we stood, and behind it, huge and menacing, stood Everest, no longer squatting half out of sight but now dominating the scene. Summit pictures were taken. Barry unfurled the National Geographic flag and was photographed with it. Before turning for home I took one last look around: Everest and Makalu were now lost in the mist but between them a vista of rolling brown hills stretched to the horizon where a shaft of light through the clouds played on the snows of a range far inside Tibet.

The descent was nerve-racking. Once, 500 feet from the top, I looked up to see Barry falling towards me, an orange bundle with legs, arms and ice-axe in all directions coming down in a shower of snow. But in a moment he had recovered and braked to a halt. Somewhat shaken, we continued. The ice below the rock outcrop felt dangerous, the steps too small, the belays inadequate. Then, as we approached the traverse past the dablang, Barry slithered on the snow. For one agonising moment I thought he was going over the precipice, but again he braked easily. With a dry mouth, and shaking, I completed the traverse. We arrived back in camp just as it was too dark to see the steps.

The descent to Camp III next day with heavy loads was equally demanding. Mike and Wally brought up the rear collecting the pitons, fixed rope and ladder. Luckily the bad weather which had been threatening came to nothing and when we staggered in to camp the Sherpas were squatting happily in the hot afternoon sun, keeping a cup of tea warm for us. Pemba Tensing grinned as if he had just climbed Ama Dablam himself. "Shabash! Very good summit, sahibs!" he cried, for they had seen the whole of our progress on the flutings of the upper face.

The next day should have been our last on the mountain. Wally engineered an overhead ropeway down to Camp II and the loads, suspended from a karabiner, were slid down. From that point on the real problems were behind us. Between Camp II and the scree slopes below there was only an hour of easy scrambling on broken rock. But we had heavy loads and this led us into trouble. While each of the sahibs carried forty pounds, the Sherpas, who had been reinforced by three new arrivals from Green Hut, insisted on taking sixty to eighty pounds rather than make a return trip the following day.

At midday they set off. When we followed half an hour later we found them halted a hundred yards down the ridge. Gumi Dorje, who had the biggest of all the loads, had stepped on a loose rock and fallen ten feet. Now he was seated on a rock, clasping his thigh, while his leg hung loose. There were tears of pain and fear in his eyes. "Broken, sahib," he whispered. "I will die." Mike looked at the leg. There was a small skin scrape and not much else to see—except that when he moved we could see that his shin was snapped cleanly across, three inches below the knee. Mike splinted the leg and gave him a shot of morphine. We began to wonder what we should do next. Let the Sherps carry Gumi down? They were all shaken by what had happened. Dawa Tensing particularly was so dazed as to be quite useless even for carrying a light load. And though the ridge below was 'easy scrambling' with small loads, with an injured man it was going to be exceedingly difficult. It looked as though we would have to carry Gumi ourselves.

Soon it was clear that the only feasible way of doing this was on our backs. Mike and I took short spells while Wally provided a belay from above and Barry organised the Sherpas carrying loads. Where we could, we moved pendulum-fashion across the steep slabs below the crest of the ridge. Seldom have I felt so keenly my dependence on a piece of rope as I did then, leaning out from the rock wall with nothing beneath me, feet pressed against the rock, while the whole of my weight, and Gumi's, passed through that thin, taut piece of nylon to Wally's belay.

At 4 o'clock, when we were less than half way down, it began to snow. We had no option but to camp—or try to, for there were no level sites on the ridge. At length we spied a ledge a hundred feet down and below that we constructed another in a debris-choked gully. In the fading light, while snow silently covered the rocks, we built a makeshift camp, short of food and with no fuel.

K

When we woke in the morning the sun was beating down out of a clear sky but it was midday before the snow-covered rocks were clear enough for us to move. Then, when we were just clear of the ridge, the weather again closed in. Now that we were on the scree the Sherps could take over the carrying, but even so we did not reach the grass-covered lower slopes before fresh snow made further progress impossible. So yet again we scratched out a bleak temporary camp.

The weather pattern repeated itself in the morning, a clear sky and hot sun, but not enough to melt the new snow before midday. Nevertheless it was our last day on the mountain. Griff sent up a strong team of porters including a big, wild Sherpa called Karma, who had the reputation of being one of the strongest men in the Khumbu. Effortlessly he hoisted Gumi on to his shoulders. In five hours we reached Mingbo. It was exactly a month from the first day of the reconnaissance.

13

*My strength is dried up like a potsherd; and my tongue cleaveth to
my gums; and thou shalt bring me into the dust of death.*

Psalm 22

AT CHANGMATANG the Spring Expedition had taken up residence:
Ed, Desmond, Pete Mulgrew, Tom Nevison and Leigh Ortenberger.
Various wives had walked in with them. Lady Hillary's journey into
the Everest region had provoked some speculative comments from the
press. A French paper, more imaginative than its British brethren,
had begun a paragraph, "Lady Hillary to Climb Everest". The text
or rather the translation of it, continued: "She lives with her husband
and family in their little cottage in Auckland. The children are the
joy of their father. Lady Hillary, who is both gracious and sporting,
will climb with three specially chosen companions, without any male,
to prove that she is as good as her husband."

The press clippings on Ama Dablam, too, when they arrived, were
read with interest. Most of them had a distinctly chauvinistic ring.
From London the news was all of Mike Ward:

"Killer Peak Conquered by British Surgeon"
"Briton Beats White Fang Mountain"
"The doctor saw the White Fang for the first time in 1953 . . .
For eight years he has waited to climb it . . . Said Sir John Hunt
last night, 'This is quite the most remarkable feat of climbing in
the Himalayas to date.'"

The Auckland headlines were more general: "Hillary's Men
Conquer Killer Peak", while in Dunedin (where I was at Medical
School) the billboards had read: "City Man's Success in Himalayas".

Wally was in the Hastings headlines and no doubt American papers
carried the amazing story of U.S. Glaciologist's Conquest of Killer.

A letter from the Nepalese Officiating Chief of Protocol, dated
March 21st, was less enthusiastic about the ascent of Ama Dablam:
"I understand that the party under Sir Edmund Hillary which was
permitted to carry on some scientific research in a specific area and

later make an attempt on Makalu has climbed without authority
another peak called Ama Dablam . . . His Majesty's Government . . .
feel compelled, though reluctantly, to withdraw the permission
granted to it to make an assault on Makalu in March–June
1961."

At first we were inclined to make light of this apparently minor
misunderstanding, but it was soon clear that His Majesty's Government was in earnest. The late arrivals of the Spring Party, John
Harrison and Bhanu Bannerjee, were detained by the Captain of the
Namche check-post, who then issued an order that we should leave
the country without further delay. Ed, with his face longer than I had
ever seen it, returned to Katmandu by plane and began a grim circu-
mambulation of the Government offices, most of which at first kept
their doors resolutely shut. True, we should have applied for permission to climb Ama Dablam, but the thought had not occurred to
any of us, and Ed had known nothing of the climb till he heard the
news at Changmatang. It was unfortunate too that the first news
should have reached the Nepalese by way of the headlines of foreign
newspapers, as had happened on a more famous occasion, when
Everest was climbed for the first time. But there was another reason
for the hostility of the Nepalese. Two months earlier there had been a
revolution in Katmandu. The King, disenchanted with his country's
faltering steps towards democracy, had taken power into his own
hands. The British Foreign Office, whatever its private thoughts
might have been, had felt bound to disapprove of this undemocratic
action, and Anglo-Nepali relations had cooled as a result. Our blunder
could hardly have come at a more unfortunate time.

In the end the Nepalese relented. Various diplomats intervened as
best they could. Something was made of the illegal detention in
Namche Bazar of John Harrison, a British subject. The Government
liaison officer for the expedition, who had spent the winter in Katmandu instead of keeping an eye on us in the Mingbo, was sacked,
and the Captain of the Namche check-post was recalled. The expedition paid a small fine and Ed returned immediately to resume the
organisation of the attempt on Makalu. But those nine disquieting
days in Katmandu had taken their toll and Ed never fully recovered
his fitness or acclimatisation. When eventually he fell ill on the
mountain, that unhappy event, which marked the beginning of our
troubles, could in part be traced back to the illegal ascent of Ama
Dablam.

Makalu lies thirty miles east of the Silver Hut. The French, who
had made the first ascent of the mountain in 1955, had reached it up
the Barun Valley, which runs from the south directly to the foot of

the mountain. For us, established in the Khumbu with all our equipment, the lower Barun was too devious a route. Instead we chose the direct line from the Silver Hut, across the intervening Hongu Valley and over three 20,000 feet passes. Over this route, which in parts was dangerous, more than 200 loads had to be carried. Fortunately there were only two accidents and neither of them serious. The first was when Pete was struck on the side of the head by a rock carelessly thrown by a Sherpa. The second was more dramatic. One of the high passes was the col immediately behind the hut, 500 feet of steep fluted snow. One of the Sherps was beginning the descent when he slipped, spun down its full length and was swallowed in the crevasse at the bottom. Jim Milledge, who had watched this performance was rushing over, horrified, to recover what he presumed would be a corpse, when a dazed figure crawled over the lip of the crevasse and staggered on downwards, apologising for his carelessness.

By mid-April the loads had been carried to the foot of Makalu and Base Camp established in a moraine trough beside the Barun Glacier. More than a dozen red, yellow, blue and green tents were scattered amongst the piles of grey rock rubble, and the cooks had built for themselves a stone-walled shelter roofed with a tarpaulin. It was a dusty place and as often as not there was a wind whirling clouds of grit back and forth. But if one looked beyond the moraine the scene was grand enough. A few miles north were Lhotse and the unfamiliar Kangshung face of Everest. Makalu lay to the south-east, presenting from this aspect an immense flank of bare brown rock, with a superb buttress-like ridge running to the summit. Farther round to the right was the gentler northern face; the French had used this as their route and so would we. A short open tributary of the Barun led up to a névé at 21,000 feet, site of Camp III, our Advance Base, and this gave easy access to the northern face. The physiologists played no part in establishing the route either from Silver Hut to the Barun, or from there to Camp IV. All this was done, under Ed's leadership, by the Spring Party: John Harrison, Pete Mulgrew, Tom Nevison and Leigh Ortenburger.

Even when Jim, Mike, John West and I arrived, instead of being recruited for work higher up we were sent down-valley for a rest. Within four hours we had left behind us the ugly slag-heaps of the glacial moraine and were walking at 15,000 feet, down open grass flats towards a yak-pasture called Sershong. At 14,000 feet we were in pine forest and rhododendron which in a fortnight would be in full bloom. For a few days we lay about, talking and sunning ourselves. There were a few low stone huts, not yet occupied for the monsoon grazing season. In one was an old fore-leg of yak, its meat dark, dry and strongly-flavoured after hanging for six months from a roof-beam, but we ate it, leaving behind in payment fifteen shillings. The weather was fine each morning but by mid-afternoon the clouds had closed in, bringing snow at higher levels and on Makalu the clouds were driving hard across the summit. Seldom have I felt less of an inclination to climb a peak than down there at Sershong, looking up at the huge mountain rising almost to 28,000 feet. The French, with a powerful team, had climbed it easily. But they had used oxygen day and night above 23,000 feet. By then I knew enough about high altitude to have a fair idea of what the last thousand feet to the summit would be like without oxygen. And in a high wind? In deep snow? It didn't bear thinking about. As I look back, I see Sershong as a green oasis on the fringe of a grey world of storm, exhaustion and eventually disaster.

When we returned to Base-Camp we were directed almost immediately to Camp II. The route ran past an old French camp littered with rusting cans, to where big prowling tongues of ice descended from a névé and broke into ice-falls. Beyond was Camp III. We set up the bicycle ergometer and put ourselves through the old routine, surprised that we could still work at half our sea-level rate. In the days that followed, the next phase of the assault plan was carried out with completion of the route to Camp V on Makalu Col at 24,300 feet.

And then things began to go wrong. Ed had just come down from directing the moves to the Col. During the day he had had a headache and he retired to his tent feeling unwell. Mike, Jim and I were sitting in another tent after dark when we thought we heard a faint voice. We listened. Silence. "Is that you Ed?" shouted Mike, puzzled. No reply. "Ed!" he shouted. "Ed! Can you hear me?" Again, no reply. Slightly alarmed now Mike crawled out into the night to see if anything unusual had happened. He found Ed sitting up in his sleeping-bag, unable to speak. There was no doubt what had happened: Ed had suffered a slight stroke, perhaps a small clot blocking a blood vessel in his brain, perhaps a temporary spasm of an artery. By morning he was well again but who could say that worse would not follow? Eric Shipton had had a similar attack on Everest without after-effects but that had been on the way down the mountain. There was no option but to advise retreat to a lower level as soon as possible. For Ed no more galling thing could have happened. He was fit and well, if not at the top of his form. He had manœuvred the expedition into a strong position for the assault and though he would be surrendering control of the expedition by going down, he would still feel responsibility for the party. Yet he could hardly disregard the advice of Mike and Jim, the party's two medical officers. In the end, reluctantly, he accepted the bitter decision. After handing over the leadership to Mike Ward he set off for the lower Barun accompanied by Jim.   _ 1961

On the 11th of May, the first assault party, Wally, Leigh and I, set out from III for the summit. Our task was clearly mapped out: to IV on the first day, V on the second, establish VI at 26,000 feet on the third, VII at 27,000 feet on the fourth, and on the fifth day, the summit, 27,790 feet. I thought we had a good chance of making it.

We were still acclimatising and the climb to IV was easier than it had been the first time. On the second day of the assault we reached V at midday as planned. With us, as well as a large group of Sherpas for carrying loads, were John West, Mike, Tom and the bicycle ergometer. What the Sherpas thought of the bicycle I can only guess. That we should be climbing without oxygen when we had large stocks of it (for emergency use) must have seemed strange enough. But that after struggling up to Makalu Col, we should assemble a bicycle and ride till we dropped from exhaustion—truly the ways of the sahibs must have have seemed strange.

Though there was a bitterly cold wind blowing across the Col, the tents acted as heat traps in the way that a glass-house does and we were comfortably warm inside as we pottered about completing physiology tests. In the evening as the sun was setting, I dressed up in wind-proof jacket and down-trousers and went outside with the movie camera. The Col was as desolate a place as one could imagine, yet there was a kind of beauty about it. Kangchenjunga stood out clearly a hundred miles to the east; by crossing the Col we had entered Tibet and again I saw that vast and mysterious plateau of brown hills rolling to the horizon. Our camp was on snow whose surface had been carved by the wind into grotesque stalked structures like huge toadstools. Just below us was the gully in which the French had camped, now an inaccessible trough of wind-polished ice. The route to the summit was visible for the first time: an ice-fall enclosed between two rock ridges one of which came down to the Col. On either side of the ice-fall were snow-gullies, the farther one being the route to the top and the site of Camps VI and VII. To reach it we had to make a level traverse across snow, skirting promontories of decaying rock rubble coming down from the ridge, then cross the ice-fall in its lower easier part. In the bright yellow light of the sunset the summit rocks looked hardly more than a stone's-throw away.

The weather next morning was better than it had been for a long time. Even the clouds, which had been humped over the summit for weeks past, seemed to be thinner and woollier as if a spell of fine weather had set in. Breakfast was slow because our propane cookers had blocked jets and for an hour or two we lay about in a state of lethargy till the time came to force down some food. Our eight Sherps set off first, led by Pemba Tensing who thought he remembered the French route. We could catch them easily we thought for our loads were much lighter than theirs. But it was not easy at all and as I struggled after them, panting desperately in the thin air, I was again made aware of the enormous physical superiority of the Sherpas at high altitudes. For me to have carried one of their thirty-pound loads to 26,000 feet would have been almost impossible; I could only just keep up with them when I was carrying no more than a movie camera.

By the time we joined them the Sherps were already several hundred feet up the gully on the wrong side of the ice-fall. There were two ways of crossing it. Either we dropped 400 feet to the easier crossing lower down or we attempted a more dubious middle path. Unwilling to lose our hard-won height, we decided to attempt the middle crossing next day. After climbing a little higher we pitched Camp VI at 25,800 in the lee of an ice-pinnacle.

In what was left of the afternoon we settled ourselves in the two tiny assault tents, three sahibs in one and four Sherps in the other. We went through the familiar routine of collecting samples of alveolar air for the physiology programme and sealed them in glass ampoules. Though my appetite had gone completely I ate as much of the dehydrated stew and biscuits as I could before retching made it impossible to take more. The night seemed endless.

By morning the wind had risen. We looked out to see dense clouds of powder snow whirling amongst the seracs and hiding the summit, and we knew we could never get to the top in such conditions. Nor at that late stage could we retreat, for close behind us were the second and third assault teams waiting to use our line of camps. But we could establish VII and hope for an improvement in the weather. One of the four Sherps refused to move. Though he claimed to be ill, we had doubts for he looked well and was as strong and experienced as any Sherpa we had. It seemed more likely that he sensed trouble and preferred not to be involved. Persuasion was useless however, and we set off, Wally and I sharing the lead on one rope while Leigh led the three Sherps on the other.

The crossing of the ice-fall began with a rope-length of step-cutting across a bulge of steep polished ice, a wretchedly bad route but there was no other. Our rate of climbing was pitifully slow. I found that at rest I felt comfortable, but the first two steps, the first few blows of the ice-axe, used all my tiny reserve of oxygen, leaving me fighting for breath. Another five steps and I would sink to a halt. A rest, recovery, and the struggle would go on.

Early in the afternoon we were clear of the ice-fall and climbing a gully in knee-deep snow. The wind, now a blizzard, was beating at our backs. At just over 26,000 feet we called a halt with the weather getting worse. Should we go on? It seemed certain we would not be able to make an attempt on the summit next day and to be storm-bound in a camp at 27,000 feet would be dangerous: we made a dump of food and equipment and turned back to VI, our only achievement the stocking of what later became Camp VI½.

We found ourselves descending into the teeth of the gale. Driving snow sheathed our faces in ice and filled the steps. Half-way across the ice-bulge just above the camp I placed a foot on a patch of snow which I thought was a step. It wasn't, and in a flash I was hurtling down the steep ice trying desperately to brake with the ice-axe. There was a sharp tug as the rope tightened on Wally. For a second he held me, then he too was falling. Fifty feet down I landed in soft snow. I saw Wally coming head-first towards me. He shot past, the rope tightened, I was pulled down a few feet and then we were both at rest, buried in the deep snow, our lungs screaming for the oxygen we had used in our frenzied attempts to halt ourselves. We staggered back to camp while the Sherpas, who had watched us in silence, numbly began to move again.

Phu Dorje was waiting. He looked at us with concern then lighted the primus and began melting snow for a hot drink. My cheeks and nose were cold and heavy and when I put a hand to them I found thick plates of ice; I leant over the primus, the ice loosened and fell with a clatter on to the billy of melting snow, but my nose remained a solid block. Phu Dorje looked at me and shook his head. My nose, it seemed, was frozen through, frost-bitten, and with horror I realised that the whole thing might turn black and drop off, like the nose of a leper, and I wondered vaguely if plastic surgeons could fashion new noses.

After a brew of tea, Leigh, Wally and I retreated to our tent. A ventilator left open had let in a mound of snow at one end and the floor was thick with ice crystals which had condensed on the roof during the night and fallen off. Scraping the snow clear of our sleeping-bags we crawled into them.

It was 5 p.m. Fourteen hours before we could move again. What the others did I do not know. There was enough to keep me occupied, for my fingers and toes had lost all feeling. At 26,000 feet a man's hands and fingers are starved of blood for the heart has more than enough to do supplying such vital organs as the brain. Slowly warmth crept down my arms and legs. By tucking a hand under each arm-pit I brought feeling back to my fingers. The logical extension of this, tucking a foot into the warmth of my groin, ended in an agonising bout of cramp and I reflected ruefully that in eight months in the

Himalayas I had mastered neither high altitude nor the lotus position.

Next morning the gale was still blowing full force. We dragged ourselves outside, fought with frozen crampon straps till I could have cried with frustration, packed our few belongings, including the precious alveolar air samples, and set off back to V, 1500 feet below. Even going downhill I became breathless and had to stop. When we reached the level traverse half a mile from the Col I was asking for a rest every hundred yards. The wind, which was driving into our faces with such power that it was hard to keep a footing, had stripped away the loose snow, leaving polished ice so hard that our crampons jittered across its surface. Though the powder had gone there was still, in parts, a thin layer of compact snow, and slabs of this, caught by the wind, were being whipped into the air and sent spinning towards Tibet like huge autumn leaves. There was a cry behind us, and turning, we saw Ngima Dorje on his back being blown across the ice. The rope tightened, he clawed his way on to his knees, to his feet, then continued on unsteadily in the slow motion that is the normal speed of high altitudes.

The big tent at Camp V was surprisingly warm. All the sahibs were now at V, Pete and Tom forming the second assault party and John Harrison and Mike the third. Leigh, who was less exhausted than Wally or I, decided to join the third assault. As we sprawled amongst the litter of sleeping-bags and down-jackets we told them of our two days on the upper slopes of the mountain. The altitude was much tougher than we'd expected. There was no hope of any of us reaching the summit unless he were spared the task of breaking trail except on the final push to the top. If the second assault did no more than establish Camp VII high on the mountain, they would have done as much as could be expected and the way would be open for the third assault.

The wind next day, May the 16th, had dropped. While Pete and Tom and a fresh group of Sherps launched the second assault, Wally and I, and John West who had completed the physiology, returned to III. From that day on I was little more than observer. Things went wrong for the second assault, badly wrong, but down at III we were cut off from them so that at first we had little idea of what was happening. Fragments of news came crackling over the radio from the higher camps but not till several days later did we piece together a coherent picture of events. Even then, there were gaps and inconsistencies. We all had high altitude sickness in some degree and to that extent our vision was distorted. Skin divers talk of 'the rapture of the deep' when they are overcome by the effects of pressure and lose their judgement, and I imagine the exhaustion of high altitudes is akin to this 'rapture'. One retreats into a muffled, self-centred world, conscious mainly of one's own suffering, with little awareness of what is happening outside. From Camp III we watched helplessly the struggles above. There was little else we could do.

For several days we heard nothing from V and we soon realised that the radio there was out of action. There was a radio at VI however, and on May 18th we heard the first news of the second assault. Ang Temba had broken his ankle—how, we had no idea. Mike had gone up to VI to help him down and it was Mike who was speaking to us over the radio. He sounded distraught, in a way that made us feel uneasy.

On the following day we heard from VI again, this time from Leigh and John Harrison who were starting on the third assault, Mike having retired unwell. Nor were John and Leigh in good shape. John had vomited during the night and had still not recovered while Leigh had found the climb a much greater effort than on the first assault.

But what was happening to Pete and Tom on the upper slopes of the mountain? At 2 p.m. we heard the first of the bad news. Annulu had just staggered into VI after traversing the ice-fall by himself. On May 16th while climbing up to our dump at VI½ six Sherpas had fallen and it was during this that Ang Temba had broken his ankle. Nevertheless VII had been established and Annulu had stayed with Pete and Tom for the summit assault. Next morning, said Annulu, they had set out for the top, but before going far Pete had collapsed. They returned to VII, stayed there that day, and next morning began the descent. At 26,000 feet, the highest point of the first assault, Pete could go no farther and Annulu had been sent down for help. They needed a tent urgently (their own had been left at VII) and oxygen.

John and Leigh debated what they should do. It seemed likely that Pete was just exhausted and would get back with the help of oxygen so their first move was to send Pasang and Pemba Tensing, who were both working magnificently, to VI½ with the tent and oxygen. When they returned that night they said that the two climbers were still alive though their position was desperate. Meanwhile, Leigh and John had tossed (using a throat lozenge instead of a coin) for who would go up to help Pete the following day. Leigh 'won' and John returned to V to direct a rescue operation, if necessary, from there.

Next morning, May 20th, we established a tenuous radio contact with Desmond who had settled into the Silver Hut and was transmitting to Katmandu. With Ed's 'stroke' world headlines, several journalists were now said to be pursuing him as he worked his way back to the Khumbu across the lower foothills.

And then at 5 p.m. we heard from VI½ over the radio which Leigh had taken with him. Tom had returned to V. Pete and Leigh would follow next day, provided more oxygen reached them and some

Sherps to carry loads. Pete spoke and to our relief sounded reasonably normal, better in fact than Leigh who had lost most of his voice, leaving him with a rasping, death-like whisper.

During the afternoon, we had seen two figures moving slowly down from the Col with frequent rests. Mike perhaps? But it turned out to be the indefatigable Annulu along with a young Sherpa (classified as a low-altitude porter) who had also been to 27,000 feet. Annulu, for the first time since I had known him, was exhausted and depressed. "Ward sahib, Mulgrew sahib, very sick," he said. He had a note from John Harrison, our first news from V. Mike was seriously ill and delirious much of the time. They needed oxygen and some Sherpas to help him down.

John West decided to climb to the Col next day to help Mike, who had to be brought down urgently. The morale of the Sherpas at III was now sinking fast. Many were sullen and arguing amongst themselves but with Annulu as sirdar there was unlikely to be an open mutiny. John used an oxygen set for the climb to V and made fast time. He arrived to find Mike stuporous in a sleeping-bag, and Tom wandering about in a daze, saying that he didn't feel too well and maybe he'd rest up for a day or two before moving on. And a week at 24,000 feet had taken much of the drive out of John Harrison; he had something wrong with his feet which mysteriously had become almost too painful to walk on. West swept through Camp V like Christ casting the money-chargers from the Temple: Mike and Tom were sent down to IV each with an oxygen set, and the propane burners, which had ceased to function to the extent that no one was getting enough to drink or eat, were unblocked by the ingenious adaptation of a blood pressure measuring device.

It was expected that Pete would reach V from VI½ that evening but at 2 p.m. all hope of this was abandoned. Leigh came on to the radio with the news that three Sherpas with oxygen had just reached VI½. The news about Pete was frightening: even with oxygen it was doubtful whether he was capable of traversing the icefall. "Pete's mind is sort of wandering," said Leigh. Both hands, both feet and parts of his face were frostbitten. But they reached VI. Even though he was rapidly losing touch with reality, Pete was lucid enough to know that if he didn't make the crossing then he never would. No one could have carried him across the steep ice. The only oxygen bottle he had left was a faulty one and within half an hour it was empty leaving him to struggle across on his own, with nothing but Leigh's encouragement and his own determination to keep him going.

At dawn next day they prepared to move. Urkien and the other two Sherpas were now so weak and demoralised that they decided to hurry down to V for help. Probably they would have been more useful had they stayed with the two sahibs, but before Leigh had realised what was happening the Sherps were vanishing into the distance. To Leigh it seemed that they had been left to die. All that day he encouraged Pete who was crawling, slithering, lapsing into unconsciousness, occasionally staggering to his feet. I had thought our return from VI to V bad enough but by comparison with that nightmarish descent it was like a walk in a city park on a summer afternoon. For Pete it was the last effort of a dying man, for Leigh, who carried the responsibility for his companion's safety, it was a tremendous effort of courage and determination. Without him Pete would have died on that desolate, wind-swept snow-slope below Camp VI.

They reached the level traverse leading to V just as it was growing dark. The wind had been bad all day but by then it had risen to gale force, worse than it had been during the return of the first assault party. The situation was desperate for on the level ground Pete no longer had gravity to help him down. And then out of the gloom five figures appeared. It was Urkien with four of the strongest Sherps from V and they hoisted Pete on to a headband and carried him. V was blotted out by the dark and for a while they thought they were lost. But Urkien, after hunting about on his own, found the tents and led the party in.

Pete was an appalling sight. In the past six days he had changed past recognition. The flesh had shrunk beneath his skin leaving him gaunt and cadaverous; his colour was an ashen grey and his eyes had sunk back into their sockets; black patches of frostbite were showing up on his face and hands, like the plague, and his feet, though not black, were a pale lilac colour and cold as ice from the ankles down. Whenever he moved an agonising pain shot through his chest. By piecing together the story John realised that Pete had had a pulmonary embolus or thrombosis on the day he had collapsed, depriving him of the use of one lung. Little wonder he had had so much difficulty in getting down.

That was the worst day. The trip down from the Col was not easy but by making a stretcher out of pack frames the move was completed and Pete carried down to Base-Camp on the Barun moraine. Because of poor reception we had lost our radio contact with Desmond but one day we got through to him. A helicopter was requested urgently: it would fly in to the yak pasture near Sershong on May 29th. The 29th came. Pete was waiting down at 15,000 feet. The rest of us were lying around Base-Camp enjoying the thick air and comparative warmth when from down valley came the heavy beating of a helicopter. Then we saw it, a shining bubble of Perspex and red struts, fluttering towards us a thousand feet above the glacier. For a while everyone went mad, Sherpas dancing about and the rest of us pointing urgently down valley to where Pete was waiting to be picked up. The pilot circled twice, coming lower each time, and then grasping our message flew back towards Sershong.

For us that was the end of Makalu. For Pete it was *mulgrew* just the beginning of a long ordeal of shifting from one hospital to another till in the end he lost some fingers and had both legs amputated below the knee. We had come with the idea of finding out how easily a high mountain could be tackled without oxygen, and we had learned with a vengeance. Pete's survival was a tribute to his own courage and that of Leigh and the others who had rescued him; above all, perhaps, to the Sherpas, to Urkien, Annulu, Pemba Tensing, Pemba Tarkay, Siku and all the others who had toiled and risked their lives. When Ed decided later to help the Sherpas by building schools and a hospital he was repaying a debt that we all acknowledged.

Hillary

14

THE RAMSAY FACE OF WHITCOMBE

Time was pressing us now. We were very tired and there was still no hint of an end. Looking down we could see Ian using his knees. Mike rebuked him, saying that even if he were bone-weary there was no excuse for such bad technique when climbing. Ian looked up with a mystified air. "Climbing? Who's climbing?" he said. "I'm praying."

Phil Houghton.
N.Z. Alpine Journal, 1962.

I CAME back from the Himalayas in June, resolved at first to give up climbing altogether. But the grim memory of Makalu faded and summer drew near. I wrote to Phil, who replied that he had grown weary of working a hundred hours a week as a house surgeon and that a trip into the hills would be a good start to the year or two of beach-combing he planned. And Ian Cave and John Nicholls, they too were keen. Where should we climb? Nicholls was adamant. The Ramsay Face of Whitcombe had to be climbed. "This year," he wrote, "it's the front pages or the back," the front pages of the *Alpine Journal* being for the more spectacular climbs of the season, the back pages for the obituaries.

Mt Whitcombe is in the Rakaia country, the land of Samuel Butler's *Erewhon* and of John Pascoe's mountaineering classic *Unclimbed New Zealand.* The approaches to it are through the Canterbury foothills, a landscape as different from Fiordland and the Darrans, as Tibet is from Nepal. Just as the Himalayan Divide and the Nepalese foothills break the force of the monsoon, so do the West Coast and the Southern Alps bear the brunt of the recurring nor'-westers so that a few miles east of the Main Divide the winds are dry. There the hills and plains are carpeted by brown tussock and only the flooding of the great rivers draining east gives notice of the rain and snow beating on mountains enveloped in the gloom of a storm.

We had made an attempt on Whitcombe in the Easter of 1960, Ian Cave, John Nicholls and I. When we set off from the end of the road it was late on a fine autumn afternoon. The low sun moulded the soft contours of the hills on either side of the Rakaia Valley, down which as Butler wrote "the river ran in many winding channels, looking, when seen from above, like a tangled skein of ribbons, and glistening in the sun." In the folds of the hills golden poplars flickered like flames, and across the horizon, etched in black and white, were the snow-covered peaks of the Divide, sharp against the luminous blue of the sky.

We walked till nearly midnight, and all next day we tramped steadily up-valley, feeling on our faces a soft breeze already nipped by the cold of approaching winter. Dust blew across the shingle flats, forcing us to shelter behind drift-wood when we lit a fire for a brew. At length we reached the source of the river where it emerged from a black cavern in the terminal ice-face of the Ramsay Glacier. We looked up-valley. It was a bleak and gloomy place, a corridor enclosed between the Divide on one side and a lesser range to the east; forming the floor of the corridor was the glacier covered by grey hummocks of loose moraine through which no white ice was visible, nor was there any vegetation. Beyond, an immense rock-face bulged out, cutting off our view of the upper névé. It was the Ramsay Face of Whitcombe.

In 1866 Sir Julius von Haast said of Whitcombe, 'It can scarcely be surpassed by any other mountain," and in *Unclimbed New Zealand* Pascoe wrote when describing the view from a near-by peak: "To the west Mt Whitcombe rose sheer from the Ramsay Glacier and so held our attention that we were unwilling to dwell on the view of the lesser mountains of the Lyell valley. With a last glance at the immense Whitcombe buttresses we began the descent . . ." It was from Pascoe's book we had the idea of climbing the face for the cover photo shows, on a jagged rock ridge, two climbers, one with ice-axe aloft, against the back-drop of the Ramsay Face. In an early guide book to the region he thought the face was "likely to remain inviolate" but in a later edition he spoke of "new challenges awaiting the coming generation".

That was us. Sitting on our packs we looked more closely at the face. The most clear-cut routes and those which had caught our attention on Pascoe's photo, were two magnificent buttresses on the southerly part of the face below the Low Peak, each 4,000 feet high. Segments of the left-hand buttress had fallen away leaving big steps but that on the right rose steep and direct, complete except in the uppermost part where it ran into a vertical wall two or three hundred feet below the summit. Probably the key to the climb lay in the forcing of those last few pitches. The lower part, where big scree fans lay against the face, looked easy.

We talked about the route as we hopped from boulder to boulder

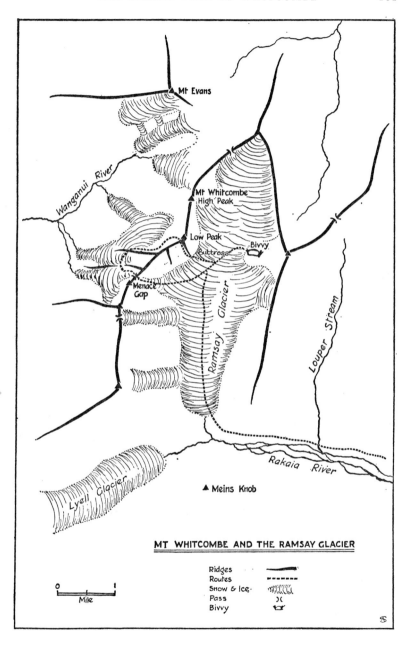

MT WHITCOMBE AND THE RAMSAY GLACIER

Ridges
Routes
Snow & Ice.
Pass
Bivvy

up the moraine. "You know where this stuff comes from, don't you," said John, kicking at a heap of shattered rubble. "From the face. The whole lot of it."

"It's too steep to be really rotten," I replied, developing a theory of mine that the steeper the angle, the sounder the rock. Judged by this the Ramsay Face should be like diamond; but in the event the theory was proved conclusively wrong.

Late in the day we pitched camp near the foot of the buttress. There were signs of a nor'-wester in the offing and when we woke next morning, cloud was settling down over the tops. Before mist swallowed the face completely we climbed a thousand feet, enough to confirm that the lower part was easy. Then the winter set in. When we caught a glimpse of the face two days later through a break in the clouds, fresh snow was plastered everywhere and we knew that for that year the climbing season was over.

That was in 1960, so when we laid plans for our climb in 1962 we knew something of what lay ahead of us. We arranged to meet up the Rakaia in February. While hurrying down the North Island on a motor-bike to keep the appointment, I was involved in a collision with a larger vehicle, a miscalculation which knocked the back end off the bike, leaving me intact but two days behind schedule. Phil waited for me and together we tramped up the Ramsay hoping to find the other two comfortably dug into a snow-cave. But there had been no suitable snow and instead they had camped under a previously undiscovered bivvy rock, about a thousand feet up-valley from the foot of the buttress. They showed us two cramped sleeping-benches at the end of a narrow tunnel.

"Fairly snug under here," they said, "but not a lot of room for four people. You might like to have a look for something better. Plenty of rocks around here."

There were indeed, and 200 feet farther up we found an overhanging boulder facing north-west, giving a good view of the storm that was rolling in from that direction. In thickening cloud we blocked in the entrance with a rock wall and watched the first of the rain blowing through cracks on to our sleeping-benches. When we went down to the other bivvy for the evening meal, Phil wisely took his sleeping-bag with him and stayed there. Very early next morning, wet if not soaked, I joined him, thinking regretfully of easier times when there had been Sherpas and water-proof tents.

The nor'-wester was short-lived and that evening the wind swung south. When we woke at 6 a.m. the sky was clear. Within two hours we had eaten breakfast and crossed the glacier to the foot of the buttress where it rose out of the heaps of rubble cast off from the crumbling face.

The climb began up a scree fan followed by a succession of debris-strewn ledges which led to an alcove, a hole left in the side of the buttress by the subsidence of a pocket of loose rock. We were almost at the highest point of our abortive attempt two years earlier. This was where the real climbing started. We roped up, Phil and I sharing the lead on one rope, Ian and John on the other. A few runners and a camera around my neck, pitons clanking from a waist-loop and I led off.

The first pitch though steep and exposed was made easy by an abundance of good holds. It was a fair sample of the sort of rock we encountered on the whole of the first two-thirds of the climb. We zig-zagged up the line of the buttress following inter-connecting ledges which seldom made us think twice about where the easiest route lay. Falling rocks were mainly a problem for John and Ian who were having to dodge rocks sent down by us, as well as those from the upper parts of the mountain. More of a problem was the cold. There was little sun on the face and last night's southerly had sprinkled the holds with crystals of sago snow, so that intermittently we were sucking at numb fingers to restore feeling.

At 12 noon we called a halt for lunch, just over half way up the face. "Is that where you usually carry your camera?" someone said, pointing to my feet. Looking down I saw that the strap had broken, leaving the camera dangling from a buckle jammed in my waist loop. I had been too intent on the climbing to bother about photos anyway so I stuffed it away in a rucksack. We chewed biscuits and chocolate, shared a quart of orange-juice and looked uneasily at the weather. Streaks of high cloud showed overhead, and gathering around the summits farther south were ominous shreds of grey vapour. The Ramsay Face was no place to be caught in a storm.

When we set off again there was a feeling of urgency creeping into what had so far been an easy climb. The ledges, which had felt so secure, now vanished almost completely leaving us on smoother rock rising sharply upwards. Where before we could look down on comfortable shelves of rock, spread below like a net, now there was nowhere the eye could rest on. One's gaze swam about in the dizzy void opening below. On either side were flanks of smooth grey wall, while above, the upper part of the face looked dark and menacing.

I began to use pitons, at first as anchors, then for protection between belays. We came to a point where the buttress was too steep for a frontal assault and followed a line of holds on to the open face on our right. Seldom have I felt so small and insecure as there, clinging to that vast, featureless face.

"I think this is going to be my last climb," said Phil quietly as he came up to the belay position. "This is getting too bloody dangerous."

The other two were close on our heels but we were too preoccupied with the climb to carry on a conversation. There was the occasional warning cry of "Rock!" as we knocked something down in their direction, and a few comments on the ones we sent down without warning. Mostly we climbed in silence. And then the light began to go. We had forgotten the weather, till suddenly, like a clammy hand, the mist enveloped us blotting out the sky, and in the grey twilight the sense of urgency became more acute. We were committed now, as surely as if in a small boat we had sailed out of sight of land and found ourselves in a gathering storm.

At 4 p.m. after clambering up a rotten gully to the left of the buttress, we anchored ourselves to a piton at the foot of the final wall. The top was close now, perhaps 300 feet. This was the crux of the climb. There was no problem about choice of route. There was only one: a steeply rising slab slanting upwards with a narrow crack where it was welded to the black, vertical rock of the face. Snow filled the crack, and the small holds on the slab were greasy. I began climbing, jamming the finger-tips of one hand into the crack on one side, and gripping the outside of the slab with the other, while my feet slithered on uncertain holds. I ran out ten feet of rope, twenty feet, and still there was no big hold where I could stop and secure myself with a runner. I grew less and less happy, but forty feet up the slab came to an end as a sharp crest standing out from the wall. Closing both hands over it, I hauled myself up and swung a leg over the top to sit astride; secure at last, the tension gone for the moment, I put in a belay and called to Phil to come up.

Looking downwards I saw the other three crowded under the wall. Behind them grey mist eddied back and forth, and through it I saw, two hundred feet away, the profile of the other of the twin Ramsay buttresses, a chaos of loose rocks piled one on the other in a tottering heap. Neither the top of it nor the bottom were visible in the mist and I wondered uneasily whether the rest of our own buttress was like that. Phil and the other two followed up the slab so that all four of us were crammed against the wall, with a vertical drop below and an apparently vertical face above. I tried tackling the face direct but even in the first few feet felt too insecure.

There was an alternative: a rubble-covered ledge running out to the right at a lower level. Climbing down, I worked along it for twenty feet with the leaning face pushing me towards the edge. I hammered in a piton for a runner. Then the ledge came to an end. Precariously on balance I reached up, feeling for holds. A pile of rubble tottered off balance, tugging at the rope as it fell away past me. When I took weight on a hand-jam, half the face seemed to shift towards me and a few boulders spun off into the mist. I realised that any moment now the same thing might happen to me. I tried pitons but each time the rock fractured. The ring of steel on steel echoed across the face, a rising note and then a sudden fall as the crack broke open. And then one of them seemed to bite. I felt desperate—we had to get up.

Reaching high, I took hold of the piton with one hand and the firmest piece of rock I could find with the other. What if that piton pulled out? For a moment panic rose within me as in imagination I fell backwards into the mist. Then I swung out and up, scrabbling for a foothold and frantically searching above as rock tumbled from around me. Then I was up and secure. Another runner and I moved back to the left on a higher ledge.

I climbed higher on the rotten face till there was so much friction on the rope dragging through pitons and over sharp edges that I could no longer move upwards. Nevertheless I was close to the foot of a small gully with plenty of room in it. It might lead to the top. After anchoring to a rickety piton I belayed Phil up to a position above me. Only then did I realise that the others, crouching under the face for the last hour with a shower of rock pouring past them, had been having no easy time of it either. Phil untied and dropped the loose end to John who climbed the face direct. He was still amazingly cheerful. While Ian came up, I followed the small gully above, turning a corner out of sight of the others. Fearful of what we might find, I looked up—and then I felt my heart thumping with excitement and I let out a wild yodel. We were at the top.

It was 6 p.m. We were on the summit of the Low Peak. There was no wind but light snow was falling and the High Peak was hidden in the mist. I hunted for a parka. No parka. Apparently I'd left it behind.

"How do we get off this mountain?" asked someone. We looked blankly at each other.

"Who's got the guide-book?" None of us had it. We all had a vague idea that there should have been a big flat snowfield running up to Whitcombe from the west; that we had only to amble south along this till we reached a low point on the Divide, cross it and drop down to the Ramsay moraine. The trouble was, there was no snow-field, nothing but a steep rock face dropping into the mist. Perhaps we could traverse south along the crest—but there were too many rock towers on the ridge for that to be an easy alternative. I peered down the Ramsay Face for the last time and for a moment felt fear prickling through me. There was only one thing certain—we weren't going back down there.

We began traversing south along the western face hoping that eventually the crest of the ridge above would become easier. Un-roped, we moved quickly in a slanting line down and across the face, kicking across narrow snow couloirs and swinging from hold to hold down the rock. There was no wind. Big snow-flakes fluttered silently out of the mist, settled on the rocks and melted; rocks clattered away from under our feet and for a long time we heard them bounding down the mountain-side till their noise was smothered. It was a strange silent dream-world, isolated and calm, with no sign of the storm we had feared. At times we ran up against big towers in the mist, or the steep wall of a couloir, and each time we lost more height and swung farther west. When at length we regained the crest of a ridge, though we were unaware of it at the time, we had left the Divide behind us and were on a side-spur running to the west.

Down the ridge we hurried expecting at any moment to catch sight of the Ramsay moraine on our left. But when the mist began to thin, it was not the Ramsay we saw but a wild mountain landscape which was completely unknown to us. Ahead and to the right, a great ice-fall loomed out of the mist, its terminal face tumbling over a ledge into a deep valley. Then, with a growing uneasiness, we saw on our left the upper reaches of a high unfamiliar névé. And when a few minutes later, as we dropped below the cloud ceiling, the whole of the landscape was revealed to us, we stopped short as if we were seeing a vision of another world. On either side névés and huge ice-falls unfolded, and ahead, in the distance, radiant in the soft light of late evening, we saw a great valley, its walls steep and clothed in bush, snow on its upper slopes; through the clouds shone shafts of light, eery, lime-green, luminous; we had stumbled into Erewhon itself.

There was no sign of the Main Divide and for one wild moment I thought we might make a break for the West Coast by plunging down that valley. But when later the clouds lifted further, we saw far to the left across the névé, a gap in a rock ridge which might be the Divide. Sliding down a rotten rock-face we raced across the snow to the gap only to find beyond it yet another névé draining to the west, and at its head, showing briefly through the cloud, yet another rocky gap. We turned towards it, this time uphill, and in the gathering darkness scrambled up the final stretch of rock.

Without doubt we had reached the Divide at last and dimly below we saw the Ramsay. A black steep-sided cleft fell away at our feet and into it we hurried, spidering our way downwards, slipping and knocking rocks on to each other. When we were blocked by a fifty-foot drop we rappelled off it to a tongue of ice, working as much by feel as by sight for it was now dark. And that was the end of the climb, for though there was still a long descent on crampons, a tortured stumbling traverse of the moraine and the final climb to the bivvy, we knew that we were safe. The anxiety and excitement that had kept us going at fever pitch all through the day, faded, leaving only weariness.

At midnight, under a sky clustered with stars, we staggered into the bivvy.

One day the Ramsay Face will be climbed again. More pitons will be left there, loose rock will be cleared from the holds and the newcomers will laugh at our difficulties. But they will not see those last pitches, unknown and swathed in mist, as we saw them, nor will they rejoice as we did as they step on to the summit; they will not walk home in a dream; for that sort of experience comes only once in a mountaineering lifetime.

15

1963: TAWECHE AND KANGTEGA, SMALLPOX AND SCHOOLS

... I was afraid you would imagine that I wanted to reach the highest peak, which is still virgin and will, I expect, remain so eternally, like your friend Mademoiselle M.

de Saussure c. 1765

SIR EDMUND HILLARY'S 1963 expedition was called the Himalayan Schoolhouse Expedition. The title conjures up a vision of a group marching through Nepal with blackboard and chalk, but the observant eye might have noted that of the nine members seven were mountaineers. A mountaineering expedition in disguise? Not altogether. We hoped to climb Taweche, and maybe, with luck, Kangtega, but we were there mainly to help Ed with the Sherpa aid programme he had begun in 1961, after Makalu. Then, he had built a small school in Kumjung and arranged to pay the salary of a teacher from Darjeeling. Pessimists had predicted that the experiment would fail, that the new school would end up as the only pre-fabricated aluminium yak-stable in the Khumbu. No such thing happened. The initial burst of enthusiasm grew into a deep-rooted faith in education, school attendance increased, and headmen of other villages wrote grave and eloquent letters asking for schools in other parts of the Khumbu.

It is so easy to be sentimental about the Sherpas, to throw up one's hands in horror at the thought of changing the smallest part of their lives. We sit back in our city homes with our books and television, water on tap, electricity, fresh food in the deep-freeze and cans from the four corners of the earth in our cupboards—and we think mistily of those happy, healthy Sherpas living simply in their picturesque stone houses and tending their yaks amidst the finest mountains in the world. Why give them schools when any new knowledge, any ideas of change, will only leave them dissatisfied?

The Sherpa has a more realistic view of his life: he knows that if blight strikes the potato crop he will have a hungry winter; he knows that his only source of fuel is the pine forest a thousand feet below the village and that his water has to be carried from the nearest stream a mile away; his picturesque stone house, in winter, is bitterly cold. He has no control over disease or injury: when he walks down to lowland Nepal he risks being struck down by a mysterious fever; his wife may die in child-birth, his sons be born deaf or cretinous.

Up till 1949 most Sherpas had little opportunity to learn about the rest of the world: now the rest of the world is coming to them. In that year, when Nepal opened its frontiers to foreigners, the first Europeans entered the Khumbu. And soon afterwards the Communist régime of China, with its roads, hospitals and radio stations, moved into Tibet. Mountaineering expeditions came to the Himalayas in increasing numbers and in recent years tourists, old and young, have been walking to the Khumbu simply to see the place. Change and education of a sort have come to the Sherpas whether we think they need them or not. They look at these people who have so much more than they have, aeroplanes, helicopters, powerful medicines, so much money that they can afford to do useless things like climbing mountains. They look and find that these foreigners are not obviously more able or intelligent than they are—the difference is one of education.

"I do not want my sons to spend their lives carrying loads as I have," said Ang Temba, one of the best of our Sherpas. "I want them to learn what you sahibs know. I want to send them to school."

What should one teach them? Reading, writing and arithmetic for a start, but where does one go from there. What future can they be trained for? There are a few areas of knowledge of obvious use: agriculture to help them grow as much as they can from their inhospitable land; an elementary knowledge of medicine so that someone in the community understands the use of such things as iodine to eliminate goitres and cretinism, or vaccination to prevent smallpox epidemics.

What else? There is one way in which Sherpas can be helped to develop a skill they have already discovered. Visitors pour into Nepal, a few to climb mountains, many just to look, and the Sherpas are unsurpassed as professional guides and companions. Their ability to establish an easy rapport with Europeans is unique and they know by now the sort of assistance a visitor needs. By teaching the Sherpas to read and write English they will be assured of work for so long as Nepal remains open to foreigners. The prospect of commercialisation of the Khumbu makes many of us blanch but already it is on its way. We can only hope that with Sherpas participating in the change themselves it will come in an acceptable form; that by learning in schools run by their own people, they will have some chance of directing their future within the culture they have established over the centuries.

The expedition assembled in Katmandu early in March. Desmond Doig was back with us to act as interpreter and add that touch of colour that without him would have been missing. Bhanu Bannerjee was there too, now a fully-fledged, frost-bitten mountaineer, for he had been in the summit party of a successful Bengali expedition to another part of the Himalayas. In charge of the construction gang was Murray Ellis, a 36-year-old engineer from Dunedin whose hard-bitten practical approach to the business of school-building was leavened by flashes of wit. Phil was the expedition doctor and we had two Americans, Dave Dornan and Tom Frost, both of whom had risen to fame in the American climbing world through their ascents of the big rock walls of Yosemite. Then there was Jim Wilson, one of New Zealand's top climbers. Jim immediately established himself as a good expedition man; that is, he was genial, unselfish, a tireless worker and liked by all. At that time, after taking an M.A. in philosophy, he had been ordained in the Presbyterian Ministry. Anyone who had just been told of this would look at Jim's robust and exuberant exterior, chuckle heartily, and say: "Yeah! that's a good one that is—but what does he really do?" Since then Jim has taken a Ph.D in Benares and returned to philosophy as a lecturer in religious studies—but people still occasionally ask what he *really* does.

Money for the expedition was provided on a generous scale by World Book Encyclopaedia, the sponsors of the 1960–1 expedition. Ed had by then joined the firm of Sears Roebuck as their adviser on camping equipment and from them we received tents, sleeping-bags, clothing and a cash donation. They suggested we make a film of the expedition and because I had used a movie camera in 1961 I was appointed photographer, a job which carried with it a trip through Chicago, home of Sears, and London where the B.B.C. had bought television rights.

The week of organisation in Katmandu passed in much the same way as it had three years earlier. There was bargaining in the bazaar, cocktail parties at the embassies, a round of the temples, and a bout of dysentery. When Ed said he wanted someone to clear equipment through the Nepalese Customs, a dangerously frustrating job, everyone dived for cover; being slower than most, I was chosen and for a few days spent most of my time at the airport. It was a tedious business, made more difficult by the perspicacity of a lively young Customs Officer who ferreted out undeclared goods with humiliating ease. We had forgotten to mention our walkie-talkie radios and as a start these were confiscated. And then he discovered our freeze-dried beef, hurriedly relabelled as mutton. We had been told just before leaving New Zealand that Nepal had suddenly decided to enforce the Hindu prohibition on the import of beef. What we had not been told was that almost as suddenly they had relaxed the law for foreigners. "This is very unhappy for you," said the Customs man. "Since one month my government allows beef into Nepal, but now you try to deceive me, therefore I must confiscate your goods." In the end, however, we parted on good terms and in possession of all our supplies and equipment.

The walk-in this time was in early spring, in contrast to that of 1960 when we started in autumn. Summer is the season of the monsoon. Where before the hills and terraced valleys had been lush and green after the damp warmth of the monsoon, now, at the end of winter, they were bare. It was different too in that now I had the film to worry about. Through the view-finder I began to see the expedition more selectively, each scene and event to be sifted for material that might be built into the story. I filmed camps in valleys, camps under huge banyan trees, camps on bare hill tops in sight of the mountains; there were bare-footed Nepalis carrying aluminium roofing, tiny Sherpanis with kitbags as tall as themselves, sahibs with umbrellas, and the first red rhododendron was an exciting find. On the chain bridges, slung high above the rivers, the porters prayed and the sahibs quoted uneasily the proverb about the weakest link, for the chains are of locally-forged iron and are repaired only when they break. At times living with the camera was a chore but more often it added a new dimension to the already fascinating business of being part of an expedition.

Then, a week out from Katmandu, I fell ill: an obscure Asiatic virus which had been lurking inside me causing headaches and strange pains, finally settled in a lung as pleurisy. The treatment is rest. While the expedition carried on to the Khumbu I stopped at the village of Jiri with a tent to live in and Ang Karmi to look after me. Jiri is the site of a Swiss agricultural aid project. Pine-covered hills surround a gentle valley in which there are Swiss-style farmhouses and barns made from stone, locally sawn pine and shingles. The weather was fine and for two weeks I stayed there, lazing in the sun while each day the grating sensation, where one roughened lung was rubbing, grew less.

As well as the farm, the Swiss had a small hospital run by a doctor and a nurse. Through working with them at their clinics each morning I began to learn the Nepali language. When I had first attempted this in 1960 Griff Pugh had advised me to learn Urdu. "Urdu is the language of Pakistan . . ." began the teach-yourself book I bought. "Learn Hindi," Norm Hardie had said when I went looking for further advice. "All the expedition Sherps understand it," and he lent me *An Introduction to Hindi*. For a while I wrestled with the language, but though in some mysterious way the Sherps understood Norm, my own attempts were greeted by incomprehension. I tried to pick up the Sherpa language through those of our porters who spoke English but none was able to give me the verbs, not even 'I am'. I found a textbook of Tibetan (Sherpa is a dialect)—in 300 pages there was no mention of the verb 'to be'. Finally in desperation I wrote to the London School of Oriental Studies for advice. "In Nepal," came the reply, "the most useful language is Nepali ..." So in 1963 I acquired a handbook of Nepali by a Major Meerendonk. For six months 'The Donk' was a constant companion and though I could never follow a group of Nepalese chatting amongst themselves, I made myself understood wherever I went. There is no surer way of winning the confidence and gratitude of a Nepali than by speaking to him in his own language.

At the end of two weeks Ang Karmi and I hired three porters and left Jiri. Without the inertia of the 200 porters of the main expedition, we chose a more circuitous route. We began with a visit to a Swiss cheese-plant, a cottage in a high open pasture on a hill called Pikay three days from Jiri. Though the Swiss had begun the plant, by then it was in the hands of Pasang, a Sherpa who had learnt the art of cheese-making partly in Nepal, partly in Switzerland. He spoke English well, the dairy was immaculate, the cheese excellent—the Swiss run their aid programmes well.

Nor had I seen the last of the Swiss. From Pikay we dropped down 4,000 feet into the Solu valley. Here the true Sherpa country begins, but the villages are lower than those of the Khumbu still four days' walk away, and the living easier; too easy to breed many of the hardy mountaineers who take part in expeditions. Spring had come to the Solu. Snow was retreating from the tops of the ridges, willows were green with young shoots and the peach trees were covered in pink blossom. Climbing up the far side of the valley we came to Jahlsa, a Tibetan refugee centre run by the Swiss. When these refugees arrived in Nepal most of them had nothing. Traders working from India and Katmandu soon deprived them of their few precious gold, bronze and silver images, their scroll paintings and the other objects with which they decorate their shrines. At Jahlsa huts had been built, a dispensary opened under the care of a doctor and a carpet-factory started. It was not as good a life as they had had in Tibet but at least they were not begging in Katmandu or dying of heat and dysentery in India.

In Dorpu below Jahlsa it was market-day and the street was full of swaggering Tibetans (no one swaggers quite so heartily as a Tibetan) selling carpets, felt boots, striped aprons; Nepalis had kukris for sale, rice, barley and corn, butter, chickens and eggs, limes, pork, chillis and peanuts, and raw tobacco leaf which only a Nepali would smoke.

We moved on up-valley for there was no time to linger. Beside the track were two palatial Sherpa houses, one of them four stories high. The owner, Ang Babu, was said to be the wealthiest of all the Sherpas and he owned much of the rich land of the valley. Two hours farther on, high above the floor of the valley we came to Chuwong Monastery, bigger even than Tengboche. The monks, after showing me the frescoes and images in the main temple, fed us on pastries and buttered tea, then set us on the shortest route to the Khumbu.

Upwards we climbed, through forests of pink and crimson rhododendron and magnolias, huge naked trees bearing waxy-white blooms a foot across. Crossing the dividing ridge we descended into the Dudh Kosi valley; our next climb, out of the head of the valley, would take us to the Khumbu itself. Up in the woods I encountered a mastiff. I knew of these animals, that their only friends are their owners, that a drunk Nepali in Katmandu had been savaged by one and lost a leg, that in Tibet, with their throats protected by thick collars, they can drive off wolves. I was approaching a Sherpa house with a Nepali porter close behind, when one of these thickset shaggy creatures came cantering purposefully down the track towards me. Uncertain whether to make friends, throw rocks, or run, I turned to ask the Nepali. He was ten feet up a tree and still climbing. The mastiff was close—I leapt for the nearest tree, a spindly rhododendron, and clung there while the mastiff leapt and growled. I wondered which of us would tire first. Then a little Sherpa girl, no taller than the dog, came down from the house, dealt the animal a great blow on the snout and called me down. Travelling through Nepal is never dull.

I remember too that first night in the Dudh Kosi. I had been sleeping in houses rather than our tent and that night we were staying in a place which served as the local inn and chang-shop. It was a typical Sherpa house, with yak-calves in the basement and the main room above thick with smoke. That night it was full. I joined a dozen drunk Sherpas drinking chang around the fire, one of them making monstrously witty comments, apparently about me. My grasp of Nepali fell short of repartee and being tired I retired to a sleeping-bag in one corner. The fire died down and with it the party. Most of the others had settled themselves in various parts of the room when a small, silent, bird-like creature flitted into the room, darting backwards and forwards at great speed, yet miraculously touching nothing.

"Pum-tok-tok," said Ang Karmi.

"Pum-tok-tok?" Then I realised it was a bat. I had never seen one before.

"Pum-tok-tok!" shouted one of the others and suddenly the room was alive with drunken Sherpas pursuing the bat. They crashed into each other, they fell over me, they knocked huge brass bowls off the shelves, they upended the last of the chang. One of them fell down the stairs where he lay helpless with laughter amongst the yak calves. They abandoned the chase but still there was no peace. One had a tuberculous cough, another stumbled below and was sick, several began to snore. A sheep tethered in one corner emptied its bladder with a noise like the bursting of a dam; ribald comments followed and laughter.

At length I fell asleep. I was woken at midnight by a painful sting-ing near the middle of my belly and lighting a match I discovered a bed-bug the size of a one-cent piece. And no sooner had I disposed of him than I became aware of a large, black mastiff chained to a pillar six feet away; or rather the mastiff became aware of me. When I moved he growled, low and menacing, and neither of us had much sleep in what was left of the night. By five o'clock in the morning I'd had enough. I woke Ang Karmi and the three porters: "Let's get out of this," I said. "We'll have breakfast in the next village."

Two days later we walked into Kumjung. The expedition was an encampment of orange and blue tents, beyond which the rows of grey stone houses climbed up the hillside. The first project, the improve-ment of the village water-supply, was already half-completed. The Khumbu villages are sited according to the availability of potato fields rather than of water and the women of Kumjung, to reach the nearest stream, had to walk a mile. Their loads of water when they returned weighed ninety pounds. Ed had realised that by merely laying a mile of alkathene pipe alongside the track, water could be brought to the village. It was a simple enough idea yet by themselves the Sherpas could never have known of alkathene pipe, let alone obtain it.

On the following day more than 400 people turned out for the com-pletion of the job, the building of a permanent stone wall on which the pipe could be laid. Most of the day there appeared to be chaos: small children staggered about under loads of rocks, ex-expedition Sherpas were grubbing out a ledge round the hillside with ice-axes, schoolboys were cutting juniper scrub with kukris, groups of pretty young Sherpanis giggled and chattered while a shouting headman threatened to cut off their breasts unless they did something useful, lost babies were crying for their mothers and a group of the village strong-men were striding purposefully about, shifting apparently immovable boulders. Directing operations in a set of startling blue windproofs was Murray Ellis. By the end of the day the work was done and water flowed freely into a temporary tank at the edge of the village. Singing and chattering in the fading light the Sherpas ambled home, carrying huge piles of cut scrub so that from a distance they looked like a small forest on the move.

The pessimists of the party, including me, made gloomy predictions that the pipe would be frozen half the year or knocked apart by yaks, but now, five years later, the same old pipe is still running. On a cold night, and most are cold, the water freezes, but by mid-morning the black plastic has trapped enough heat from the sun to melt the ice. The only problem arising out of the Kumjung project was the flood of requests for pipe-lines in other villages.

While I was in Jiri there had been a smallpox epidemic in the Khumbu. A porter with the American Everest Expedition, which had come in just ahead of us, had fallen ill on the march-in and dropped out with smallpox, two days short of the Khumbu. He had stayed in the house of a friend in one village, staggered on to the next and there he had died. Smallpox is one of the most contagious of all diseases: some of those who had been in contact with the sick man fell ill and they, by moving, had carried the disease further. By the time I arrived Ed and Phil had had vaccine flown in from Katmandu, several thousand people had been inoculated and the epidemic had not spread nearly as far as it might.

One day I came face to face with the disease. I was returning from Thami where I had been vaccinating the few who had missed Phil a week earlier. As I passed through the little village of Themo I asked Ang Karmi about a cluster of new huts surrounding a larger building whose terracotta-painted walls proclaimed it a monastery.

"New gompa, Mike-sahib. Lamas, lamanis coming from Tibet one year. No liking Chini. Head lama very good man, very big lama. All Sherpas much liking. Some lamas sick, sahib. Hlendum," he said, using the Sherpa word for smallpox.

"Have they had medicine?" I asked, pointing to the ampoules of vaccine.

"I not knowing sahib. I asking."

We walked up the dusty track to the huts and the few tattered black yak-hair tents amongst them. Tibetans gathered around, some with the shaven heads and dark red robes of monks or nuns, others were laymen.

"Who is sick?" I asked.

One of them beckoned and led me to a tent which was dark except where sunlight slanted through the entrance. Half-wrapped in a dirty blanket, in the sun, was a child who was dying: his face, trunk, arms, all that I could see of him, were thickly covered in the sores of smallpox and his mother who squatted beside him held out a hand to me as if entreating me to do something. I stayed in the entrance trying to explain that there was nothing my medicine could do. And I realised that I was afraid that that festering disease might take hold of me too, even though I was vaccinated. Again she beckoned and turning into a corner away from the sun she lifted aside a blanket to show me a young girl, so covered with disease that she was barely recognisable as a human being.

And then a man of my own age stepped forward and taking my hand passed it across a crop of nodules on his face. "Is it the hlendum, sahib?" Horror rose within me and involuntarily I pulled my hand away and stepped back. For a moment I felt as if I were back in medieval Europe at the time of the plague, or as if I were facing one of the lepers of the New Testament.

"Tell these men," I said to Ang Karmi, "that I cannot cure those who are sick, but I will give medicine to the others so that the disease will not spread to them."

By now a crowd was gathering, some with their faces daubed green as a protection against the evil disease that had come amongst them. I opened an ampoule of vaccine and showed on my arm the sore where I had recently been revaccinated. Ang Karmi spoke to them in Tibetan but they shook their heads and drew away. Desperately I tried to convince them myself, in halting Nepali, feeling, as I spoke, like an evangelist preaching some new salvation. Then one came forward, a shy soft-spoken man who had lived in Kalimpong and had faith in Western medicine. He tried to persuade the others but still shook their heads.

"They will take your medicine if the Head Lama gives it his blessing." I was led into the courtyard of the monastery, up a flight of narrow stairs to where a very old man was sitting cross-legged in a tiny room just big enough for the two of us. He had mild eyes, a gentle smile and the soft, slim hands of one who has never worked. When I presented the traditional offering of money he waved it aside. Through Ang Karmi as interpreter I explained how I could help his monastery. He listened, nodding at intervals, and then replied.

"He saying you are good man," said Ang Karmi, "but your medicine not good."

My vocabulary had already been stretched to its limit. There was nothing I could say. He gave me tea, clasped my hands in his and placed a white scarf around my neck. Then he said goodbye.

But before I left I was taken down to one of the houses. My guide knocked and the door was opened by a woman whose face and hands

Kangtega from the south. The route runs up the ice-fall, behind the rock ridge, and finally up the summit snow-face

Sir Edmund and Lady Hillary, and the Head Lama of Tengboche. At the opening of the Thami school

At Kangtega Base Camp: Pemba Tarkay, Mike Gill, Jim Wilson

Kangtega (left) and Thamserku from Kunde village

Sherpas in the Kangtega ice-fall

Yaks and a Tibetan trader

Ceremony at Tengboche

A child reincarn-
ate lama

The Head Lama
of Themo
monastery

A Khumbu river in the monsoon

Three little girls from Thami

Pemba Tarkay, mountaineer

On the Milford Road, 1965: Mike Hutchins (left), Jim Wilson, Ed Hillary, Mike Gill

Penguins on the sea-ice

Murray Ellis, the Weasel, the Snowmobile, Norm Hardie, and Ed Hillary

Adélie penguins

"Pete Strang was beating out a wild reveille on an empty jerry-can"

Bruce Jenkinson at the foot of the summit cone of Herschel

The downhill run to Moubray Bay

Herschel, Moubray Bay and the Adélie penguin rookery. Hallett Station is on the left

were covered in smallpox. Someone spoke to her and plucking up the sleeve of her gown she showed me her arm; it was almost an accusing gesture. Amongst the rash of the pox was a sore marking the vaccination she had had from us a week earlier. Then, at last, I understood their mistrust. But how could I explain that our medicine had not caused the disease? That before she came to us the disease was already in her blood?

Before I left the village I washed my hands and arms, still afraid that I might have picked up the virus. I felt sure that many more of those in the monastery would die. But when I returned two months later everyone was well. There had been no fresh outbreak and only the two children had died.

The Kumjung pipe-line having been completed, we shifted to Pangboche to start work on two larger projects, the building of a school, and the attempt on Taweche, a peak of 21,460 feet with the village on its lowermost slopes. Taweche is one of the inner circle of Khumbu peaks which came to be Ed's by right of conquest. Of the other three, Ama Dablam had been climbed in 1961, the apparently impregnable Thamserku was climbed by an expedition of Ed's in 1964, and in 1963 we had permission to attempt Taweche and Kangtega.

Taweche is less spectacular than the other three, as a square fortress is less spectacular than a cathedral, but the climbing of it is no easier. Grass slopes led from Pangboche to a Base Camp beside a lake at 17,000 feet. Above this, for 3,000 feet, rose an encircling ring of cliffs, guarding access to a snow plateau above. On the far side of this rose the summit slopes, a thousand feet of steep snow supporting a corniced ridge of ice. The key to the climb, we thought, was the forcing of those 3,000 feet of rock; once camped on the plateau the summit would be ours.

If the weather had been clear, as it was in late winter on Ama Dablam, the climb would have been easier, but I can remember only one wholly fine day while we were on the mountain, the day we attempted the summit. Spring in the Himalayas, except towards the end of the season, brings snow showers most afternoons. We expected this but Taweche attracted more bad weather than the other peaks. I remember in the Mingbo seeing the whole of the region bathed in sunshine except Taweche where a neatly-placed grey cloud smothered our route on the South Face. It was as if the bad weather came from the bowels of the mountain itself.

Base Camp beside the frozen lake under the cliffs of the South Face, was never a pleasant spot for there was always fresh snow on the ground. A few miles to the east was Everest where the Americans

M

were beginning their long (and later successful) struggle to the summit. Already we had heard the tragic news of the avalanche which
had killed one of them. Looking at the rearing face of Taweche,
loaded with snow, it was easy to imagine the same thing happening to
us. The only feasible route up it involved too much time in gullies
and on avalanche fans.

Dave and Jim were the first two on the mountain. By the time
Murray and I joined them they already had the route through to
19,000 feet, with rope fixed on the upper steep section. We suggested
that Camp I be placed on a patch of snow at 18,000 feet at the foot
of the fixed ropes but Dave's principles were against this. He was a
thoughtful, scholarly person, sparing of words, and bore no resem-
blance to the caricatured American of the tourist trade-routes.
Through him we built up a picture of American climbers, or some of
them, as a small, ascetic community whose code of ethics was better
defined than ours. Littering the mountain-side with camps and fixed
ropes troubled Dave. It was the difference between the man who
goes trout-fishing with a fly-rod and the one who uses a charge of
gelignite. Besides, our site for Camp I was quite clearly an avalanche
fan. Dave was outvoted however. Our more primitive New Zealand
approach was to reach the summit by any method offering and had it
been feasible we would have drilled a hole up the centre.

With four Sherpas we carried two tents to the site of Camp I, dug
them in under the partial shelter of an outcrop of rock and tethered
them to pitons. The danger of the place was underlined the following
day. We had just returned from a long day of route-finding and rope-
fixing. Ang Temba, who had stayed in camp, handed a large rock to
us and pointed reproachfully up the face. A jagged tear in the roof
of the tent told the rest of the story.

Before we had completed the route to the plateau on top of the
cliffs, the weather deteriorated even further and we retreated to
Pangboche to help with school-building. When we returned to Camp
I a week later we found one tent flattened by an avalanche, leaving
two poles poking gauntly through the torn fabric. The establishing
of Camp II on the plateau became a matter of urgency. It was more
difficult than we had first thought. Higher up there were three big
problems: two rock steps, each requiring pitons and later rope ladders,
and a steep broken ridge of bare ice. Each one was a day's work and
each afternoon we returned down frozen fixed ropes in a snow-
shower. On May 6th, with five Sherpas, we carried Camp II to the
open spaces of the plateau. Four of us stayed there, Dave, Jim, Ang
Temba and I.

The summit day was our best on the mountain. We began early
with a long trudge across the powder snow of the plateau to the foot

of the perilously steep fluted face leading to the summit ridge, whose overhanging cornices leaned out as if to watch our progress. And our progress was frustratingly slow. Thick powder snow lay on a deeper icy layer and had to be threshed away before we could cut steps. At times the hard layer vanished leaving us floundering to our waists in snow like quick-sand. Hour by hour we worked upwards leaving behind a long straight trench. When I could I used the movie camera but cold had crept into the mechanism, slowing it down to an erratic grind. Like us, the camera was feeling the altitude.

The last fifty feet to the summit ridge, round the edge of a massive, poised block of ice, was the steepest pitch of all, a wall of snow and ice requiring handholds as well as steps. Dave led on to the crest of the ridge.

"How does it look?" I asked. We still had no idea of what that final hundred yards to the summit was like. Dave thought for a while before answering.

"Looks O.K. for the first part. It's kind of difficult after that."

The three of us climbed up to join him. Dave was right. The first part was broad and almost flat but beyond it the ridge narrowed abruptly to an irregular line of huge blocks balanced along the crest. Wind had carved and eroded it to the point where light was visible through the thin ice twenty feet below the crest. We sat down to rest and consider the situation. Time was no problem for it was still only one o'clock. Nor was the weather, for though towering piles of white cloud rose above the foothills to the south, dwarfing even Everest just along the range, around us the sun was shining. Dave was keen to go on but he had no one to go with him. I looked along the poised ice and I remembered photos of Himalayan cornices, of foot-steps leading to gaps where the ridge, and the climber on it, had dropped into oblivion. To reach the top of Taweche looked more a test of luck than skill. Jim agreed. Ang Temba? "Taweche no good, sahib."

The decision made, we began to relax. The Sherpas say that on the mountain dwells the god Taweche. I could almost believe it: that some hoary, ill-tempered spirit had been retreating before us, summoning up those snow-storms on the face, hurling rocks and avalanches on Camp I, softening the snow. And now, backed into his last stronghold, he was tempting us to destruction along that last tottering crest to the summit.

To placate Taweche the monks of Tengboche had made for us two prayer-flags and the Head Lama had blessed them. Before we left, Ang Temba performed a simple ceremony. He had carried the prayer-flags with him and now he climbed slowly upwards to the point where the ridge narrowed. There, on a small mound of snow, he planted the two flags. As we turned to begin the descent, I looked back at the meandering line of steps, the flags idly stirring in puffs of wind, the untouched summit beyond, and I felt a quiet glow of satisfaction. The climb could not have had a better end.

It was mid-May by the time we had removed the pitons from Taweche, stripped the cliffs of their fixed ropes and returned to Kumjung. There were still several things to be done including an attempt on Kangtega, and with the monsoon due in a fortnight there was not a great deal of time to do them in. The Pangboche school had been completed, blessed by the Head Lama, and it had taken in its first pupils. The school at Thami was still only half finished. While we had been on Taweche, Louise Hillary and Ann Wilson had walked in from Katmandu. Sherpa households began to vie with each other in entertaining us, the expedition became more and more a social occasion and Kangtega receded into the background.

One of the happiest occasions was a 'sports-day' organised by Desmond, ostensibly for the children but in fact for everyone. It was held on the flat sandy area by the school and the surrounding slopes provided a grand-stand on which the Sherpas perched like roosting birds. The entertainment was of a high standard. For a while there was a pandemonium of small boys and small girls in races of all sorts: three-legged races and ordinary races, egg-and-spoon, thread-the-needle and obstacle races. Then came the major events. Jim won the shot-put against strong competition from Phu Dorje, Pemba Tarkay and Murray Ellis. Ang Temba won the steeplechase-cum-climbing race, a strenuous event which the sahibs wisely kept clear of. With some confidence we challenged the Sherpas to a tug-of-war contest: in Desmond we had a first-class anchor man and the rest of us had the advantage on a weight-for-weight basis. But at the crucial moment a fresh group of lusty Sherpas rushed to the assistance of their fellows, too late the sahibs cried out for reinforcements, and the Sherpas won decisively.

The opening of the Thami school was a more solemn occasion. It was a handsome building. Since the rush-job on the pre-fabricated Kumjung school in 1961, Ed had brought the style of his buildings more into line with that of a Sherpa village. The walls were of stone, the timber locally sawn in the pine forests, the design close to that of a Sherpa house. To this were added glass windows, an aluminium roof (pine-shingle roofs, though the delight of the aesthete, are the despair of those who maintain them)—and a coat of gleaming crimson paint for the woodwork.

The Head Lama conducted the ceremony of dedication. The scented smoke of juniper fires hung in the air as the villagers crowded round the central figure of the Lama, cross-legged on a low throne.

He swayed as he chanted Buddhist incantations, there was sprinkling of holy water, ringing of bells and burning of incense. Speeches in three languages followed, the Nepali flag was unfurled and the national anthem sung. Finally, with the Head Lama taking her by the arm, Louise cut the ribbon across the door and declared the school open.

At noon on May 29th, the tenth anniversary of the climbing of Everest, we set out on the long approach march to Kangtega with eight days allotted to us to reach the summit. Besides the string of porters there were nine of us: Jim, Dave, Tom and I, Ang Temba and four good high-altitude Sherpas. I doubt whether any of us thought we had the ghost of a chance on Kangtega—I felt as Chiang Kai-shek might embarking with his army to retake the Chinese mainland. The monsoon, which traditionally starts at the end of May, seemed to have broken in earnest, and at that time we had only a vague idea of our route on the mountain; we knew only that the Khumbu face of Kangtega, towering over Tengboche, was unassailable, and that our only hope was a southern approach to the back of the mountain.

To reach the south side we had first to dip down to 9,000 feet in the Dudh Kosi Valley, cross a high pass to the parallel valley of the Inukhu farther east, and from there move north again to Kangtega. In the first three days we passed rapidly through a variety of terrain, corn-fields in the Dudh Kosi bright with new growth, wet forest swarming with leeches, high pastures and rocky ridges. On the Inukhu side we dropped through a hillside of rhododendron in full bloom into the twilight of the rain-forest lower down. And all the time it rained.

But on the fourth day a miracle happened. The rain stopped and the sun shone, through mist at first, then stronger and hotter, from a blue sky. It was as if we had somehow rolled back the monsoon into India to give ourselves that one last chance. We climbed gently north out of the forest into sub-alpine scrub, and beyond that into open pasture where yaks were grazing and gambolling, whisking their brush-like tails and throwing their hind-legs into the air as if to welcome us. On the fifth day, still in fine weather, we pushed on into an increasingly barren landscape of moraine, ice and high mountains. Late in the afternoon we turned the last corner and there, close to us, was Kangtega.

It was the view we had been waiting for and it looked promising. The final 1,500 feet looked easy, a steep summit cone of snow rising out of a plateau. The lower part looked reasonable too, a thousand feet of icefall rising to join a gentle smooth-surfaced glacier. The only unknown was the middle section, the point where glacier and plateau joined, for this was hidden behind a rocky spur. There were three problems, the finding of a route through the ice-fall, the uncertainties of the middle section—and the approaching monsoon.

Next morning, our freakish run of fine weather still holding, Jim and I and two Sherpas set off up the icefall. After casting about amongst the slots and seracs we picked up a lead which led us through the jumble of broken ice to a point where only a single huge crevasse barred our way to the smooth glacier above. There was no snow-bridge. We could reach the open going on the far side only by climbing down one side of the crevasse and up the other.

"Can't even see the bottom," muttered Jim peering over the edge. We walked along the lower lip till we came to a slanting passage-way down which we climbed into the depths of the crevasse. Big blocks of ice were jammed there, and from them we had access to the foot of the wall opposite. Inside, the crevasse was like a tomb with walls of ice. Icicles clustered on the lips of the crevasse overhead framing a strip of blue sky and the blocks beneath our feet, lightly covered in soft snow, felt curiously unstable as if at any moment they might suddenly crumple and vanish into an underground cavern.

There was a route up the opposite side, a drift of snow easing upwards to a fifteen-foot wall of ice, beyond which a shallow gully led to the glacier. Jim was starting up the drift when without warning he broke through, coming to rest on his outstretched arms with his legs dangling free in a gaping hole beneath. Pemba Tarkay, I noticed, was glancing nervously around, wondering as I was whether we too were standing on a shell through which we might plunge at any moment. Jim extricated himself, anchored to an ice piton and began cautiously to hew a line of holds up the wall. An hour later the crevasse was safely behind and we were looking ahead up the glacier. But the upper part of it curved out of sight—the middle section would remain unknown till next day.

We were away by 5 o'clock in the morning, moving fast in the hope that we could climb the glacier before the sun had softened it. But the sun moved faster, climbing swiftly above the eastern peaks till it shone down into the great snow corridor up which our route lay. The light was blinding, the heat so intense that the backs of my hands puffed up as if burnt in a fire. For six hours we floundered upwards in deep snow till we could go no farther. There, at a height of 20,300 feet we pitched Camp I in sight of the unknown middle section. Separating us from the plateau was an open ice-fall but there was a route through it. Given the weather and sufficient strength—it was our seventh day without a rest—we thought we could make it.

During the night the weather changed. When we woke at 2

o'clock for an early start, snow was pattering on the tents and outside the stars had vanished in thickening mist. It seemed the monsoon had caught us at last. And when four hours later the mist lifted a thousand feet, we set off only because it was our last chance. We climbed through the icefall to the big plateau. At first our main worry was the weather, but as the hours rolled by we wondered whether we had the strength. The summit was 2000 feet above the camp, a day's work at that altitude. But it was the snow that held us back, not the height or the distance: breaking crust on powder snow is a trial at any altitude but up there it was a nightmare. Jim and I shared the lead, counting steps, 150 each, and soon we could manage only 100 between rests. The plateau, desolate under the grey sky, stretched ahead of us, seemingly endless. But at length we stood at the foot of the summit cone. The weather had closed in again, blotting out our tracks and smothering the mountain in flurries of light snow. Should we turn back . . . ?

"We're going to the top," said Dave.

The slope was steep, and as on Taweche soft snow lay on top of a firmer layer. Then, half a rope-length up, the surface changed. Wind had had cleared away the powder leaving crisp snow and as we gained height our spirits rose. Kangtega was ours . . .

But not quite. 150 feet below the summit we came to a schrund running across the face. Jim found a bridge and began cutting a line of steps up the slope above. Twenty feet up he struck soft snow. It was steeper now, perhaps 60° and to beat a trail upwards in this slush, where no step could be relied on, was a task almost beyond us. In a last despairing surge of energy Jim flailed a precarious trail upwards. We had forgotten about the possibility of an avalanche till thirty feet short of the summit, Jim came to a halt. There had been a sharp ominous 'whoomph' and in the white surface above, a thin, irregular crack had opened up. Eyeing it uneasily he dug down to a harder surface for a shaft belay.

"It's wind slab," he said. "You'd better come closer—if we're not careful we'll have the whole slope on top of us."

We should have retreated and tried another route but by then exhaustion had made us almost indifferent to the risks of the situation. And there were, after all, only thirty feet to go. I led past Jim and immediately found myself threshing a trench in a morass of soft snow. And then there were was a smooth 'swish' behind me and a foot of snow peeled off from below the line of steps, as though sliced with a knife.

"Hang on a minute and I'll dig down to a better belay," Jim called out grimly. The bigger part of the potential avalanche was still poised above and between us.

"O.K." said Jim and I started again. Only ten feet to go. Then a crunch cut through the air. Jolted by a spasm of fear I plunged the ice-axe deep into the snow, burying my arms to the shoulder. There was a deep-throated rumble, the slope shook and from the corner of an eye I saw a white wave surging down the mountain. Tensely I waited for Jim's weight to come on to my makeshift belay.

Down the slope Jim had thrown his weight forward on to his belay, head down, while the surging snow ran over and round him and he waited for my fall. But the dust settled, the silence returned and we found we were all still safe on the mountain. Dave and Tom had dug in to one side of the avalanche; the sliding mass of snow had no more than brushed them. Jim chipped some steps across the firm surface laid bare by the avalanche and we crept up to the crest of the ridge. The summit was still half a rope-length away and a few feet higher but so far as we were concerned we were close enough. There was a cornice on one side of the ridge and still a small area of wind-slab on the other. We'd pressed our luck far enough and we cut back down to the schrund now bridged by several tons of fresh avalanche snow. Dave carried on past us to the summit from which dimly through the mist he could see the outline of the Low Peak, easily accessible from where he stood. We had climbed Kangtega; it was the eighth day out of Kumjung, exactly as we had planned.

When the expedition departed for Katmandu a few days later, Phil and I stayed behind. Neither of us felt the need to return urgently—hospital work in New Zealand could wait till next year. Ed had become interested in extending our medical work beyond the end of the expedition with the idea that one day he might build a small village hospital. He left us food, equipment and living expenses, and through the monsoon months of June, July and August, Phil and I lived in Kumjung as general practitioners to the Khumbu.

We lived in the village monastery, not in the main temple but in two rooms opening off the walled courtyard in front of it. The words 'monastery' and 'temple' give too grand a conception of the place. It was no Tengboche: no monks lived there permanently, there was no Head Lama, no splendid frescoes. The roof leaked and the dusty Buddha images, gazing indifferently into the gloom of the temple, were visited only on special occasions. Ed had already improved our living-room almost to the point of rebuilding: a new wooden floor, a tarpaulin on the roof, woven bamboo mats as wall-coverings, a wood-burning stove, a big bay window overlooking the village—it suited us perfectly. For $3.50 a week we kept one of our Sherpas, Khancha, to cook for us, and for $1.50 we bought a mastiff pup called Setuk. Khancha was strongly critical of the purchase of Setuk.

"Three months coming—Setuk big dog. All small boys biting. Much trouble making."

Our superior knowledge of psychology told us that with a gentle upbringing in civilised surroundings, Setuk would never learn the savage habits of his fellows and we lavished our affections on him. I had found him in Thami one day early in the expedition, a small ball of black fur curled up in the dust. When I bent down to pat him he sunk his teeth into me, but that was a reflex common to all Sherpa dogs, and not I thought an indication of his personality. In the end Khancha was right—he usually was—and though Setuk became devoted to our own household, he never gave up his habit of biting strangers. It was an instinct and one of our more painful duties as doctors was to dab gentian violet on teeth-marks in the bottoms of small boys who had not run fast enough.

Each morning Sherpas would drift in with their problems. There were innumerable teeth to be pulled, belly-aches in those who ate too much chilli, boils on unwashed Tibetans, running ears and noses in most of the small children. Hangovers were a problem in the festive season. There were more serious problems too: TB was a scourge and even in the three months we were there at least three people died of it. One leper came to us and we saw his sores heal miraculously with treatment. The familiar conditions of heart failure, pneumonia, chronic bronchitis, gall-bladder trouble were there too, and we had one broken leg to look after.

As the weeks went by we became familiar with most of the one hundred or so households of the village and we made friends with Sherpas who because they had no connections with the expedition were unknown to us. There was the Lama Karma for instance, an affable Sherpa who was our nearest neighbour. He had long ago abandoned religion as a vocation and with a small income from his land and three strong daughters to work for him he was free to spend his time with friends, playing dice or sharing a pot of chang—more than once he borrowed expedition funds to help himself through a bad day.

Each week I did the one-hour trip to the village of Namche Bazaar, the trading centre of the Khumbu and the place where the few Nepalese administrators of the area live. Namche is a dusty village crowded into an alcove in the hillside with little room for growing crops. It was always an interesting place for the traders of Namche are a different breed from the land-owners and small farmers of Kumjung—they were more shrewd and careful, unaccustomed to hard physical labour, and a few of them were much wealthier. With each yak-train returning from Tibet over the Nangpa La there might be artefacts for sale, gold and turquoise ornaments, silver butter lamps, and bargaining for them added interest to the business of examining and treating the sick. They were aware of the significance of the Chinese presence in Tibet but being equally aware of the possibility of Chinese entry into Nepal, they were careful in their opinions. The Chinese have declared that Nepal is one of the five fingers of her hand in the Himalayas, along with Sikkim, Bhutan, NEFA and Ladakh, and the demoralised handful of Nepalese soldiers in Namche with their ancient carbines and shotguns are unlikely to delay them in the Khumbu. The Chini, they said, are good to poor men but not to the rich. The monasteries were allowed to go on but not to accept money as they had before.

In Kumjung we became aware of social strata where before we had seen none. June is the month of the festival of Dumje, a whirl of entertaining, and a season for propitiating the gods that the harvest be a good one and the yak-calves be healthy and numerous. In their entertaining the villagers of Kumjung formed three groups. There were the wealthy upper strata who owned much of the land and had large houses, most of them with a shrine in a separate room; their food was more varied, with more meat, and their chang was the superior variety made from rice. Below them was the middle group, with small land-holdings or none, and smaller houses. Their chang, often made from corn, and their rakshi distilled from fermented potatoes, was less palatable. Many of our expedition Sherpas, grown newly rich from expedition earnings, belonged to this group. Then there were the poor—the refugees, the landless, the widows; their houses were small and of only one storey, their possessions few and their food unpretentious. The differences were not great but they were there nevertheless.

The concluding ceremony of Dumje, in Namche Bazaar, was impressive. It was late in the afternoon, and mist cast a gloom over the courtyard of the monastery. The Head Lama of Tengboche was there for the occasion, around him a few monks, and villagers crowded in on all sides. In the prelude to the ceremony, which seemed to be an exorcism of evil spirits, there was blowing of horns, the slow crash of drums and cymbals and the muttered chanting of the monks. Then the Head Lama, cross-legged on a dais, cast grain and oil on a burning pyre of split pine. An assistant placed before him a triangular tray on which there was an effigy of a human figure. At the climax, after an elaborate ceremony, the Lama leaned forward and with a three-edged knife, stabbed the figure again and again; red dye gushed from the belly and the severed pieces were thrown on the fire. Then an iron dish containing butter was placed on the fire. The butter melted, boiled yellow then black, smoke rose from it and a flame flickered across the surface. A monk stepped forward with a bowl of rakshi and with a ladle hurled the spirits into the smoking dish. Sheets of bright flame exploded upwards in the half-light and a long pleased Ah-a-a-ah broke from the crowd.

With Dumje concluded the villages were suddenly half-empty as the Sherpas left for the high pastures with their yaks. To visit a grazing village, after having seen it dead and deserted two months earlier, was a revelation. Thick grass was bursting from the ground and everywhere there were flowers, blue and purple poppies, fields of yellow primulas, daisies and gentians. Sherpas bustled around the tiny stone houses and shouted after their yaks on the hillsides. There were calves to be attended to and everywhere an abundance of good food: fresh curd, cheese, and bowls of creamy nut-flavoured milk. Much of the time mist obscured the mountains but through gaps there were fleeting glimpses of glaciers and ice-covered rock like huge paintings hung in the sky.

At the end of three months we loaded twelve porters with our gear and set off, for the last time, down the winding muddy path that runs amongst the walled fields and houses of Kumjung. To say we would rather have stayed would be a romantic distortion, for there seemed to be more important things to be done in the larger world beyond the Khumbu. But we were sorry to leave people who were now our close friends and in growing familiar with the landscape we had not lost our delight in it. The Khumbu is not Shangri-La but there are moments when one can believe that it is.

16

THE TUTOKO TENT-TESTING
EXPEDITION, 1965

Full many a glorious morning have I seen,
Flatter the mountain-tops with sovereign eye
William Shakespeare

FOR TWO months more Phil and I travelled in the Himalayas, through the hills of Nepal, North India and Bhutan. Then we went our separate ways, Phil back to Dunedin, I to Chicago where Sears were editing the movie of the school-building and the climb on Taweche. But that was only for a month and on January 1st, 1964, I began work as a house surgeon at the Auckland Hospital. Psychologically, the unfettered life of a medical student is a poor sort of preparation for the rigorous routine of clinical work. I needed the experience, a year of it was compulsory anyway, but I regretted the loss of my freedom. When Phil suggested I join him in Dunedin at the end of the year I applied for a job forthwith. So in 1965 I was a demonstrator in physiology at the Medical School. For six months Phil and I shared a flat and the late summer and autumn were like old times. We spent long weekends in the Darrans or down the Hollyford, we went fishing and looked for new climbs.

At Easter we returned to Moraine Creek to attempt the first ascent of the South Ridge of Revelation, a small climb we had talked of for years. With us was Mike Hutchins, an English lecturer who two years later sailed with Phil on a trip around New Zealand in the wake of Captain Cook. The Darrans, that long weekend, were at their most summery with only the mildest of easterly breezes rustling the tussock. It was bliss to walk again in the beech forest and tussock. Across Lake Adelaide rose the familiar bluffs and ridges of Sabre and by climbing Revelation we could see again the Central Darrans. The ridge itself was of hard granite, the holds small, and the face below steep enough to keep us alert. In the cool of the late afternoon we strolled down the Korako Glacier and descended the bluffs to the hut with a couple of hours of daylight to spare. The Darrans we felt were giving of their best.

With the coming of winter we climbed no more and I settled down to work. Phil, in his vagrant way, moved on to Christchurch and for a few months I was on my own. Then I had a letter from Ed. Would I be free for a week or so in December? He had a tent to test for Sears, a model comfortable enough for the American camping public yet strong enough to withstand a storm. The Darrans being a range he'd not been in during his climbing days before Everest, he wondered if we might combine a trip to Tutoko with the testing of the tent. The expedition budget was $300. Jim Wilson was free to come along with Barry Smith an old climbing friend of his; and Max Pearl, who had been medical officer in the Himalayas in 1964 was prepared, as ever, to abandon his practice for a trip in the hills. Nothing could suit me better. Turner's Bivvy was the obvious site for a Base Camp. Nor'-westers being a speciality of the place, it should be possible to test any tent to breaking point—the usual problem in December is to find the good weather, not the bad. Thus was born the Tutoko Tent-Testing Expedition.

We arrived in Milford at the tail-end of a long spell of bad weather. The rivers were high but dropping fast and the cloud-level in the gloomy but majestic Sound was lifting. Jim and Barry were already on their way to Turner's to receive the air-drop we planned for the following morning. There was no question of carrying in the tent or the bulk of the food—Sears expeditions aren't run on shoe-strings. The Darrans were fresh and clear next morning, a perfect day for flying. Our plane hopped over the nearest pass from Te Anau, banked steeply over the small Milford air-strip and landed with a flourish. Bill was one of the more dashing of the local pilots, a dangerous sort of temperament to have in Fiordland and a few weeks later he was climbing out of the wreckage of his plane after misjudging a take-off from one of the smaller lakes. Nevertheless, he was a good pilot and the air-drop was perfect. There was an unbelievable pile for a short trip, more than one plane-load. Ed and I climbed aboard to point out the site of Turner's Bivvy and push the loads through the dropping hatch when the time came.

The plane took off and began to circle and climb, as insignificant as a fly between those encircling ramparts. As we gained height waterfalls and small lakes came into view below and a couple of crayfish-boats traced straight lines on the surface of the Sound as they steered for the open sea. Then we were turning north up-valley towards Tutoko. The route to Turner's Bivvy looked ridiculously steep, a wall of bald bluffs with only the merest smear of green to suggest there was any grass on them. The bivvy rock itself seemed to have vanished. This was puzzling, and to me, a self-proclaimed expert on the Darrans, humiliating. Climbing parties had quite often failed to find the rock but I thought I knew every foot of the country below. Nor was there any sign of Jim and Barry. It didn't matter, however, for there was only one place flat enough for an air-drop, a snow gully on the edge of the Madeline Plateau a thousand feet higher.

Bill lined up on the gully, throttled back and the plane, suddenly quiet with the engines silenced, whirred down like a duck coming in to land. "Now!" The first load spun down and buried itself 200 feet below. Then the plane was surging up under full power and banking tightly to come in again for the next drop. Meanwhile, down below, Jim and Barry were toiling up the lower bluffs. They counted the loads. "Can't be much more now," said Jim after the fourth, but the plane kept circling. Six loads . . . eight . . . ten . . . Jim was frankly incredulous. "What's Ed doing? Bringing the family up for the summer?" After the eleventh load the plane straightened up and shot off down-valley.

Twenty minutes later there was the buzz of an engine. "Tourists," said Jim, and happy to find an excuse to rest they lay back in the tussock to watch. Again the plane climbed up to the Madeline Plateau and again swooped low. Hardly able to believe what they saw they watched the load drop: twelve . . . fifteen . . . there were nineteen altogether. And shaking their heads they set off upwards, pondering the problems of collecting the stuff.

The rest of us caught up with Jim and Barry two days later to find them sun-bathing amidst the collected litter of the air-drop carried down the previous day. Turner's itself was still buried beneath spring snow—no wonder I'd not seen it. The site Jim had chosen was beside a near-by cluster of moraine boulders we had seen from the air and there, on a grassy ledge, the tents were pitched, naked and new, proudly facing the north-west whence the storms would come.

The days that followed were, for a trip in the mountains, strangely inconsequential. Usually there is a mountain to climb: one climbs it and moves on. But we were looking for a storm and no positive action on our part was likely to change the course of the weather. We could only wait. Not that we found the waiting difficult. We sunbathed in the tussock, we slept and read, we ate like kings. At various times we climbed Madeline and Syme and explored the approaches to Tutoko. In the evenings while the sun set behind Grave in the west, we watched with never-ending fascination, ice break away from the face of Tutoko and talked about Himalayan expeditions past and to come. And day after day the mild east wind blew from a clear sky.

One long day Mike and I traversed Tutoko, up the familiar granite of the three buttresses of the south-east ridge, up the snow-face to the summit and down the far side. At dusk, bone-weary, we were plugging steps up a six-foot deep trench scoured by avalanches in the steep slope leading to Turner Pass, hoping as we climbed that at that hour we would meet no new avalanche, for in that pre-formed track it would have thundered down like an express train. Because I had forgotten to bring torches we crossed the Madeline Plateau in darkness, finding our old tracks by feel more than by sight. We had almost reached camp which was hidden in the night when we found ourselves trapped on a bluff unable to climb farther. A sleepy voice from close below answered our shouts.

"Who's that?" said the voice.

"Hutchins and Gill."

"Well come on down. Don't just sit up there making all that noise. We've kept a meal for you. What do you think you're doing anyway?"

"Trying to find a crack for a piton. We're going to have to rope down this bit," and an appreciative laugh floated back up to us. By feeling the rock carefully I located a crack, pushed in a piton and aimed the hammer at it—inaccurately, for a moment later the piton was tinkling down the bluff. There had been silence from the tents but now a low voice came up to us.

"Goddam! Those two idiots *are* using pitons up there," and in a few moments two figures with torches came up and rescued us.

At length our time was up. We packed loads, eighty pounds each, and tottered off down the bluffs, lowering the packs on ropes where the going was steep. Mike added a dash of excitement when he tried dropping his pack six feet on to a ledge too small to hold it. The pack rolled slowly at first, then faster, thudding through the tussock, and finally, exuberantly, in great leaps, spraying out food and clothes and climbing gear with each bound. Most of it we recovered later, from the lower reaches of the Age. We camped on Tutoko Flats. And the following day, our packs being too heavy, we made two trips down to the road before we had everything out. No sooner were we clear of the valley than the heavens opened. The wind swung to the northwest, gale-force winds drove across the tops, and the mountain-sides, where they could be seen through the curtains of rain, were spouting water, and the rivers in high flood.

The expedition purse was lighter than it had been but we drew on it to the extent of a couple of meals at Milford Hotel. Over the wine we discussed, without too much regret, our failure to carry out our major objective. We had not, after all, tested the tents. But in other ways the expedition had been a success. We had established some records which are likely to stand unchallenged. Probably, we decided, we were the first expedition ever to carry twenty-pound loads up to Turner's and have to double-pack out. And certainly the first to go into the Darrans, praying for bad weather, and come back disappointed.

17

THE ANTARCTIC

Lands doomed by nature to everlasting frigidness, and never once to feel the warmth of the sun's rays, whose horrible and savage aspects I have no words to describe; such are the lands we have discovered, what may we expect those to be which lie more to the South, for we may reasonably suppose that we have seen the best as lying most to the North. Whoever has resolution and perseverance to clear up this point by proceeding farther than I have done, I shall not envy him the honour of this discovery but I will be bold to say that the world will not be benefited by it.

Capt. James Cook,
on leaving the Antarctic regions, Feb. 1775.

IN HIS canny way Cook was almost right for the world has derived no great benefit from the Antarctic. There are some who believe that those great epics of exploration, the journeys of Amundsen, Shackleton and Scott, are of lasting significance, and there has been a plethora of scientific programmes in recent years whose value will be vouched for, no doubt, by the scientists. But for the most part the great continent remains as it has been from earliest times, a vast sterile waste of ice more hostile to habitation than any other part of the globe. Though the seas abound with life and there are penguins and seals along the coastline, in the interior there is nothing. No workable mineral resources have been found and it seems unlikely that anyone will choose to live there permanently, no matter how crowded the rest of the earth may become.

Yet the Antarctic is a place one does not easily forget. It is a land of great beauty. Snow, sea and sky blend in the soft summer light and there is colour everywhere. Penguins, seals and snow petrels add life where one expects to find none and the intense cold can be exhilarating. When I was invited to join the Mt Herschel Expedition for five weeks in the spring of 1967 I had no hesitation in accepting. It was, of course, one of Hillary's expeditions. An intriguing part of being on one of Ed's expeditions is the possibility of being invited on another. And there always *is* another. At some low-point on the trip

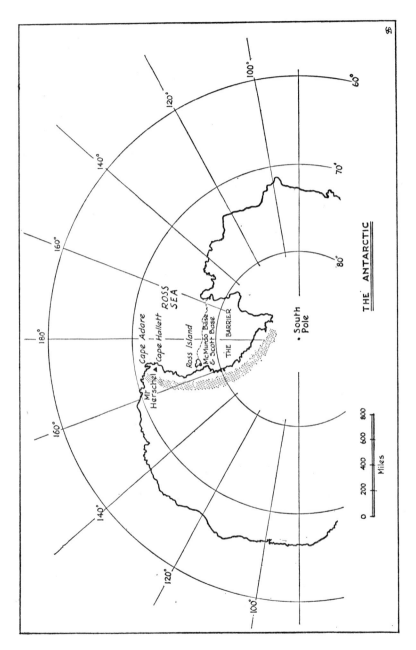

THE ANTARCTIC

N

he might mutter 'never again'—transport has broken down or some petty official has flung a spanner in the works—but before the trip is over, ideas for the next are simmering to the surface. One might have expected he would have sat back and lived on past glory at some point in the last fifteen years, but the old compulsion to be out doing things is still there as active as ever; the same restlessness, I suppose, that took him into the New Zealand mountains in the first place, and to the Himalayas in 1950; that made him seize the chance of joining Shipton on the Everest reconnaissance. I remember someone saying at the time of the climbing of Everest that Hillary was just lucky. There is a half-truth in this, but it was the sort of luck that lead Fleming to discover penicillin. Each of them saw the opportunity in a situation and followed it up. When Ed was chosen with Tensing to make the main attempt on Everest, it was not luck that gave him the favoured position but simply that he, of all those present, possessed the most formidable combination of skill, strength and tenacity and of these qualities the most important, I suspect, was tenacity, the determination to complete what he had set his mind on.

The tenacity is still there, the restlessness, the imagination to see where possibilities lie, and so the expeditions, a bewildering variety of them, go on. Those who take part do little or nothing towards the preparation: Ed raises the money (for Herschel, from newspaper articles), prises permission from the authorities, assembles, packs and ships the gear—the tedious part of the business falls on his shoulders. Little wonder that those who go with him are enthusiastic. But Ed is more than just a good leader, someone who can organise well and push an expedition through difficulties to a successful conclusion. There are other qualities less easy to define: a real humility, blunt honesty, a spontaneous generosity and warmth of spirit—a combination of qualities that gives him stature above those around and inspires loyalty.

The climbing of Herschel was something Ed had thought of for a number of years, ever since he had first seen the mountain from Hallett Station. Twenty miles away across the bay, Herschel rises steeply from the coast, a dramatic pyramidal rock peak with no easy route on it. Most of the more accessible peaks of the Antarctic are gentle enough to be climbed in passing by geological or survey parties but Herschel, and the other big peaks of the Admiralty Range in which it stands, are tougher than that.

The expedition gathered in Christchurch—called Chi-Chi by the Americans who use it as a base for the Antarctic—on October 16th. There were nine of us. Ed was leader; Norm Hardie, who had led the Silver Hut advance party in 1960, was deputy leader. As keeper of the two Snowmobiles we had Murray Ellis who had helped drive and maintain the Ferguson tractors that Ed had taken to The Pole in 1957. Bruce Jenkinson, one of New Zealand's few professional alpine guides, added fibre to the climbing team, the other three members being Pete Strang, an exuberant ginger-haired medico, Mike White, engineer (an expert on central heating), and me with the veteran Bell and Howell movie camera. There were two geologists, Graham Hancox, and Dr Larry Harrington, but Larry was not due to join us till later in the trip.

The planes flying south were either Super Constellations or Hercules, commonly known as Connies and Hercs. One of the Connies, ominously called Phoenix, had an engine which lately had been bursting into flame and we were delayed while it was being repaired. But at 7.30 p.m. on October 18th, after a nine-hour flight, we landed on the Barrier Ice-shelf near the big U.S. base at McMurdo. My first look at the Antarctic: a great snow plain bathed in muted light, blue and soft in the distance where long lines of mist ran across the mountains, and orange where the sun lay low on the horizon. Standing beside the landing strip were several Hercs. and some tracked vehicles waiting to collect us, and beyond them was a small village of half-buried huts. A few miles away the great bulk of Erebus filled the northern horizon, with a spur running to Observation Hill, topped, as we discovered later, by a wooden cross bearing the names of Scott and his party. A sub-zero breeze nipped our faces painfully but soon we were in a warm vehicle rattling across the ice towards the flat green buildings of New Zealand's Scott Base.

Three days later with our gear packed on four sledges we were on a Herc bound for Hallett, 500 miles north. We stopped out into air that was noticeably warmer—"It's called the Banana Belt," said Murray—and the mountains were closer and more spectacular than those around Scott Base. Herschel, on the other side of the frozen bay, was excitingly close. Hallett Station itself looked scruffy, an assortment of orange and green huts sprawled on a flat shingle spit jutting into the bay. In the nesting season 100,000 penguins share the spit and though the rookery was almost empty when we arrived, straggling black lines of birds out on the ice showed where they were starting to come in. At the Station were thirty American sailors under the charge of a tough little Chief Petty Officer who, according to those who disliked adding work to the hardships of the Antarctic, was a demon of a man. To us he was more a good angel, even if he didn't always look the part, and we came to regard him almost as the tenth member of the expedition. No one could have been more hospitable and we slept, ate and worked at the Station as if it were our own.

In keeping with the times, we were using Snowmobiles to drag our sledges. The days of dog teams in the Antarctic have all but gone, motorised vehicles of varying sizes having taken their place. Ours were of the smaller variety sometimes known as 'tin dogs', about seven feet long, two and a half feet wide, and painted red. A pair of short skis supports the front and provides steering while the bulk of the machine rests on a single wide rubber track driven by a two-stroke motor. Originally these had been designed as toys for wealthy Americans at ski-resorts. Under ideal conditions they reach forty miles per hour and can drag a 1,000 pound sledge. The trouble was that conditions were seldom ideal. Had there been four Snowmobiles instead of two, life would have been easier both for them and for us.

It was early afternoon on October 21st when we set off with the sun slanting across the ice from the north. There was no wind and to start with at least the machines chugged eagerly across the hard surface at a steady ten miles an hour, with two people on each Snowmobile and two perched astride each sledge. Herschel was across the other side of the bay, seemingly no more than a couple of hours away. But before long conditions changed. Crumpled pressure ridges broke up the flat surface and fresh snow lay thickly across the corner of the bay we were now entering. By some trick of topography the area around Herschel acts as a collecting-ground for the wind-drift snow, which in the Antarctic is ceaselessly on the move. The Snowmobiles slowed down as they nosed their way through the soft drifts, the ploughed trail behind us became deeper and more tortuous as we wound back and forth hunting for the best way through; sledges capsized as they struck buried chunks of ice, one of them smashed a runner—by 6 p.m. when we camped we were little more than half-way across the bay with worse to come.

It was one of the gloomiest of all our camps for we were cold and had not yet fallen into the routine of sledging life. The minor discomforts of cold are legion: bulky down clothes make every movement awkward, bare fingers stick to metal so one wears gloves and fumbles, motors refuse to start, foods freeze into solid blocks, toothpaste won't squeeze, medicines crack their ampoules, film becomes brittle and snaps; the movie camera, though it had been treated for low temperatures, refused to run at its proper speed unless kept warm inside a down-jacket and for four weeks I lived with a seven-pound camera slung round my neck. But within a couple of days we had slipped into a routine. The two-man pyramid tents went up in a matter of minutes regardless of the weather. One man would crawl in first while the other stayed outside, handing in gear, collecting snow for cooking, filling the primus. And then inside, with the primus on a cook-box

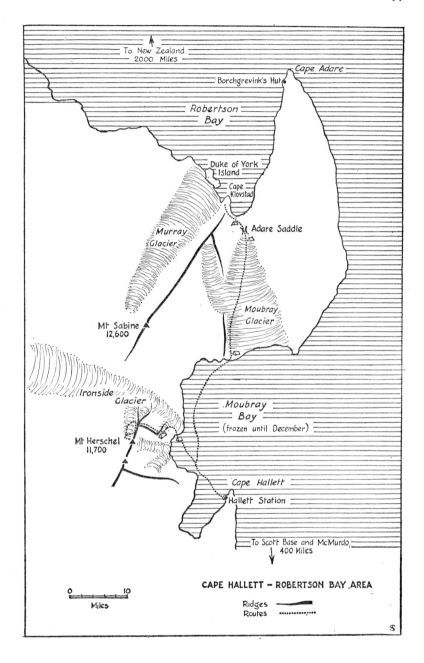

CAPE HALLETT – ROBERTSON BAY AREA

Ridges
Routes

as the centre-piece and a sleeping berth on either side, soon the tent was warm and the meal cooking. The primus is the source of all comfort in the Antarctic. Without it clothes would stay sodden or frozen and the intense cold would make life a misery.

It took us the whole of the following day to establish a Base Camp on the sea-ice at the foot of Herschel. We chose a more methodical way of breaking trail: four of us went ahead on skis selecting the best route amongst the low pressure ridges, and an unladen machine followed behind compacting a trail. Then we returned for the gear. We moved more slowly and the Snowmobiles gulped through our petrol but it was the only way. We made Base Camp beside the tide-crack where the floating platform of sea-ice rubs up and down against the ring of ice-cliffs, skirting the coast.

Our route on to Herschel was an East spur abutting on to the long North ridge of the mountain and we knew from aerial photos that the easiest approach to the crest of the spur, where we hoped to place Camp I, was by way of a side-valley on its flank which looked smooth and easy. But first we had to find a way up the coastal ice cliffs. Beside them we saw our first seals, huge blubbery creatures, who glared at us balefully or lolloped across the ice to drop through the tide-crack like jellies down a hole. Many had new pups, soft creatures with liquid black eyes, and the ice was stained with blood where the cows had been in labour.

The ice-cliffs were high and for the most part unclimbable but at length we found a precarious route through a shattered area where the Ironside Glacier grinds against the coastline. On the mainland at last, we worked our way round to the entrance of the side-valley. In photos it had looked easy but not so in reality, for it was heavily crevassed, steep at its upper end and waist-deep in new snow. To find a route through to the site of Camp I took us the best part of two days and at no time did we feel safe. There was always the possibility of being obliterated by a soft snow avalanche but worse than this were the crevasses. We could never be sure, either there or in any other part of the Hallett area for that matter, that we were not poised on top of an abyss. In warmer regions a crevasse is usually marked by a depression, but not in the Antarctic, where a vast underground cavern can be roofed by the most fragile of ice-shells that one finds only by systematic probing or by falling through. More by good luck than skill, none of us had a major fall but we all at times had the frightening experience of dropping through waist or shoulder deep.

On the fifth day out from Hallett we all braced ourselves for the carrying in of Camp I at 3,000 feet on the crest of the spur at the head of the side-valley. Those with Himalayan experience talked regretfully of Phu Dorjes and Pemba Tarkays while others repented not

having trained more conscientiously at home but at length the
moment came when everyone slung a fifty-pound load on his back.
Everyone, that is, except Jenks and me who were carrying lighter
loads, for we were to stay at Camp I and pursue the assault on the
following day. The plan was to place a Camp II at 7,000 feet and
attack the summit from there. But we began to wonder. Why Camp
II? Why not strike out for the summit from Camp I itself? We
talked with Ed. "Why not?" he said and we decided that we would
go for the top.

With the others gone we settled into camp and sorted out some gear
for the climb: rope, ice-pitons, spare clothes, altimeter, movie camera,
still cameras, film, primus and enough food and fuel for a couple of
days. We spoke little, both being of taciturn disposition. Perhaps
there was more to our silence than that for we knew there would be
nothing easy about the next day's climb. The summit was still 8,000
feet above us and this alone meant that we would be stretching ourselves to the limit. A long climb of moderate difficulty can be more
dangerous than a shorter more severe route where one is often so
laced to the mountain by ropes and pitons that falling off is impossible.
If we moved fast on Herschel it would be at the expense of safety;
one false move, a stumble, a loose crampon strap, might be the end
of both of us. At least there'd be no chance of spending a night out—
the next night wasn't due for four months.

That night I slept fitfully with vivid dreams between periods of
wakefulness. Then it was morning. We cooked a breakfast of steak,
biscuits and coffee, and stepped outside. It was the best day we had
had yet, perfectly still and the sky clear. Our camp was still in shadow,
the valley below ghostly in the pale Antarctic night, but behind Cape
Hallett was an orange glow where the sun was swinging northwards
from below the horizon. The early light crept across the sea-ice and
caught the East face of Herschel towering above us. We began climbing. At first we moved clumsily on the steep ridge for there was soft
snow lying on ice and loose rock. Then the sun was on our backs and
with the angle easing we moved more quickly. Higher we could see
the spur steepening again and there was a glint where ice showed
through.

"I don't like that much," said Jenks. "Looks like the edge of an
ice-wall—we might yet be spending the rest of the day hammering
pitons into hard ice."

Uneasy about what we might find up there we pressed on steadily
till an hour later we stood at the foot of the ice-wall, 200 feet of it
separating us from a plateau above. Broken ice-falls plunged into the
valleys on either side of us leaving us no alternative but the wall. A
curious sort of formation I thought, an ice-fall astride a ridge, but

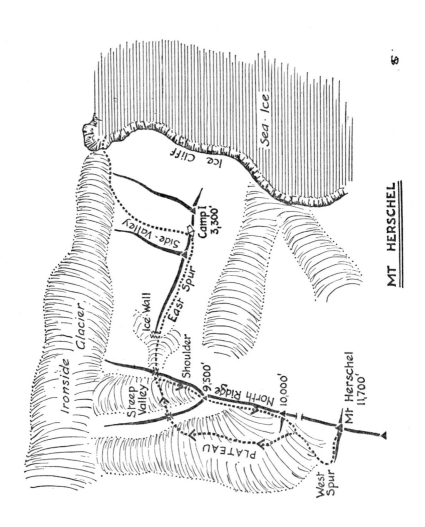

Sea Ice

Ice Cliff

Side-Valley

Camp 1
3,300'

East Spur

Ice Wall

Ironside Glacier

Shoulder

Steep Valley

9,500'

North Ridge

10,000'

PLATEAU

West Spur

Mt Herschel
11,700'

MT HERSCHEL

then in the Antarctic one gets used to the ice doing curious things. It was not impossible either—the ice of the lower half was hard and polished but tilted back from the vertical and the upper cliffs were split by crevasses up which we might find a way.

"You're the ice expert," I said waving a hand upwards, "Have a go."

Jenks began cutting steps up the line of a shallow crack, the big axe swinging rhythmically with showers of ice-chips exploding into the sunlight. It was a good lead and not easy to follow even with the support of a rope from above.

"No point in wasting time on big steps," explained Jenks. He was perched on the edge of a shallow depression filled with loose snow, the roof of a crevasse I discovered as I shot through up to my waist. There was not even the security of a good piton belay for the ice was of a strange brittle texture, too easily fractured to hold a piton.

"Try not to fall off," were my last words to Jenks as he lead off again. "I doubt whether this belay would even slow you down."

The wall was leaning out more steeply, too steep for us to be able to continue the frontal attack and Jenks moved diagonally to the left across an ice bulge. He was moving more slowly now, using hand-holds for balance while he cut across the bulge. Then he was out of sight and by the speed the rope was moving I knew he had found easier going. I followed and together we fossicked about amongst some broken ice till we found ourselves on the floor of a crevasse, a narrow corridor leading through to the plateau-like crest of the ridge above.

Ten o'clock and the altimeter said 6,500 feet. There was no wind, no cloud on the horizon and though cold crept through when we stopped, while moving we had no need of down-jackets or even gloves. We unroped, drained a thermos and ate some biscuits. Up here, wind had swept away the loose snow that had slowed us on the lower part of the mountain, and when we set off again we began to pick up speed on a crisp packed surface. Then we came to the foot of the big shoulder on Herschel's North Ridge, a long sweep of steep snow leading to the first of the rock 2,000 feet higher. To begin with we gained height easily, zig-zagging upwards on crampons but insidiously the angle steepened till suddenly, an hour later, I realised that we were launched on a dangerously exposed piece of mountainside without even a rope between us. Jenks was poised above me on the toe-claws of his crampons, leaning against a slope so steep that he was using hands as well as feet as he climbed.

"Would you like the rope?" I asked.

"Not unless you do. But I think I might chip a few steps. I'm getting into ice up here."

The next hour was painful with ankles on the stretch and weariness slowing our progress so much that we wondered if the climb wasn't defeating us already. But soon after midday, the sun at its highest point on the northern horizon, we hauled ourselves to the top of the shoulder at a height of 9,000 feet. Behind a sheltered outcrop of brown rock we lit the primus. The lower mountains were below us now leaving the highest peaks of the range in full view, but we were in no mood to spend time gazing at the scenery—there was too much uncertainty in the hours ahead. It was my turn to lead and I set off along the jagged crest of the North Ridge. Sheer on our left was the immense precipice of the East Face and the ice on our right dropped from sight at an impossibly steep angle. Only the crest was climbable and that was never easy. At times I asked for a belay but mostly we moved together, conscious always of the relentless passing of the hours. It was 5 o'clock when we came to the foot of the summit cone; 1,500 feet to go and perhaps the most difficult part of the climb still above us. Here the ridge merged into a face. We drank some coffee and unloaded as much gear as we could dispense with, the first of a chain of depots leading to the summit and a visible sign of our growing exhaustion.

We began by slanting diagonally up 500 feet of snow and where this merged with the rock we left our ice-axes. Though the rock looked clean from below, we found ice and packed snow filling the holds. Tired now and increasingly aware of the exposure, we were looking up more and more often to see if the summit was coming closer. Half an hour slipped by and the view above was unchanged. If anything the rock was rearing more sharply than before. The pack, though it contained nothing but down-jackets, felt unbearably heavy. Why not another depot? Surely we'd soon be at the top anyway, and before Jenks had time to disagree I'd placed our two dirty orange jackets on a ledge with a boulder to weigh them down. "By God! You'd better remember where they are!" said Jenks for they merged imperceptibly with the rock when seen from above.

The sun was still on our backs but only just for soon it would be sliding behind the ranges to the south-west leaving us in shadow. We went on. The rock seemed interminable, gully after gully, small cracks, chimneys. We had been two hours on the face already. Then suddenly the angle eased and we were looking up to the summit only a hundred feet higher. At seven o'clock we were on top, looking along a summit ridge to a twin peak a rope-length away. It was cold up there, for the wind, though there was little of it, cut like a knife. Anxiously we looked down in the direction of our down-jackets. Not a sign of them. Below us the patches of sunlight were shrinking, the shadows darkening, and stretching to the horizon were vast anonymous ranges of mountains beset in the ice. Never have I seen so lonely a place; beautiful, yes, radiant in the soft light, but how inhospitable, how desolate these wastes of snow and ice. Sunset on a high mountain in the Antarctic is no time to linger. Shivering we turned and fled.

We moved fast on the descent. So similar were the ledges below that for a few frightened minutes I thought we had lost the down-jackets. But no, there they were and we thankfully pulled them over our heads. Then we were down to the ice-axes and a few minutes later back to the rest of our gear and a thermos of hot coffee. Instead of climbing down the North Ridge and the shoulder we had used on the ascent, we set off down a plateau to the left of them. The sun had gone. The going was easy and for a while as we ambled down we felt warm in our down-jackets and safe. Then we came to the traverse of a ferociously steep valley separating us from the route we had climbed ten hours earlier. Tensely we cramponned across the frozen surface, aware that a slip would not be easily stopped for below the slope swooped into an ice-fall tumbling 6,000 feet to the Ironside. And then the surface softened, we could dig our heels in and we moved easily across to the foot of the shoulder.

Within half an hour we were feeling our way down the ice-wall, the last obstacle and below it, for the first time in seventeen hours, the strain was off and a rare feeling of contentment began to steal through us. To set the seal on the day Jenks found a small hard orange in a pocket and cracked it in half with his ice-axe. Sucking the frozen pieces we swung carelessly down through the blue-green Antarctic twilight. It was the best part of the day. When we reached Camp I after midnight we had been climbing for nineteen hours.

It was not quite the end of Herschel: next day Pete Strang and Mike White completed the second ascent, a tribute to their stamina for they had done a good deal more load-carrying than we had. On the 29th we were back at Base Camp and there, in a tent kept swelter-ing hot by a roaring primus and two bottles of whisky, we drank toasts far into the night, to past success on Herschel and to success to come on our crossing of Adare Saddle to Robertson Bay, for that was the second part of the expedition.

On the following day we returned to Hallett to prepare for the journey north. Historically, Robertson Bay is an interesting place. Two parties wintered there. The first was the British Antarctic Ex-pedition of 1898–1900 led by Borchgrevink, a man who has received little recognition. Admittedly he accomplished little—in the course of a year he travelled no more than fifty miles from his hut—but they were the first men to live on the Continent or to attempt exploration of any sort. There is a story that their hut was of great strength because they believed savage animals were at large in the Antarctic and that these were responsible for the deep scars sometimes found on seals. They found no such animals but they proved that men can survive the Antarctic winter. At no stage however did they penetrate more than a few miles inland, nor did they reach Adare Saddle, three miles south of Robertson Bay, or the flat snowy tops beyond. Scott's Northern Party, under Campbell, did little better, and like Borchgrevink they left with a poor opinion of the weather in the area. Since then no one, except a helicopter party which touched down briefly, had revisited the area and the crossing from Hallett to Robertson Bay had not been attempted.

There were other reasons for going north besides those of exploration. At Hallett, Larry Harrington joined us. Larry, an expert on Antarctic geology, had lead the first exploration of the Hallett area; the weather had been fine that season, every peak, plateau and glacier a new discovery and now he was keen to tidy up the geology of the northern end of the range. Because of bad weather we stayed longer at Hallett than intended, but the time passed easily. For one thing there were the penguins whose numbers, in the ten days we had been gone, had swelled from a few hundred to 80,000. The rookery was always fascinating. The whole of the spit at Hallett, a few acres of undulating shingle, is crowded with penguins except in one corner where the Station has been built, though even there a few birds resolutely assemble their nests amongst the buildings. A strong fishy smell hangs over the place and as you approach the outermost pebble nests, their owners begin to cry derisively. You walk through the rookery like a boat crossing a pond, with a bow-wave of angry birds diving to either side from under your feet, and in your wake a chaos of fighting penguins. The displaced birds scramble back to their nests, squawking indignantly, running a gauntlet of cuffs and pecks from their neighbours, pinching pebbles as they go or squaring up for a fight. The rest watch attentively with their quick, white-ringed eyes, craning their necks this way and that, always expressive, always comical.

One afternoon we drove a Snowmobile out to Cape Hallett, and leaving the machine on the ice below, climbed a short distance up the rock. From the open water ten miles out the birds were streaming in, long black lines of them, walking in business-like fashion, or sliding on their bellies propelled by flippers and feet. We watched a line of about twenty approach the Snowmobile. A short distance away the leading bird scrambled to his feet and climbed a low hummock to assess the situation. The others followed. Shoulder to shoulder they stood, peering forwards or looking along the line to see what the rest were doing. "All's well," said one of them, and he tobogganed down the slope with the others falling in behind. When they return to the sea they are said to line up in just this way, waiting for the first bird to move—for there may be a sea-leopard under the ice waiting for a meal. And if no one makes the first move they gang up on the weakest member and hustle him over the edge.

Meanwhile Murray and Mike had been pulling one of the Snow-mobiles apart to replace a burnt-out condenser. It could have happened to any vehicle but there were signs that our two machines were ageing prematurely; drive belts were being replaced too often and the rubber tracks were badly worn. We knew well enough what was wrong, that we were asking them to do work almost beyond them, but it was difficult to see a way round the problem. Then the Chief, always resourceful, came to our rescue. He was a wiry little man with a grizzled grey beard, a peaked cap pulled down over his eyes and usually he was chewing a cigar.

"I got an idea," he said. "Why don't you guys take that old Weasel we got out there on the trash-heap. Maybe the tracks isn't so good but you heat her up a bit, put a bit of ether inside her. Yeah, I reckon she'll go quite a way before she breaks up."

Weasels are tracked amphibious vehicles, relics of the war in the Pacific, which have been widely used in the Antarctic. The Chief towed a very battered Weasel into the garage, ran hot air through the engine to clear it of ice, filled the cylinders with ether, and with a hiss and a roar and a fearful lot of clanking it was going. So when we left for Robertson Bay on November 2nd we had two Snowmobiles, three sledges and a Weasel. We could see most of our route from Hallett: twenty miles across the sea-ice of Moubray Bay, another twenty up the broad flat Moubray Glacier, and finally a brief climb up snow slopes to Adare Saddle at 3,000 feet. From there the bay should be in full view about five miles away.

The sea-ice was not too troublesome for we understood the prob-lems of pressure ridges and soft snow. But three miles short of the Moubray Glacier we came to a thin-edged tide-crack. The Snow-mobiles, driven fast, crossed safely, but the heavier Weasel would almost certainly have dived through into deep water, like a seal. We left it there for our return and carried on to establish a camp on the terminal slopes of the glacier. Then the weather closed in. The mountains, the blue ice-cliffs, the seaward bergs beset in the pack, all disappeared from view in a smother of drifting snow. Inter-mittently there were clear patches but for the best part of five days we lay on our backs, reading, sleeping, eating, cursing the southerly winds and occasionally wandering across to the tide-crack to look at the seals.

One hears varying reports on Antarctic weather: some people

describe it as good, others as mainly bad. The most accurate account I found in the U.S. Sailing Directions for the Antarctic: "The weather is extremely variable; usually the weather changes in cycles with the period of southerly winds lasting longer than northerly with constant breaks of periods of calms ... Local winds of great intensity are found in some small areas with calm weather existing only a few miles from the area of high winds." And of Robertson Bay, "the wind in gales is often of extreme violence".

Borchgrevink's meteorologist wrote feelingly about their weather at Robertson Bay: "Nothing more appalling than these frightful winds, accompanied by tons of drift snow, can be imagined. On ninety-two days, the wind blew with a velocity above forty miles an hour, and on two occasions above ninety miles an hour, at which stage our anemometers were demolished."

But all this I learned later, and when on November 6th, the weather looked more settled, we had high hopes that we were in for another period of calm. So with two well-laden sledges towing behind the machines, we set off for Adare Saddle. After four miles of easy going across a névé beside the glacier, we came to a crevassed area, the first we had encountered with the Snowmobiles. For two miles we kept someone in front probing for a route with an aluminium marker pole, and though we found a way through there was always a feeling of uncertainty, as if we were walking through a mine-field. When we drove through to the expansive, flat, mid-portion of the glacier, we felt happier for it seemed that until we approached the Saddle our worries were over.

As the afternoon wore on, cloud settled on the higher country ahead and spread south separating us from the sun. Steadily we chugged on across mile after mile of featureless snow. At one point the lead machine, which had been spluttering at intervals, came to a halt, but Murray, whose hands seemed impervious to cold, dismantled the carburettor, corrected something, and in less than an hour we were moving again. Over the last four miles we climbed steadily up a gentle incline leading to the steeper slope which guards Adare Saddle. At the foot of this we camped. No sooner were the tents up than a fierce wind came rattling down from the north, plucking and pushing at the canvas and building up big leeward snow-drifts. But when we turned in, though the gale was still blowing, a glimmer of blue showed through the cloud overhead and we had hopes of a fine day on the morrow.

In spite of the weather we slept soundly. A general physical well-being and a robust appetite are among the blessings of Antarctic travel and one sleeps none the worse for lack of darkness. When we rose in the morning the wind had dropped and the day was bright with sun. The climb to the Saddle had worried us for we thought it too steep for the machines. But they performed magnificently and shaking off the drift that had covered them during the night, they pulled sturdily to the top. Some big crevasses higher up had us probing for solid ground but before midday we stood on the Saddle looking north towards the open sea.

It was the view we had been waiting for. Out right the long black finger of Cape Adare pointed north, while on our left was the blunted promontory of Cape Klovstad. Between them, ice filled the sweep of Robertson Bay and spread outwards till it joined the dark waters of the ocean. We could see no way clear to the coast for though the slope immediately ahead dropped gently, a couple of miles away it fell abruptly from sight. The icy surface bore witness to the prevalence of gales, for it was polished by the wind and furrowed, and of loose snow there was little, except in more sheltered areas.

We had planned to carry a camp down to the bay and explore the geology from there, but with time running out this was no longer feasible. So we camped above, in the hope that next morning we would climb down unladen to complete the crossing. Two tents having been pitched, we walked across to Cape Klovstad in the shining afternoon light to where, on our left just beyond the cape, we could see Duke of York Island standing in the path of the Murray Glacier, which crumpled and surged around it like a river round an island in a rapid.

We returned to camp, and there we split into two groups. Norm took half the party back to the camp of the previous night, for he had a surveying programme to complete and a peak to climb. Ed, the two geologists, Mike White and I, formed the Robertson Bay party.

During the night a southerly gale blew up, so that by morning we were isolated in thick drift scudding past from the south. It was disappointing for time was running out fast, and a worry too, in that any day now the thawing sea-ice in Moubray Bay might suddenly break up in a storm and be carried out to sea, cutting off our retreat. But there was nothing we could do; in such weather we could move neither forwards nor back, and we lay in our sleeping-bags lamenting yet another lost day.

There was still wind in the morning but visibility was better. Ed decided to make a last bid for the bay, though even as we cooked breakfast we could hear the wind rising. On two ropes we set off towards the lip of the bay, with the wind driving long lines of white drift ahead of us across ice and shingle. As the angle steepened down-hill we felt the gritty patter of thicker drift striking the hoods of our down-jackets. We had doubts about going on. On crampons we strode down a gully of ice beside a rib of black basalt, but abruptly it

came to an end and we found ourselves looking down steep rock and
ice into the head of the bay. There was none of the lee shelter we had
hoped for and wind howled around, swelling to gusts of frightening
power. The climb down was not easy: to the left, tongues of ice
probed their way down steep basalt-slopes while on our right an
ice-fall plunged into the sea. Below us there was a route but we had
little inclination to use it. We had a feeling that if the weather
thickened much further, we might not return.

"We're getting out of this," said Ed. "Home to Hallett." None of
us was reluctant to turn back but it was frustrating all the same.
Robertson Bay had become as definitive a goal as the summit of a
mountain and we were nearly there. We could almost have thrown a
rock on to the sea-ice. I took the movie camera from inside my down-
jacket and finished off a film; Larry, below me, was looking sorrow-
fully at the rocks he had come so far to collect. Ed had already turned
back and was leaning forward into the wind, now pouring down the
slopes with the force of a river in flood. After two hours of beating
into the wind we were back in camp. We ate briefly, crammed the
wildly flapping tents into their long bags and lashed everything to
the sledge; mercifully the Snowmobile started almost immediately;
putting our shoulders behind the sledge we got it moving and leapt
on top. We were on our way to join the others at the head of the
Moubray Glacier.

The camp was deserted when we got there, a full blizzard blowing
and the wind strengthening all the time. A note told us that the others
had left earlier to climb a peak to the west. Time passed and we grew
alarmed, but then four ice-encrusted figures appeared out of the
flying snow. All was well. The blizzard that followed was the worst
that either Ed or Larry had been caught in. We lay in our sleeping-
bags for two days, reading books for the second time, rationing food
with increasing care and wondering whether there was still some ice
in Moubray Bay. Occasionally one was forced outside, to return
frozen, with a trouserful of drift snow. And Larry spent the best
part of a day drying his sleeping-bags after I had knocked a two-
gallon pot of water off the primus, a mishap born with the stoicism
which is the hall-mark of the seasoned Antarctic traveller.

At midnight on the third day the wind began to abate. Outside,
there was still some cloud but no drift. And then in the blue twilight
we saw a pair of snow-petrels, white except for their black eyes,
flitting silently around like two spirits. It was an omen. And though
visibility was bad, Ed decided to move. The Snowmobiles were
almost buried beneath the feathery snow and I doubted whether they
would shift the sledges. For a hundred yards we heaved and pushed
till at length we came to a steeper part of the incline where, with the

going downhill, we had enough momentum to plough a homeward track. After four miles the glacier flattened. The machines, held back by their laden sledges, sank into the deep snow and would go no farther. Ed unloaded the gear, joined the Snowmobiles, one dragging the other, with behind that a single lightly-laden sledge, and he and three others carried on. The rest of us camped.

Next morning Mike and Jenks, with the two Snowmobiles, were back to collect us. They told an epic story of how the previous day they had all but lost Ed, Murray and the two machines down one of the Moubray crevasses. Soon after leaving us they had emerged from the region of mist and deep snow on to smooth easy going with not a crevasse in sight. Murray was in the lead machine, thirty feet of tow-line separating him from Ed, when he felt the snow beneath him sinking. He knew what that meant—he hadn't travelled to the Pole and back for nothing—and he opened the throttle wide. There was enough slack to let the machine jump forward a couple of feet. Then with a 'whoosh' a hole appeared beneath the back end of the machine which was left clawing desperately for a hold on the lip of the crevasse. It paused a moment, gripped the snow and surged forward to safety. Shaken, Murray and Ed climbed out to have a look. Between them a hole had opened up, ten feet wide, twenty long, and apparently bottomless. Had the lead machine gone in almost certainly Ed's would have followed it. There was no more trouble until, a few miles short of Moubray Camp, they ran out of petrol. On skis they trekked forward to the camp, collected a jerry-can and carried it back. Finally at midnight the Snowmobiles and their weary drivers pulled in beside the tents on the edge of the sea-ice.

Now Mike and Jenks were back to collect us. Again we loaded the sledges, not much lighter than they had been yesterday; again the machines roared and skidded, and again nothing moved. That was bad enough. But there was worse to come, for while straining forwards one Snowmobile had sheared an axle. Someone commented on the superiority of dog teams, how a Husky with a broken leg is simply shot and fed to the others. But you can hardly shoot a Snowmobile, not rationally anyway, and the extent to which one can be fed to the other is limited.

I remember then despairing of returning to Hallett before Christmas. We were fifteen miles up the Moubray with a few hundred pounds of gear, and only ourselves and one battered Snowmobile to shift it; there was thick mist all around; we were late and the sea-ice was due to breakup. Yet, against all expectation, we were back at Hallett within thirty-six hours. It was as if we had left behind us, with the ruined machine, the ill-luck that had dogged us the past fortnight.

o

"Looks like we're man-hauling from now on," said Norm cheerfully when we had proved beyond doubt that the damage was irreparable. I took a last photo of the dead Snowmobile, Pete drummed out a wild reveille on an empty jerry-can, and Larry, who had been talking nostalgically about earlier man-hauling trips, began looking for the harness. We sorted out three sledge loads, the largest for us and two smaller ones to be relayed by the remaining Snowmobile.

Man-hauling turned out to be a strangely exhilarating business. Gone was the frustration of waiting for an engine that refused to start or pull its load, and instead there was a camaraderie that made light of the work. It gave us an inkling of the way a team of dogs might feel. A couple of hours down glacier the surface was firmer and the cloud began to lift. Outlines of mountains appeared through the dissolving mist and towards the south-west we looked across a typically Antarctic landscape, a great névé with humped snowy peaks rising from it, like an archipelago of islands from an inland sea. All day we pulled steadily while the machine chugged back and forth relaying its loads. At 9 p.m. two miles short of the camp we saw a lone figure coming towards us. It was Ed, certain by now that some fresh disaster had struck. And as we swung up to him, dragging our sledge easily on the downhill run, his face lit up with the happiest smile we had seen for a fortnight. Back in camp Murray was out to greet us. He watched ironically as we swaggered in, feeling as if we had just returned from the Pole.

"All you lot need is a bloody standard-bearer out in front!" he said as he handed us a billyful of orange-juice. While we snatched some sleep, Ed and Murray worked through the night ferrying gear across the sea-ice to where the Weasel was waiting three miles away. We had doubts as to whether it would keep going, or go at all for that matter, but by now there was a feeling of optimism abroad. For the last time we struck camp, and assembled everything beside the Weasel. It started effortlessly. Murray kicked a few spare cogs and wheels into place and we were off.

The day was clear and sunny, with no wind, and we romped across the sea-ice in festive mood, with four of us towing behind on skis weaving from side to side like water-skiers. The crossing went without a hitch till the last six miles, when above its own clanking and the frenzied putter of the Snowmobile, the Weasel began making more ominous noises. Then, as if it were laying an egg, the Weasel popped a wheel out on to the ice, closely followed by a few bolts and washers. A mile farther on there was a clatter and another wheel dropped out of the track system. Another tinkled onto the ice. And another. Murray stopped, struck a blow or two with the big hammer, rearranged a few loose parts—and that, apparently, was enough to halt the disintegration. Towards the end of the day, like a line of penguins, but not as clean, we staggered from the sea-ice to the shingle spit, back amongst the rookery, the oil-drums and the grubby huts of Hallett Station. The Chief and the rest of them welcomed us with a gala dinner, and that evening we were entertained to beer and movies: a forty-four gallon drum heaped with cans of beer, and four movies.

Two days later, with the weather still fine a Hercules circled in over Hallett. Someone tried to hustle from the centre of the air-strip two penguins, who, like a pair of demonstrators, fought fiercely for their right to stay there. The plane skidded in on its big skis, took us aboard, and then, with the help of some Jato bottles, we rocketed off in the direction of McMurdo.

We left for New Zealand that evening. A last glimpse of the Antarctic from the Constellation: through a gap in the clouds a bleak expanse of sunless sea-ice seamed by black leads of open water. And at home it was spring, the air warm and thick, and there was blossom on the trees.

APPENDIX FOR NON-MOUNTAINEERS

On Ropes, Belays and Other Technicalities

I once met someone who thought that climbing a mountain is like the Indian rope-trick: you cast the rope up, snag it on a rock and then shin up. Few people believe this but many are vague about the value of a rope other than as a heroic affirmation of the principle of perishing together.

A pair of climbers should rope up whenever they feel that one of them is likely to fall off and come to harm if he does so. This is no use, however, if one simply drags the other with him, so one of the two is usually firmly attached to the mountain so that he *can't* be pulled off. This attachment to the mountain (e.g. a rope tied to a piton) is called an *anchor*. The anchor man must then arrange the rope so that if his companion falls off, friction can be applied to the rope and the falling man brought to a standstill. This process is called *belaying* and the technique varies on snow, ice and rock.

On *snow* the shaft of the ice-axe is plunged into the slope as far as possible and the rope passed round it. When somone falls the friction of rope on shaft will easily bring him to a halt. *Ice* is a more difficult proposition since the ice-axe shaft won't penetrate it. The best method is to use, as an anchor, a *piton*, an iron peg with an eye at one end to which one can tie oneself. The piton is hammered into the ice and if well-placed it can be remarkably solid. Nevertheless, a long fall on ice is not something to contemplate with any confidence.

Belaying on *rock* can also be tricky. A climber who falls 200 feet down a vertical wall is moving very fast by the time his companion's belay comes into operation. Imagine sitting on the window-sill of the tenth floor of a building, belaying a large sack of coal on the fifteenth floor. The tenth floor man shouts "On Belay!" whereupon someone on the fifteenth floor cries "Hold!" and tosses the sack of coal out of the window. The sack hurtles past the belayer until it reaches the fifth floor where the rope comes tight and either breaks or cuts the belayer in half. The solution to this problem is to run the rope through a series of pulley on the eleventh to fourteenth floors: when let go, the sack falls only a short distance before it is slowed by the top pulley.

The same thing is done in rock-climbing. At regular intervals the leader attaches a 'pulley' to the mountain, in the form of a piton hammered into the rock or loop placed over a knob of rock, and the rope is threaded through this. These are called *running belays* and a loop of rope carried for the purpose is a *runner*.

Threading the rope through a piton or loop is inconvenient so a *karabiner* (snap-link) is used as intermediary. This is an oval metal ring with one side hinged. The karabiner is clipped into the eye of the piton and the rope is clipped into the karabiner.

One other technique requires explanation and that is *rappelling* also known as double-roping or roping-down. This is the reverse of the Indian rope-trick and is a useful way of getting down steep walls quickly. The rope is threaded through a piton (which has to be left behind) so that both ends hang down to the foot of the wall. One then slides down the doubled rope which is retrieved by pulling on one end. Quite often the rope jams when half pulled through and many daring climbs have been made in retrieving snagged double-ropes.

INDEX

INDEX